Dislocating masculinity

Much recent writing on and by men suggests that male prerogatives are being sustained and lent authority by the new discipline of 'men's studies'. *Dislocating Masculinity* is an original and ambitious anthropological collection which raises important new questions about the study of men and masculinities. In a sustained cross-cultural enquiry, local experiences of 'hegemonic masculinity' are deconstructed to reveal the complexities of gendering and gendered difference. The familiar oppositions are analysed – male/female, man/woman and masculinity/ femininity – as are the other apparent certainties – that 'a man is a man' everywhere and that everywhere this means the same thing.

The chapters, written by both men and women, present a multiplicity of representations of manliness in settings which range from Imperial India to rural Zimbabwe to the gay community in London. Notions of masculinity define many different male and female identities; through idioms of masculinized power, they are often potent ways of expressing inequality. The complex relations between desire, sexual orientation, potency, fertility and sexual experience are considered in different social settings, as is the relation between gender and race, class and age. In both the theoretical and ethnographic chapters, essentialist ideologies of masculinity are challenged via a focus on embodiment and agency and subordinate masculinities. By dislocating a singular notion of masculinity, particular versions of masculinity which disempower both men and women are exposed.

Andrea Cornwall is a researcher based in the Anthropology Department, SOAS, London, and is currently an Associate Fellow, Institute of African Studies, Ibadan, Nigeria; **Nancy Lindisfarne** is Lecturer in the Anthropology of the Arab World, SOAS, London.

Male orders
Edited by Victor J. Seidler
Goldsmiths' College, University of London

MALE ORDERS attempts to understand male forms of identity, practice and association in the modern world. The series explores how dominant forms of masculinity have helped shape prevailing forms of knowledge, culture and experience. Acknowledging the challenges of feminism and gay liberation, the series attempts a broad and critical exploration of men's lives as well as engaging constructively with malestream definitions of modernity and post-modernity.

Also in this series

Recreating Sexual Politics
Men, Feminism and Politics
Victor J. Seidler

The Achilles Heel Reader
Men, Sexual Politics and Socialism
Edited by Victor J. Seidler

Men, Sex and Relationships
Writings from *Achilles Heel*
Edited by Victor J. Seidler

Men's Silences
Predicaments in Masculinity
Jonathan Rutherford

Fathers and Daughters
Sue Sharpe

Unreasonable Men
Masculinity and Social Theory
Victor J. Seidler

Dislocating masculinity

Comparative ethnographies

**Edited by Andrea Cornwall
and Nancy Lindisfarne**

Routledge
Taylor & Francis Group

LONDON AND NEW YORK

First published 1994
by Routledge
11 New Fetter Lane, London EC4P 4EE

Simultaneously published in the USA and Canada
by Routledge
29 West 35th Street, New York, NY 10001

Transferred to Digital Printing 2003

Routledge is an imprint of the Taylor & Francis Group

© 1994 selection and editorial matter, Andrea Cornwall and
Nancy Lindisfarne; individual chapters to the contributors

Typeset in Times by
Ponting–Green Publishing Services, Chesham, Bucks
Printed and bound in Great Britain by
Selwood Printing Ltd, West Sussex

British Library Cataloguing in Publication Data
A catalogue record for this book is available from the British
Library.

Library of Congress Cataloging in Publication Data
Dislocating masculinity: comparative ethnographies/[edited
by] Andrea Cornwall and Nancy Lindisfarne.
    p.   cm. – (Male orders)
Includes bibliographical references and index.
1. Men–Psychology–Cross-cultural studies.
2. Anthropology. 3. Masculinity (psychology)–
Cross-cultural studies.
4. Androcentrism.   5. Feminist criticism.
I. Cornwall, Andrea, 1963– .
II. Lindisfarne, Nancy, 1944– .   III. Series.
HQ1090.D57   1993
305.31–dc20   93–13078
                             CIP

ISBN 0–415–07941–1 (hbk)
ISBN 0–415–07942–X (pbk)

Contents

Contributors

Les Back is a Lecturer in Cultural Studies, University of Birmingham. He has done anthropological fieldwork in south London and Birmingham and has written widely on the politics of racism.

Andrea Cornwall is based in the Anthropology Department, School of Oriental and African Studies, University of London, and is currently an Associate Fellow of the Institute of African Studies, Ibadan, Nigeria. She is conducting research in Southwestern Nigeria on processes of gendering over the life course. Her previous work has been on participatory research methodologies and reproductive health. She has published on both gender and development topics.

David Forrest graduated in Social Anthropology from the School of Oriental and African Studies, University of London. He lives in north London and is flattered to be called an 'unreconstructed Marxist'.

Lin Foxhall specializes in the anthropology and history of Greece and has taught both anthropology and ancient history in the US and UK. She is currently a lecturer in the School of Archaeological Studies, University of Leicester. She has published widely and is presently editing a volume on ancient Greek legal systems, to be published by Oxford University Press.

Angie Hart is Lecturer in Social Anthropology at Keele University. She has done field research on prostitution and gender in Spain and Italy and has published on a number of related topics in economic and medical anthropology. She is presently completing two books: an ethnographic monograph on prostitution in Spain, and a co-edited policy-related study on HIV and AIDS in Europe.

Deniz Kandiyoti is a Lecturer in the Department of Anthropology, School of Oriental and African Studies, University of London. She is the author of numerous articles on women in the Middle East, feminist theory and gender and development issues; her recent publications include *Women, Islam and the State* (1991).

Helen Kanitkar is Lector in the Department of Anthropology, School of Oriental and African Studies, University of London. Her main research interests are Hindu communities in Britain and the Indo-Anglian novel. She is the editor of the *Anthropological Bibliography of South Asia* and the *Bulletin of the Vrindaban Research Institute*; her publications include *Hindus in Britain* (1982), co-edited with R. Jackson.

Nancy Lindisfarne is Lecturer in the Anthropology of the Arab World at the School of Oriental and African Studies, University of London. She has done fieldwork in Iran, Afghanistan, Turkey and Syria. She has published numerous articles on gender, marriage and Islam in the Middle East and, as Nancy Tapper, is the author of *Bartered Brides: Politics, Gender and Marriage in an Afghan Tribal Society* (1991).

Peter Loizos is a Reader in Social Anthropology at the London School of Economics, University of London. His first career was as a documentary film-maker and he has recently completed *From Innocence to Self-consciousness: Innovation in Ethnographic Films, 1955–1985* (forthcoming). His anthro-pological fieldwork has been done in Cyprus and in northern Sudan and he is the author of *The Greek Gift: Politics in a Cypriot Village* (1975) and *The Heart Grown Bitter: A Chronicle of Cypriot War Refugees* (1981), and co-editor, with E. Papataxiarchis, of *Contested Identities: Gender and Kinship in Modern Greece* (1991).

Bonnie McElhinny is a linguist working at Stanford University, California. She has done extended fieldwork on the relation between the gendering of occupation and language among the Pittsburg police. She is interested in interactional and variationist sociolinguistics and the ethnography of speak-ing; her publications include works on African-American vernacular English, oral narratives and secondary and tertiary education.

Chenjerai Shire is a freelance researcher and has taught ChiShona for a number of years. He is currently studying film criticism and has also researched and translated documentaries for television.

Acknowledgements

The immediate origins of *Dislocating Masculinity* lie in a series of meetings of the London University Gender Research Group at University College in 1990 when the topic chosen for discussion was 'masculinity'. Behind this choice lay a number of pertinent questions. Why had the study of men, as men, been the object of so little anthropological attention? Why, when men's groups had become salient by the late 1970s (Seidler 1991a), did men's studies, as a discipline, take so long to emerge – particularly when it appears to depend so heavily, and anachronistically, on earlier women's studies approaches? In short, why had 'masculinity' suddenly become so fashionable?

The following year, Nancy Lindisfarne organized a seminar series in the anthropology department of the School of Oriental and African Studies, University of London. The brief of the seminar series was to seek, through ethnographic materials, ways of thinking anthropologically about 'masculinity' and to consider what contributions anthropologists could make to current debates. The popular reception of the series, and the dearth of anthropological texts which investigate different masculinities, encouraged thoughts of publication. Several of the papers from that series are included in the volume and Andrea Cornwall became intimately involved in its realization.

Our contributors have been enthusiastic, patient and unfailing in their support. All have responded graciously to our often heavy-handed editing, while Dave Forrest, Angie Hart and Deniz Kandiyoti have also played key parts in the on-going dialogue about masculinities which sustained us.

Heartfelt thanks are also due to other friends and colleagues whose curiousity, criticism, various kinds of expertise and unstinting goodwill have spurred us on: Eduardo Archetti, Clare Baker, Janice Baker, Vic Conran, Lisa Croll, Kit Davis, Dale Eickelman, Mary Hegland, Mark Hobart, Diana Jeater, Sharon Lewis, David Parkin, John Peel, Mario Sarris, Ian Scoones, Jeff Roberts and Stuart Thompson. We would particularly like to thank Ruard Absaroka, Colin Perrin, Veronica Doubleday and Sue Wright, all of whom meticulously read earlier versions of the introduction and offered us invaluable editorial and other advice; if our efforts fail to meet their high standards, the fault is only our own.

Finally, very special thanks are due to Huw Davies and Edward Lindisfarne, whose editorial skills, wisdom and companionship helped magick the final manuscript into being.

Andrea Cornwall
Nancy Lindisfarne

Introduction

Andrea Cornwall and Nancy Lindisfarne

Over the last few years there has been a surge of interest in the study of men and masculinity. We are told that on both sides of the Atlantic men are starting to respond to the challenges of feminism. Women and gay men are no longer the 'problem' to be unravelled. Now the spotlight is on the hetero-sexual male. Fresh definitions of 'masculinity' abound, affirming old myths in attempts to create new males. From the 'wounded male' to the 'new man', images of reconstructed men appear on advertising bill-boards and television and in magazines and newspapers. These responses to feminism not only attempt to 'unwrap masculinity' (Chapman and Rutherford 1988; Polan 1988), but also to reassert male prerogatives (Faludi 1992): perhaps as Brittan suggests, 'what has changed is not male power as such, but its form, the presentation and the packaging' (1989: 2).

Now, as in the past, the term 'men' is used as an unmarked universal category to stand for humanity in general. Over the last two decades, feminists have challenged the ideological and material entailments of such implicit male bias. It is ironic that the logic of feminism as a political position has often required the notion of 'men' as a single, oppositional category. Founding their position on the assertion that 'the personal is the political', feminists have consistently raised awkward questions about the status quo in both the community and the academy (cf. Caplan 1987a). More recently, however, the feminist political project has faced a number of theoretical and methodological challenges from within. Several of these challenges have had a direct bearing on the genesis of this volume.

Like feminism, anthropology can be described as an inquisitive and uncom-fortable discipline which offers theories and methods for investigating a multiplicity of interested perspectives. Yet anthropologists have been curiously silent in the recent wide-ranging debates on masculinity. In *Dislocating Masculinity*, our aim is not simply to fill a descriptive void, but to demonstrate why the premises and methods of social anthropology are important to the study of men and masculinities. The ethnographic studies we present reveal the richness of an anthropological approach to questions of gender; they raise important theoretical questions and suggest further areas for research.

In our introduction, we examine the wider academic background to our study and draw on the new ethnographies of our authors to address anthropologically some of the intellectual and political issues raised by feminist and postmodern theory. In this respect, our positions as gendered participants in current debates about masculinity are significant. We want to disrupt the premises which underlie much recent writing on and by men, whether it belongs to the canon of men's studies (cf. Brod 1987; Kimmel 1987) or is the work of anthropologists, such as Gilmore (1990). In so doing, we offer a new perspective for viewing gendered identities and subverting dominant chauvinisms on which gender, class, race and other hierarchies depend.

AN ANTHROPOLOGICAL INVESTIGATION OF MASCULINITY

A basic precept of anthropological studies is that new insights into social relations follow the investigation of cultural categories that have previously been taken for granted. This process is interactive and comparative and, of course, it can only ever be partial. Such investigations depend on anthropologists finding ways of learning how others see the world. New, and often very different, vantage points offer anthropologists opportunities to gain a greater understanding of their own cultural biases and how these are often imposed on others. Three basic steps are intrinsic to anthropological strategies to view the world more reflexively.

The first is to try to dismantle the conventional categories which dominate thinking on a particular subject. Thus anthropologists may ask themselves what they mean by their use of the terms 'man' or 'woman' and to what extent their own notions of gender are likely to intrude in their attempts to understand gender relations among others. Or they may start with a notion such as 'masculinity' on which everyone seems to agree. By looking in detail at everyday usage and the contexts in which people talk of masculinity, its complexity soon becomes apparent.

The second step is comparative. Comparative enquiries rely on detailed descriptions of social interactions and how social labels are used in different social contexts. By examining the difficulties of translating particular meanings of masculinity from one social setting to another, anthropologists challenge the existence of any apparently straightforward universal category and raise questions about the social contexts in which such categories are used.

The third step occurs when anthropologists draw on the insights of ethnographic studies to examine their own preconceptions. Here, through ethnography, we ask to what extent the familiar oppositions – male/female, man/woman and masculinity/femininity – are everywhere belied by a much more complex social reality.

Much of this complexity hinges on the way people understand the relation between gender and power. One aim of *Dislocating Masculinity* is to offer an approach that responds to the problems posed by the use of western gender categories *and* addresses people's experiences of inequality. In this respect, our focus on masculinity is deliberate.

Though it is obvious that all men are not equally powerful, in the west being male is often associated with the power to dominate others. As anthropologists we want to investigate this association. Just how accurately does it describe people's everyday social lives? How are ideas of power connected with maleness? Or, conversely, what attributes of maleness are seen as empowering? What happens, for instance, when a man perceives himself as weaker than others?

If unquestioned, a cultural premise that associates men with power amounts to a mystification, benefiting some people and disadvantaging most others. Following Carrigan *et al.* (1985), it is useful to think of those ideologies which privilege some men (and women) by associating them with particular forms of power as 'hegemonic masculinities'. Hegemonic masculinities define successful ways of 'being a man'; in so doing, they define other masculine styles as inadequate or inferior. These related masculinities we call 'subordinate variants'. As we shall see, one reason the rhetoric of hegemonic versions of masculinity is so compelling is that it rests on an apparent certainty: that 'a man is a man' everywhere, and everywhere this means the same thing.

Essentialist interpretations of the male/female dichotomy are a major problem in comparative studies of gender. In any given setting, gender differences are often presented and perceived as absolute and dichotomous. Moreover, such gender differences, when viewed from an historical or cross-cultural perspective, often appear stable or repeat themselves as variations on a single theme. However, essentialist explanations cannot explain variation and the fact that cultural forms are never replicated exactly. An essentialist male/female dichotomy cannot account for the ways people are gendered in different places at different times. Once comparative studies expose a diversity of meanings, the idea of 'being a man' can no longer be treated as fixed or universal.

If notions of masculinity, like the notion of gender itself, are fluid and situational, we must consider the various ways people understand masculinity in any particular setting. And we must explore how various masculinities are defined and redefined in social interaction. How do individuals present and negotiate a gendered identity? How and why are particular images and behaviours given gender labels? Who benefits from such labelling? And how do such labels change before different audiences and in different settings?

Examining how notions of masculinity are created and presented through interaction reveals clearly the relation between a multiplicity of gendered identities and power. While ideas of 'male dominance' and 'patriarchy' are neither sensitive nor appropriate tools for analysis, we argue that relations of power are an aspect of *every* social interaction. By dislocating any single notion of masculinity, we see that particular versions of masculinity emerge in tandem with particular perceptions of equality or inequality. This means that people's experiences of the intersecting relation between gender and power are socially constructed and historically located.

The first chapter of *Dislocating Masculinity* is an extended introduction to an anthropological investigation of masculinity. The assumptions English speakers often make when they talk about masculinity are explored through the multiple identities conjured up by the notion of the 'macho man'. We then examine the assumptions which link attributions of masculinity with power. The links between gendered power and social and material privilege often appear compelling and 'natural'. We suggest that this persuasive rhetoric can be dismantled, first, by treating power as immanent in all social interactions and, second, by viewing inequalities from the point of view of *subordinates*. From this vantage point we offer a brief outline of the history of gender studies in anthropology and relate this history to themes which reappear anachronistically in the new discipline of 'men's studies'. We suggest that an emphasis on the social construction of sex and gender has now become a stumbling block to new approaches to gender studies and masculinity in particular. However, feminist interpretations of postmodernism seem to offer a productive way forward. They focus on the fluidity of processes of gendering and, when they are linked to the new feminist politics of location, they offer ways of using comparative insights to combat inequality. This chapter ends with the suggestion that if we locate and describe the multiplicity of competing masculine identities in any given setting we automatically begin to dislocate the hegemonic versions of masculinity which privilege some people over others.

COMPARATIVE ETHNOGRAPHIES OF MASCULINITY

Anthropologists can make a major contribution to the study of masculinity by asking new questions. Here, in a preview of the ethnographies collected in *Dislocating Masculinity*, we suggest how the variety of comparative issues they raise illuminate wider theoretical debates and the relation between gender and power in specific cases.

The first three case studies, all of which have a Mediterranean focus, raise important methodological issues through the new ethnographic materials they present. Each illustrates how theoretical positions with their attendant western forms of male bias reproduce the illusory unity of dominant versions of masculinity. In Chapter 2, Angie Hart notes the considerable semantic difficulties which are raised by treating 'masculinity' as an analytic term and then importing it into other settings. Her study of the male clients of female prostitutes in Alicante makes clear how and why most of the few ethnographies of 'masculinity' (of which a disproportionate number seem to have been done in Spain) reproduce the preconceptions of the anthropologist.

Most studies of prostitution have focused on the sex-workers themselves, while, typically, their clients have been ignored or treated as 'everyman'. Hart's study of how these clients/men define themselves and are identified by others introduces us to the many ways maleness and personhood may be construed in everyday life.

In Chapter 3, Peter Loizos examines the considerable ethnographic literature on Greece and describes a fundamental problem with much of this ethnography: the tendency to generalize and write of 'Greek society' or 'Greek men' as if such labels refer to homogeneous groups and are meaningful categories for analysis. Loizos' re-reading produces a far more interesting picture. He describes how a range of hegemonic masculinities (and their subordinate variants) are produced when various national institutions (such as the army and the Greek Orthodox church) intersect with regional differences (concerning, for instance, inheritance rules and attitudes to authority) at different stages of men's lives. The matrix of variant masculinities is further complicated by the other attributes of hegemonic masculinities, such as taking the 'active' role in sexual encounters.

Nancy Lindisfarne (Chapter 4) also treats theory and ethnography in tandem. She challenges the homogeneity of what have been called 'honour and shame' societies, arguing that such apparent unity is the product of a bias towards the rhetoric of male 'honour' and the hegemonic masculinities this rhetoric supports. She reverses this bias: by problematizing gender, it becomes possible to ask how people make gender known to themselves and how gendered identities may then be reified to sustain inequalities. Drawing on Strathern's work in *The Gender of the Gift* (1988), she considers how people are gendered through interaction: that is, how anatomical and physiological notions of difference are construed, literally embodied and transformed through sexual intercourse and/or parenthood. A range of ethnographic and other materials from the Middle East illustrates how ideas about female virginity and defloration create and confirm a variety of masculine identities.

Hegemonic versions of masculinity frame relations of inequality. However, hegemonic forms are never totally comprehensive, nor do they ever completely control subordinates. That is, there is always some space for subordinate versions of masculinity – as alternative gendered identities which validate self-worth and encourage resistance. Chapters 5 and 6 consider both the ways dominant forms may 'emasculate', 'femininize' or otherwise diminish subordinate men, and their responses to domination. David Forrest (Chapter 5) examines in detail the social entailments of what has been called the 'butch-shift' (Segal 1990) – the emergence of a particular accentuated form of masculinity among gay men who choose to present themselves in terms of body images, sporting activities and clothing which in earlier stereotypes were associated only with straight men. In effect, the butch-shift has dislodged the association between macho masculinity and heterosexual men. Forrest offers an explanation for the changing images of gay men in terms of

the wider political economy. Those with commercial interests have bene-
fited from the commoditization of men's bodies generally and encouraged
the emergence of the gay community in particular: 'A buck is a buck. Who
the hell cares if the wrist holding it is limp?' (Altman 1982: 18, quoted in
Forrest, here).

Masculinities vary not only over time but according to setting. Andrea
Cornwall (Chapter 6) describes how the identities of *travestis* in Salvador,
Brazil, are multifaceted, emerging through their activities as prostitutes and
through their participation in religious cults known as *Candomblé*. Looking at
the ways in which *travestis* are gendered within these different domains,
Cornwall raises a number of questions about 'sex' and 'gender' which
challenge taken-for-granted ideas about what it is to be a 'man' or a 'woman'.
Travestis, she argues, have both a 'male' and a 'female' body depending on
which parts of the body are considered significant in determining 'sex' at any
particular moment. That is, they can be 'women' or 'men' according to the
setting and the activities in which they take part.

Cornwall's detailed and subtle ethnography locates processes of gendering
in the interactions between actors in particular situations. These interactions
establish the gender of the actors within different domains of discourse.
Within *Candomblé*, alternative versions of both gender and agency provide
different ways of thinking about masculinity and femininity. These are not,
however, independent from hegemonic versions of masculinity and femininity, which continue to impinge both within and outside *Candomblé*.

Though women as both authors and subjects are virtually absent from the
historical sources on ancient Greece, in Chapter 7 Lin Foxhall takes women
as her point of departure for rethinking masculinity. She describes the
hegemonic masculinities which are documented in terms of 'monumentality',
a strategy by which adult male citizens publicly associate themselves with
immortality. Other data suggest not only that men were dependent on women
in the domestic terrain, but that their location in the kinship system and their
experience of genealogical continuity were far more precarious than those of
women. By focusing on what has been omitted from previous accounts of
ancient Greek masculinities, Foxhall challenges classicist stereotypes which
have been reproduced by Foucault (1978–86), among others.

Chenjerai Shire (Chapter 8), like Foxhall, considers how different masculine identities are constructed through time in different social spaces.
Shire writes autobiographically of his childhood in rural Zimbabwe. He
describes how boys were gendered in different settings: they were taught to
be fluent in a men's language in the male meeting place of the *dare*, tips for
successful love-making were imparted by senior kinswomen in the women's
space of the kitchen and other aspects of sexuality were learned through play.
Shire draws attention not only to the situated masculinities of young boys, but
to how these are related to the repertoire of adult male identities defined in
terms of heterosexuality and fertility. Shire's chapter also has an historical

dimension. He describes how the 'tribal' and 'national' identities of the people who now know themselves as the Shona of Zimbabwe were created through colonialism, which also transformed idioms of hegemonic masculinity in radical ways. Earlier versions which depended on totemic kinship relations lost ground as senior men adopted the militaristic styles of their tribal neighbours, yet simultaneously the exodus of young men to the mines and cities eroded other attributes of rural patriarchy.

Shire links specific masculinities to particular places and shows how activities and occupations can be gendered. This theme continues in Chapter 9. Bonnie McElhinny, writing of female police officers in the United States, shows how in some situations work identities may take priority over gender in defining personhood. Thus, the female police officers describe themselves as learning 'to be hard' and 'unemotional' as part of 'doing their job'. To understand why impassivity is seen as an aspect of the masculinity of male police officers, but transforms women into police professionals, McElhinny distinguishes between referential (that is, direct) associations and those which are indexical (that is, contingent). She shows that masculinity is contingently associated with emotional distance. This allows female police officers to intrepret behaviour that is normally and frequently understood as masculine (such as a lack of emotionality or displays of physical violence) as occupational.

The distinction between direct (referential) and contingent (indexical) markers is a useful one for exploring the complexities of gendering. Direct markers of gender are unequivocal and unambiguous: the categorical symbols of gender, such as the gendered pronouns 'he' or 'she', or abbreviations like 'Mr' or 'Ms'. By contrast, contingent markers are *non-exclusive*, and are linked to other ideas in a probabilistic rather than determinate way. So, for instance, baldness or aggressive behaviour are often seen as masculine attributes, but both may also be associated in quite different ways with attributions of age, health and personality which are not necessarily gendered at all. Or, as Cornwall (Chapter 6) shows in the case of *travestis*, there is only a contingent link between the penis and maleness.

Les Back (Chapter 10), like McElhinny, provides examples of the gendering of occupations. From his study of white working-class youth in south London, we learn how the masculine identities of apprentices are mocked by senior workmen: apprentices may learn a trade but they also have to 'qualify as men'. He shows how various forms of aggressive play are used to negotiate relative status, while words such as 'wanker' and 'poofter' can emasculate, imply homosexuality and/or feminize those who are deemed losers in any particular interaction. Elsewhere, elements of exaggerated macho sexuality, such as those associated with black (heterosexual) masculinities, are adopted by working-class white youth. As Back shows, the appropriation of these images can produce new, popular, anti-racist masculinities, yet simultaneously reinforces racist stereotypes in the wider society.

The greater the disparity between superiors and subordinates in any particular setting, the more ritualized and masked are relations between them. Social boundaries which protect material and other privileges of superiors are often defined by gender markers. The effects of colonialism have often been described in gendered terms; those who are ruled are feminized and portrayed as 'of inferior vigour' in relation to the dominant masculinities asserted by the colonizers (Stoler 1991; see also Kandiyoti, Chapter 12 in this volume). However, the rhetoric of the dominant culture hides the complex processes of negotiation and multiple, contested gendered identities *within* the spheres of both colonizers and colonized.

Helen Kanitkar (Chapter 11) describes how the 'ripping yarns' of the British Empire introduced boys to an idealized, hegemonic masculinity associated with white racism, muscular Christianity and colonial power. The audience for these stories were young boys and youths whose masculine identities outside the fictional setting were defined by their subordination to adult men with whom they shared identities defined in terms of class, nation and race. Dependants are often characterized as childlike and immature sexually and socially. While idioms of childhood defined the relation between the schoolboys and adult British men, these same idioms also defined the far greater subordination of adult 'native' men – 'boys' – whom the British boys saw as their inferiors and had no hesitation in dominating.

Kanitkar draws attention to the ways in which masculinities produced within colonial discourses impinged on relations *between* colonizer and colonized and *within* each category. In this way, her account complements that of Shire (Chapter 8). Thus we learn how the hegemonic masculine styles of the British, regarding sportsmanship or Christianity for example, were reworked by colonized men to characterize and control their fellows. To regard the colonized as simply the passive victims of colonialism would obscure processes of resistance among men and women as well as the active redeployment of hegemonic colonial masculinities.

The salience of representations of black male (hetero)sexualities was a dimension of race relations in colonial settings (see also Back's account of contemporary race relations, Chapter 10). Indeed, images of rampant black male sexuality, of the rape of white women, and of black women's sexual availability to white men are used by dominant groups to maintain 'racial' differences. However, such themes may coexist with quite different discourses on racism and sexuality. For instance, in the *Boys' Annual* stories the sexuality of 'native' men is never mentioned, 'native' women rarely make any appearance and 'white' women are present only in supporting roles. Though adult colonial men are portrayed as heterosexual, the 'imperial cadets' were the chaste inhabitants of a homosocial world where homosexual desire was unacknowledged and heterosexual desire was stigmatized as belonging to the kind of youth that can be seen, with pale and pimply face, sucking cigarette or cane-top, loafing around and ogling the girls, instead of joining in the sports of their more *manly* fellows.

(Mee 1913a: 293, our emphasis; cited by Kanitkar, Chapter 11 in this volume)

Notions of difference operate in many dimensions and produce complex identities. In the last of our ethnographic chapters (Chapter 12), Deniz Kandiyoti touches on virtually all the major themes which run through *Dislocating Masculinity*. Kandiyoti has already explored what she has called 'the patriarchal bargain' (1988a; 1991), suggesting that an important but neglected point of entry for the identification of different forms of patriarchy was through analyses of women's strategies of accommodation and resistance. As she shows here, her argument is widely applicable to all kinds of gendered subordination, including those associated with childhood, social class or single-sex institutions such as the army. She also writes of the dependency created by desire in the extraordinary homosocial and sometimes homosexual environment of the Ottoman fire department in Istanbul. Drawing on historical sources, ethnography, biography and fiction, she discusses the limitations of psychoanalytic explanations of the dynamics of family relations. Her starting point – her disquietude with the ostensible motivations of the 'enlightened, pro-feminist' male reformers in the Middle East – is not dissimilar to the contemporary feminist unease at the pro-feminist stance of 'new men' and many men who are writing within the genre of men's studies.

TOWARDS DISLOCATING MASCULINITY

The many themes which link the ethnographic chapters anticipate directions that anthropological studies of masculinity may take in the future: these include a focus on the processes of gendering, the metaphors of gendered power, and the relation between dominant and subordinate masculinities and other gendered identities in any given setting. In *Dislocating Masculinity* our argument rests on five premises. First, we argue that the male/female dichotomy has no intrinsic biological or other essential reality. Rather, this dichotomy is a potent metaphor for difference in western cultures whose import must be understood in terms of historical and ethnographic specificities. This is not to say that dichotomous gender attributions are not available elsewhere, perhaps even as near-universal metaphors for aspects of human sociality. However, there are no fixed ways these metaphors are grounded or employed in social life. They are only one among many other sets of metaphors used in the construction of human identities.

Secondly, we suggest that the oft-used analytic categories 'gender role', 'sexual orientation' and 'biological sex' have little explanatory value, since they too imply a false dichotomy between the sexed body and the gendered individual. Though this biological/social opposition has been the basis of most studies of gender, we insist that both the sexed body and the gendered individual are culturally constructed and that biology is no more primary or 'real' than any other aspect of lived experience.

Thirdly, we argue that the conflation of the notions male/men/masculinity and female/women/femininity in western constructions of difference must be investigated and documented historically and ethnographically. We suggest that the three terms do not necessarily overlap and that each term of the two triads has multiple referents which blur, qualify, and create the possibility of ambiguous interpretations in any particular setting. Thus notions of maleness, designations of manhood and attributions of masculinity have no essential referent, nor even a finite range of referents. Rather, each of the three terms can be used to describe a wide variety of different and even flatly contradictory aspects of human bodies and human behaviour.

Fourth, we argue that interpretations of maleness, manhood or masculinity are not neutral, but rather all such attributions and labels have political entailments. In any given situation they may align men against women, some men against other men, some women against other women, or some men and women against others. In short, the processes of gendering produce difference and inequality: and nowhere more obviously than in the versions of masculinity associated with (masculinized) notions of power.

Finally, we suggest that ethnographic studies of the production of gendered difference offer new ways of looking at 'masculinity' which take us beyond the strictures imposed by continued use of a single category, 'men', on the one hand, and the endless play of fragmented identities on the other. In its hegemonic forms, masculinity privileges some people and dislocates and disadvantages others. However, such hegemonic discourses may themselves be dislodged over time. The shifting and contingent relation between 'masculinity' and 'men' and power becomes clear when we examine the *enactment* of hegemonic and subordinate masculinities in a single setting.

Our aim in *Dislocating Masculinity* is to pose a series of open-ended questions in a cogent and radical way. Our explicit focus is on the negotiation and plurality of masculinities, while our theoretical premises are processual. We argue that indigenous notions of gendered difference are constantly created and transformed in everyday interactions. Relations of power are constituent parts of these interactions. The experience of hegemony lies in the repetition of similar, but never identical, interactions. This experience is never comprehensive; it changes over time and space. Multiple gendered (and other) identities, each of which depends on context and the specific and immediate relations between actors and audience, are fluid and they are often subversive of dominant forms.

Chapter 1

Dislocating masculinity
Gender, power and anthropology

Andrea Cornwall and Nancy Lindisfarne

In this chapter we locate our studies of masculinity. Our perspective draws extensively on anthropological accounts of gender and feminist theory, and our ambition is to establish a framework for comparative analyses in general and for our ethnographic chapters in particular. Indeed, one of our introductory obligations is to present important aspects of this work in a manner which is both accessible and intellectually challenging.

We begin with a paradox that is at the heart of all anthropological analyses. Though we seek to question taken-for-granted social categories, we can only do so in terms of our own experience. Imprisoned as we are in the strictures of our language, it is difficult to escape using the terms 'men', 'male' or 'masculinity', and 'women', 'female' or 'femininity', without implying a binary notion of gender (cf. Threadgold 1990). To use complex circumlocutions instead merely side-steps the problem, providing no adequate solution. Accordingly, we use these terms reservedly.

A preliminary step to ethnographic comparison, then, is to examine the categories of our language more closely and to sharpen our critical awareness of ideas about 'men', 'maleness' and 'masculinity'. The *Shorter Oxford English Dictionary* (1973) offers definitions of the adjective 'masculine' as 'having the appropriate excellence of the male sex; virile, vigorous and powerful'. 'Masculine' may describe attributes, actions and productions as well as certain inanimate objects which are connected with the male sex because of some essential quality, such as relative superiority or strength (1973: 1284). The primary definition of 'male' is simpler: 'of or belonging to the sex which begets offspring, or performs the fecundating function' (1973: 1265). Yet the apparent certainties of such definitions are themselves contradicted: 'masculine', when used of a woman, suggests that 'she has the qualities proper to a man' (1973: 1284).

Conventional usage depends on a series of explicit and implicit premises. First, masculinity and maleness are defined oppositionally as what is not feminine or female. Second, gendered identities implicitly depend on the social acquisition of appropriate attributes. Third, anatomy, learned behaviour and desire are conflated so that 'normal' sexual orientation and identity are heterosexual. And, lastly, through biological, sexual and social connotations, the idea of masculinity is reified and universalized. Masculinity appears as an essence or commodity, which can be measured, possessed or lost.

However, masculinity is neither tangible nor an abstraction whose meaning is everywhere the same. In practice, people operate according to many different notions of masculinity; closer inspection reveals a cluster of wide-ranging notions with certain 'family resemblances' (Wittgenstein 1963). Masculinity draws and impinges on a number of different elements, domains, identities, behaviours and even objects, such as cars and clothing. The notion of masculinity and what are described as masculine attributes can be used to celebrate and enhance normative maleness. However, such ideas can also unseat any straightforward relation between masculinity and men. Accordingly, we ask questions which aim to disrupt conventional understandings. How and when do 'boys' become 'men'? What makes someone a 'man' in some settings and a 'client', 'pimp' or 'person' in others? Is a man only, or always, a 'man'? Are only men 'masculine'? When a man is exhorted to 'be a man', what does this entail? Is a man always the same kind of 'man'? If so, what do men have in common? How and where are these commonalities constructed and used? And, if a man fails to do 'what a man's gotta do', does he cease to be a man?

The many different images and behaviours contained in the notion of masculinity are not always coherent: they may be competing, contradictory and mutually undermining. Moreover, completely variant notions of masculinity can refer simultaneously or sequentially to the same individual. Meaning depends on who is speaking and who is being described in what setting. Masculinity has multiple and ambiguous meanings which alter according to context and over time. Meanings of masculinity also vary across cultures and admit to cultural borrowing; masculinities imported from elsewhere are conflated with local ideas to produce new configurations. The popular notion of 'the macho man' provides us with a vivid example of the complexity of notions of masculinity and their intimate connection with particular social settings.

MASCULINITIES AND 'THE MACHO MAN'

The term 'macho' is a fairly recent importation into colloquial English, from Mexico via North America. It is used widely, in very different ways, to present multiple masculinities. Though macho derives from the Latin *masculas* and the Spanish term *macho*, both of which denote the 'male sex', Chambers' Dictionary has recently defined macho as 'ostentatiously virile' (1986: 578). In Britain, the macho man is not everyman; he is less a stereotype than a caricature in which distinctive attributes are selectively presented. Some aspects of usage carry with them accretions from their etymological source, echoing essentialized images of the Latin male as vigorous and often violent. However, in Britain, Latin men are also portrayed as romantic and emotional, although such expressiveness (and perhaps dependence) is deeply at variance with popular images of the macho man: thus, images of the 'soft' Latin appeared in the racism directed at Argentinian soldiers during the Falklands War. In short, there is no singular notion of macho masculinity, but a cluster of elements which may be contradictory or oppositional according to context.

Consider, for example, two settings in which the macho man may be found. In a rugby club, men who present themselves as macho may be valorized for displaying physical prowess and unflinching toughness, as well as a virility which is always heterosexual. The macho man should be successful at 'scoring' women and tries, though the epithet 'rugger-bugger' does suggest further questions. Thus, a British women's rugby song ridicules yet reinforces the theme of heterosexuality: the couplets of the children's song 'Knick-Knack Paddy Wack' run: 'they can't get a good hard-on; . . . they can't get it up to screw;. . . . they can't have it off with me; . . . they can't get it up to score; . . . they are lacking in sex drive; . . . little boys with little dicks; . . . masturbation is their heaven', etc. Yet, as an American men's rugby song has it: 'when I was young and in my prime, I used to butt-fuck all the time. Now I'm old and turning gray, I only butt-fuck once a day'. In another all-male setting, that of a gay bar, the archetype of the macho man is of the physical body moulded to perfection, but has little to do with other conventional 'masculine' attributes. Indeed, a markedly different macho masculinity emerges. As Forrest (Chapter 6 in this volume) suggests,

> Inside some pubs or clubs the gay 'macho man' might be seen holding a bottle of mineral water, rather than a pint of strong lager; his perfectly sculptured chest may be meticulously shaven and well oiled; his hair gelled; he might own the most fabulously camp flat off the King's Road, complete with a designer multi-gym.

To the rugby players the gay macho man may be a target for heterosexist abuse because of his presumed *lack* of masculinity.

To talk, as Blanchford (1981) does, of the 'masculinization of the gay man' implies that there are uncertainties about the relation between 'masculinity', 'men' and 'gay men', and that masculine identities are changing in complicated ways. The message of a 1979 Gay Pride poster which announced that 'Not all boys dream of being a marine' (Pollak 1985: 40) is not necessarily contradicted by the recent changes implicit in the 'butch-shift' (see Segal 1990), while macho identities in general have been sent up by Julian Clary in a camp version of *How to be a Real Man* (1992). Such a repertoire of masculinities clearly dislocates familiar assumptions.

Conventional notions of the macho man conflate (hetero)sexual orientation and 'masculine' identity, physical appearance, attributes of personality and behaviour. The macho gay man challenges this problematic conflation. The heterosexual desires and orientation of the stereotyped macho man with his bulging muscles can no longer be presumed. Macho gay men have become more explicitly objects of homoerotic desire, but so too have popular figures like the Chippendales, who have marketed an exaggerated macho image for both homoerotic and heterosexual titillation. In both cases there is an increasing focus on the objectification of the male body, a focus which is also evident in the increasing use of silicone to augment the 'maleness' of calf and pectoral muscles and the penis (cf. Bowen-Jones 1992). Forrest argues the new emphasis on macho styles is associated with changes in women's identities and behaviour *and* the fact that *all* men – gay, straight and bisexual – continue to benefit from sexist bias. As Forrest points out, homophobia is a construction which effectively distinguishes a 'man's man' from a man who is 'interested in men' (Sedgwick 1985: 89, quoted in Segal 1990: 143). However, because heterosexist prejudice also exists in most social settings, the fact that today's 'muscle queens' are indistinguishable from their heterosexual companions at the gym must alter the ways in which macho identities are presented in the future.

Let us examine two other aspects of the macho stereotype: the use of physical force and the concealment of 'soft' emotions. For our caricatured rugby player (whom we need not assume is straight), idioms such as 'to fight like a man' or 'to take it like a man' are likely to imply specific kinds of behaviour whose absence 'emasculates' or 'feminizes' a man. Such idioms are often used metaphorically by both men and women and vary in their meaning. So, for instance, some elite masculine styles in Britain require that violent personal confrontation be avoided (except on the rugby pitch), but favour professional coups and financial killings.

However, idioms like 'to fight like a man' can also refer to the literal use of physical force. Consider one such instance: a punch on the jaw. Clearly, attributions of masculinity depend on who throws the punch, who receives it and who is watching. Displays of violence may serve as markers of masculinity in distinctly different ways. Even in a boxing ring, things are not necessarily straightforward: a victory may be explained by a boxer's sexual abstinence as well as by his speed and strength.

Physical assault may be a response to a personal insult. An able-bodied man who throws a punch may be seen as affirming his masculinity, particularly if the recipient is also an able-bodied male of a similar age. In this situation, however, the masculinity of the victim is also being negotiated. He may fight back, run away or break down in tears. Or he might fight back and lose, or simply stand, with his arms folded, and refuse to fight. Any one of these responses may be interpreted as enhancing or diminishing the masculinity of either or both parties. Or as Kanitkar points out (Chapter 11 in this volume), attributions of masculinity may hinge not on the act of violence itself, but on the style of the confrontation. As Back's discussion of the 'wind-up' illustrates (Chapter 10 in this volume), every interaction allows for a variety of interpretations. How people explain what has happened depends on the circumstances, which means that no single episode is ever judged in isolation.

Rather, each episode is part of a continuing process whereby people negotiate relative positions of power as individuals and as representatives of social categories such as those based on gender, age, class or ethnicity. Interpretations of violence – in racist attacks, domestic battering, child abuse or queer-bashing – depend on preceptions of legitimacy and provocation. Not only will some people applaud a violent response which others deplore, but an individual's reactions are not necessarily constant. At different stages in the process of negotiating masculinities, and according to the different perspectives of the actors and their audiences, attributions of masculinity can and do change radically.

Resorting to physical violence can be interpreted as potency, brute ignorance or a pathetic fragility, depending on the perspective. As McElhinny describes (Chapter 9), the relation between force and emotion is contingent. Refusing to fight can be regarded as 'cowardly' or as a demonstration of qualities of self-control or 'reason', of not 'giving in' to emotion. Taking up the challenge and fighting may be considered 'manly' and as an appropriate expression of 'macho emotions' (cf. Skynner 1992: 14), yet losing a fight may be more diminishing than not having become involved in the first place. Of these possible outcomes, conventionally only one seems clear-cut and direct: bursting into tears. In physical confrontations such behaviour is likely to be unacceptable in a 'real man'. A man who cries may be called a 'poofter' or a 'big girl's blouse', or accused of 'crying like a baby'.

However, nothing should be prejudged. Being masculine can involve a range of behaviour which elsewhere would be termed feminine or not considered relevant in gendered terms at all. While some people ridiculed the well-known footballer Paul Gascoigne (Gazza) when he wept publicly after having been barred from competition, others understood his tears as evidence of deeply felt, and acceptable, emotion. And when the tennis star André Agassi 'wept tears of delight' after winning the Wimbledon tournament, some people denounced his behaviour as 'all that could be expected' of someone who 'wore an earring and a necklace and had a pony-tail', yet others found Agassi's tears 'very sexy'.

Being masculine need not be an exclusive identity. It can involve self-presentations which include behaviour conventionally associated with *both* masculinity and femininity. Such, of course, is the case with the so-called 'butch', as opposed to 'femme', lesbian (cf. Wieringa 1989). There are male *and* female versions of masculinity and, equally, female *and* male versions of femininity.

While his gay counterpart has been and is maligned for being effeminate, the sensitive and caring heterosexual male has recently been celebrated as a 'new man'. Indeed, some heterosexual men have confessed to feelings of inadequacy before the models of macho masculinity which have been thrust at them since the late 1970s (cf. Seidler 1991a). They have rejected the macho image and appropriated attributes conventionally associated with femininity. This new man is often associated with an inverted stereotype of the macho man: he has a puny frame (though perhaps he is not quite a 'seven-stone weakling'), an unassertive manner, a desire for nurturant activities and a wish to express emotion. However, the limits of 'feminized' self-representations are seemingly defined by the new man's perception of the 'emasculating potential' of the new woman.

In Britain both macho and new-men stereotypes are now prominent in the media, and are part of a repertoire from which masculine identities can be assembled. Bly's popular book *Iron John* (1991) seems to resonate with the fashionable angst of the new man, while simultaneously celebrating a version of macho masculinity. Bly offers a recipe for 'recovering' the ability to express those softer emotions which he claims have been 'lost' by men over the course of human history. Seen in this light, our stereotyped macho man, who is often presented as the quintessence of masculinity, is clearly judged not nearly 'man enough'. Many current advertisements play with new combinations of machismo and sensitivity; yet elsewhere the tensions between the two images are an endless source of jokes and heart-searching feature articles. Arguably these competing representations have less to do with redefining masculinity than with realigning the general association of maleness with power.

In English, the adjective 'macho' is one of a large number of idioms used to attribute masculinity, and it is the nuanced differences between alternative attributions which impart meaning to the idiom 'macho' in any given setting. When we attempt to compare the ways 'macho' is used cross-culturally, its meanings multiply exponentially. For instance, in Spanish- and Portuguese-speaking settings, the noun *macho* is often used as a term for 'man' which expresses something fundamental about 'being a man'. Thus, in Alicante, the term *macho* refers specifically to an 'instinctive', animal-like quality of male sexuality rather than to the Anglo-American family of resemblances described above. However, as Hart (Chapter 2 in this volume) shows, *macho* acquires meaning through its contrast with other terms which in English would also be translated as 'man'.

Eduardo Archetti has described the complex use of the term *macho* in Argentina. It includes images of virility and force, but a *macho* can also be generous, be controlled and use seduction, rather than violence, as a tool for domination. And, though a *macho* should be heterosexual, he will not lose his masculinity if he is the 'active' partner in homosexual relations. Viewed by other Latin American males, Argentinian football stars are among the most envied of *machos*, but in general Argentinian men are not associated with a particularly *macho* national stereotype. Conversely, Argentinian men regard the Mexican *macho*, for instance, as exaggerated in his swagger and bravado.

Finally, the term *macho* is also used as a form of address, in such expressions as '*que cuentas, macho*' ('tell me about it, *macho*') where it establishes an opening and interest between two male speakers (personal communication; cf. Archetti 1991, 1992). The term *macho* is exclusive to men, while the term *hombre* may be used as much between women as between men: only compare the ungendered use of 'guys' in American English.

Yet elsewhere the idea of the *macho* can involve deliberate artifice and parody conventional sexual imagery through both exaggeration and inversion. Cornwall (Chapter 6 in this volume) considers how, in Salvador, Brazil, *bofes* present a highly sexualized masculinity for sale to male clients, while the *travestis* attract male clients by adorning themselves with the physical trappings of 'femininity'. Yet, in the context of the sexual services they offer, and their sometimes violent behaviour, both *bofes* and *travestis* may be termed *macho*.

As Cornwall demonstrates, attributes and behaviour conventionally associated with 'masculinity' or 'femininity' can be selectively asserted to mark a single individual as both 'male' and 'female', while the boundaries between the two are constantly renegotiated and redrawn in each encounter. Hautzinger (1991), in another study in Salvador, provides a very different example of the same process. Hautzinger relates how the notion of the *macho* – in the form of *machismo*, behaving as if male – is used to describe some of the ways in which female police officers are seen as 'doing men's work'. However, the female police officers' *machismo* differs in crucial respects from that of male police officers. Female police officers, like male ones, are located as agents of state 'masculinity'; however, they repeatedly engage in *both* stereotypically 'masculine' and 'feminine' activities (personal communication; cf. McElhinny, Chapter 9 in this volume, who describes how female police officers in the United States systematically resist attributions of masculinity). In both cases, because of the 'feminine' elements in female police officers' 'masculinity', it takes on a qualitatively distinct, problematic cast – as do the 'feminine' elements of the *travestis*' identity, as Cornwall describes.

Though the uses of the word 'macho' documented here are linked etymologically, the social history which connects them is impenetrable. There are of course broad family resemblances, but everyday usage stretches and transforms meaning. So, for instance, Shire (Chapter 8 in this volume) finds 'macho' an apt adjective to describe particular versions of Zimbabwean masculinity. Viewed cross-culturally, the uses of 'macho' may be seen as a range of variations within a repertoire of cultural themes, yet such 'variations' and 'cultural themes' can only be discerned retrospectively. As an exploratory device, our excursion with the macho man has exposed the differences among his fellows. However, as a general methodology, tracing the multiple uses of a single term is not the best way of understanding gendered identities cross-culturally and trans-historically.

COMPETING MASCULINITIES

What, then, do we mean by 'masculinity'? Masculinity and femininity have often been portrayed as polarized opposites which only change in relation to each other. Thus Kimmel, writing from within the genre of men's studies, informs us,

> Masculinity and femininity are relational constructs. . . . One cannot understand the social construction of either masculinity or femininity without reference to the other.
>
> (1987: 12)

Behind this popular idea lurks a number of questionable assumptions, among them the idea that these qualities cannot be ascribed to a single individual at the same time. Indeed, Kimmel's proposition suggests that there is only one vantage point from which gendered identities can be judged, thus ignoring both the ambiguities and contradictions involved in gendering human beings and the multiple perspectives from which this is done.

Certainly, an important aspect of many hegemonic discourses is their focus on an absolute, naturalized and, typically, hierarchicized male/female dichotomy whereby men and women are defined in terms of the *differences* between them. However, to adopt such a perspective to the exclusion of others is to ignore, first, how any hegemonic discourse produces subordinate and subversive variants and, second, the existence of multiple and competing hegemonic masculinities within any particular setting.

Attending to the relational character of masculine/male/man and feminine/female/woman does of course raise intriguing questions. Thus, Shire (Chapter 8 in this volume) and Kandiyoti (Chapter 12 in this volume) consider aspects of intergenerational relations, while Loizos (Chapter 3) and Foxhall (Chapter 7) look at the different ways in which men and women can be persons, householders and citizens. Or Rousseau's observation that 'The male is only a male at certain times, the female is a female all her life' (quoted in Seidler 1987: 88) can usefully be compared with Forrest's account of a comprehensive gay identity (Chapter 5 in this volume).

By attending to the relation *between* maleness and femaleness, we may also consider how hierarchical relations between men and women reproduce differences *within* those categories. A striking example of this process is when men, shell-shocked during World War I, were feminized as 'hysterical men': 'having travelled . . . through "No Man's Land" all have become not just NOT men, nobodies, but *not* men, *un*men' (Gilbert 1983: 423, quoted in Showalter 1985: 173).

The same process occurs in other hierarchical discourses on 'class' or 'race', where subordination may be represented as weakness or effeminacy (cf., for example, Jeater 1993). However, the process is never simple. As Back shows is the case in south London, racism does not create a monolithic racialized persona: black macho styles of dress, music and language may be adopted by white youths to shore up their images. Conversely, Shire (Chapter 8 in this volume) and Kanitkar (Chapter 11) both note how in racial hierarchies some blacks may adopt idioms of white masculinity to gain prestige and control over other blacks. And, from another point of view, it is notable that both these chapters show how subordination, however it is construed in gendered terms, is frequently associated with childlike immaturity.

Most importantly, a focus on the rhetorical relation between male and female encourages us to consider where, how and by whom boundaries between 'men' and 'women' are imposed, as well as the criteria by which 'sex' or 'gender' are defined in different settings (cf. Lindisfarne, Chapter 4 in this volume; Cornwall, Chapter 6; and Kandiyoti, Chapter 12). For these reasons, it is appropriate to ask why Kimmel chooses to emphasize the male/female opposition to the exclusion of other, often more interesting, issues.

As our brief investigation of the macho man has already suggested, the ways in which men distinguish themselves and are distinguished from other men must be an important aspect of any study of masculinity. As Segal points out in her exemplary study of British masculinities in the post-war period, an understanding of the *differences* between men is as important to understanding the little-explored 'riddles of "masculinity" [as] its relation to, and dependence on, "femininity"' (1990: ix, x). The contexts and criteria in terms of which men are differentiated from each other is an area which has been neglected in anthropology. It has also been neglected in much of the men's studies literature, where further simplistic discriminations generate categories such as 'gay men' and 'black men' that mask more complex relations of inequality and identity (cf. Forrest, Chapter 5 in this volume; Back, Chapter 10).

The definition of 'masculinity' offered by the *Shorter Oxford English Dictionary* is not neutral. Yet it is authoritatively presented as if it is the only correct form of masculinity. When such an idea is used to establish and enhance the relative power of some people to the detriment of others, it obviously has wider political implications. Carrigan *et al.* describe such authoritative forms of masculinity as hegemonic.

Hegemonic masculinity is far more complex than the accounts of essences in the masculinity books would suggest . . . . It is, rather, a question of how particular groups of men inhabit positions of power and wealth and how they legitimate and reproduce the social relationships that generate their dominance.

An immediate consequence of this is that the culturally exalted form of masculinity, the hegemonic model, so to speak, may only correspond to the actual characters of a small number of men. Yet very large numbers of men are complicit in sustaining the hegemonic model.

(1985: 92)

Following Carrigan *et al.*, we will call privileged forms of masculinity which masquerade as being unitary 'hegemonic masculinities'. Such dominant constructions determine the standards against which other masculinities are defined. We will refer to these latter, contingent masculinities as 'subordinate variants'. However, as our discussion of the contemporary popularity of both macho men and new men shows, various hegemonic models can coexist. Rarely, if ever, will there be only one hegemonic masculinity operating in any cultural setting. Rather, in different contexts, different hegemonic masculinities are imposed by emphasizing certain attributes, such as physical prowess or emotionality, over others. And, of course, different hegemonic masculinities produce different subordinate variants: as we know from the feminist concern with women's 'invisibility', powerlessness in one arena does not preclude having considerable influence elsewhere.

In our borrowed use of 'hegemonic masculinity', our interest is in understanding how relations of power and powerlessness are gendered, and how, in any particular setting, attributions of masculinity are assumed or imposed. However, we suggest that such attributions are neither exclusive, nor permanent. Nowhere is there ever only a single system which defines people's success and failure as gendered subjects in absolute or enduring terms.

The idea of hegemonic masculinity encourages a consideration of how power is related to attributions of masculinity. However, Carrigan *et al.* do not problematize the notion of masculinity itself. By eliding the terms man/male/masculinity, they ignore the fact that it is not masculinity but *male* masculinity they are describing. To continue the above citation, they argue,

> The overwhelmingly important reason is that most men benefit from the subordination of women and hegemonic masculinity is centrally connected with the institutionalisation of men's dominance over women. It would hardly be an exaggeration to say that hegemonic masculinity is hegemonic so far as it embodies a successful strategy in relation to women.
>
> (1985: 92)

Implicit in their argument is a contingent connection, yet the relation between men and masculinity is made to seem incontrovertible. Ironically, such a slippage is a fundamental characteristic of hegemonic masculinities!

Three kinds of mystification work to create this sleight of mind and disguise the implicit masculization of power. First, an association between 'men' and 'power' is made to seem 'natural'. Feminists use the term 'male bias', or describe as 'sexist', just such associations. This process is enacted through the elaborate etiquette of social relations in any particular setting.

Such associations are also made verbally. This can be done through assertion: 'boys will be boys', or 'men are [naturally!] more aggressive than women': or through metaphors such as those which refer to 'real men'. But, in effect, all language is metaphorical: consider how the word 'male' is both naturalized and lent authority through its association with biology, or how the abstract connotations of 'manhood' are linked with a physical referent, the penis. Or how the emphatic use of 'man' as either a noun or verb often carries with it inclusive, positive images of possession and control, as in Kipling's 'If–' (cf. Kanitkar, Chapter 11 in this volume). In this way, virile male bodies are often seen to be at one with the body politic and, in the monotheistic religions at least, even the deity is seen as stridently male.

Another device which links men with power and control is metonymy, associating men with images or instruments of power – whether Popeye's spinach, a Lamborghini Diablo or military hardware: as men in both the US and British armies put it, 'I've got a rifle, I've got a gun; my rifle's for killing, my gun's for fun!'. Such associations are naturalized by being linked to aspects of the body, and they may be transformed or inverted to produce a wide range of meanings. The gun/penis association is only one possibility. The same soldiers also link the penis with bestiality, as in the endless jokes told about 'sheep-shagging' during training exercises in the UK. Or they may ridicule inappropriate aggression by calling a man a 'penis' or a 'cock', while a martinet may be dismissed as a 'dick-head' or a 'prick'. Metonymic associations often reveal the kind of 'commodity logic' which typifies capitalist formations (cf. Strathern 1988; and below). Thus, masculine identities may be located in possessions which can be acquired or lost. Such are the implications of the aphorism, 'Clothes do make the man' or the Texas wisdom that 'a man is no better than his horse, and a man without a horse, ain't no man at all'.

Secondly, (masculinized) power is consistently associated with those who have control over resources and who have an interest in naturalizing and perpetuating that control. This means that in gender, class and race hierarchies, men *and* women who are pre-eminent may be included in particular gendered constructions of power which simultaneously disempower subordinate men and women. In Britain, elite public culture valorizes both emotional distance – 'the stiff upper lip' – and physical toughness (cf. McElhinny, Chapter 9 in this volume). The contingent link with an elite masculine style is evident in, for instance, one of the Queen's Christmas broadcasts in Britain, in which she lauded a terminally ill man's 'military bearing and silence on the subject of pain and dying' (Stevens 1992). This style is reproduced in many other contexts. Thus in a single-sex school, it is likely to be a sporty 'lad', rather than a studious, unathletic 'spod', who is a popular leader, popular with girls and a school prefect (cf. Kanitkar, Chapter 11 in this volume). And, of course, the link between elite masculinity and racism may be explicit: in the clubhouse our rugby player may be chided to be fair or generous with the phrase, 'Play the white man.'

In many cases, the 'feminization' of subordinates is marked. For instance, patronage is often associated with sexual favours (cf. Loizos, Chapter 3 in this volume; Foxhall, Chapter 7); or it is the case that men are often brutalized by their military experience, which renders them anonymous and punishes failure by labelling men 'wimps', 'women', 'pussies', 'poofters', 'wankers' or 'homos'. Often men get by 'by making themselves liked', while brutalizing others weaker than themselves (Kandiyoti, Chapter 12 in this volume). It is notable that in victory soldiers (and football fans, cf. Archetti 1992) are often extremely vicious towards the vanquished. And the gendering of inequality is rarely clearer than in the wartime rape of women by 'normal men' (cf. Brownmiller 1975; Bennett 1993) whose actions assert their (hetero)sexual male identity while imposing anonymity and a 'weaker' sexuality on their female victims and vanquishing the enemy by sullying 'his property'.

Cartoons are often particularly revealing of the gendering of political relations. Cartoons are surprising precisely when they play effectively on hegemonic idioms. Thus, during the Gulf War Saddam Hussein, the Iraqis and the allies (Arab and non-Arab) were all mocked in gendered terms. For instance, Bush's infamous 'kick-ass' comment was turned into an obscene image suggesting the rape/buggery of Saddam (Heath 1991: 18). Elsewhere, Saudi men were 'moustaches' hiding behind the bare shoulders of the American women soldiers (Trudeau 1991: 30), while a group of 'new men' earnestly discussed 'the sexual associations evoked by recent war pictures from the gulf' (Peattie and Taylor 1991: 30). Cartoonists ridicule dominant idioms, but usually remain within the limits of political expression allowed by those who dominate. However, revolutionary actions may also be constructed in terms of gendered metaphors of power: one aspect of Gandhi's protest against the hyper-masculine world view of the Raj explicitly associated non-violence with celibacy and the spiritual elevation of androgynous forms of being (cf. Caplan 1987b).

Thirdly, images, attributions and metaphors of (masculinized) power are so pervasive that they are frequently used to signify power in settings which have little to do with men. Martin's work on biological idioms – of active sperm and passive egg in conception, and the masculinized Killer T virus cells and the feminized macropages of HIV virology – provides two stunning examples of how ideas of masculinized power insinuate themselves into supposedly 'objective' research (1987, 1992a, 1992b). A more immediate example of this process can be found in Lakoff and Johnson's discussion of the ways in which we talk about argument in the language of war:

> Your claims are *indefensible*. . . . His criticisms were *right on target*. I *demolished* his argument. . . . It is important to see that we don't just *talk* about arguments in terms of war. We can actually win or lose arguments. We see the person we are arguing with as an opponent. We attack his positions and we defend our own . . . the ARGUMENT IS WAR metaphor is one that we live by in this culture; it structures the actions we perform in arguing.
>
> (1980: 4)

Winning arguments, winning wars: both define versions of hegemonic masculinity. Consider only the number of peers in the House of Lords who owe their titles to their bellicose ancestors. More generally, an understanding of how arguments – and more violent altercations – are implicitly gendered is of direct relevance to the negotiation of masculine identities.

DISEMPOWERING MASCULINITY

In social theory and everyday usage, power has been treated as if it were both an abstraction located in concepts, beliefs and ideologies 'out there' and also a substantive property which can be won, exchanged or lost. Such a concept of power focuses attention on institutions, on formal relations between the powerful and the weak, and on men. It also leads to an emphasis on social stability, consensus and the intentionality of leaders, while the compliance of subordinates is dismissed as 'false consciousness' and their agency and interests remain more or less invisible. In short, conventional perspectives on power are male-biased, riven with functionalism and unable to account for social change (Davis *et al.* 1991). If 'sexuality is the dominant discourse of power in the west' (Braidotti 1992: 185), then to dislocate hegemonic masculinities, we must find another way of thinking of power and attend to the experience of gendered subordination.

Foucault's approach to power is strictly relational. Power is treated as an elusive, negotiated aspect of all social transactions, whose existence depends on a 'multiplicity of points of resistance' (1981: 95). His broad understanding of power dislocates it from its association with social pre-eminence. Rather, power is implicated in all aspects of social life, thus focusing attention on social process, change and the ways in which people experience autonomy and efficacy.

Foucault's approach to power is compelling, yet it is not without its problems. Several related issues concern us here. The first is the implicit male bias which permeates both Foucault's notion of power and his perspective as author.[1] While Foucault's analysis can be used to disrupt the conventional hegemonic association of men and power, this association is, in fact, naturalized in much of his own work. Second, power *per se* is not dissected, nor are its gendered attributes or the implications of representations of sexual difference explored. Third, in spite of his central concern with the surveillance of desire and the sexed body as an object of power, Foucault barely considers how the body is gendered – a topic which we address below. A fourth problem lies in his lack of interest in questions of agency and autonomy in the way power is enacted between people. Foxhall (Chapter 7 in this volume) in her critique of Foucault's historical study of sexuality in ancient Greece reveals the importance of the discourses on masculinity Foucault missed.

Though resistance is central to Foucault's discussion of power, he has been rightly criticized for not adequately considering the extent to which control is exercised in particular settings, how it constrains those who are controlled, how metaphors of control are gendered and, above all, how they change (Turner 1985). Feminists and anthropologists studying gender have long been concerned with the muting of women's voices (cf. Spender 1980; Ardener 1975). Here too, our interest is in disempowerment: the association between men and power is most clearly revealed in studies that focus on the experience of subordination in hegemonic formations. In this respect, Scott's argument in *Domination and the Arts of Resistance* (1990) is directly applicable to studies of gender and masculinity.[2]

Scott follows Foucault, treating power as elusive and relational; he writes of his own project that he seeks to 'outline a technology and practice of resistance analogous to Michel Foucault's analysis of the technology of domination' (1990: 20). Scott's interest is in everyday forms of resistance – the 'weapons of the weak': in the mundane, informal, diffuse and often individualistic activities through which the relatively weak can influence and frame their responses to dominant ideologies, and perhaps benefit materially from resources which they feel have been withheld from them by those who dominate.

Scott argues that all relations of power are characterized by dual transcripts. The 'official transcript' articulates, legitimizes and constrains the position of superiors and simultaneously reinforces the mechanisms (such as imposition of a gendered or class identity) by which subordinates are controlled. It is enacted in face-to-face encounters between superiors and their subordinates. However, all official transcripts have their counterparts in what he calls 'hidden transcripts' which are created off-stage, where dissent from dominant norms can be safely expressed. Only in desperation do the weak resort to open rebellion or revolutionary activity; far more often, and far less visibly, the weak aim to restore their own sense of worth and to maximize their advantage *within* the system which disempowers them (cf. Kandiyoti, Chapter 12 in this volume).

Hegemonic and subordinate discourses are mutually constructed. Those who dominate in any particular setting are constrained by the hidden transcripts of their subordinates, while the subordinates are neither passive nor mystified, but actively negotiate their position *vis-à-vis* those who are more powerful. An understanding of relations of power depends on contextualization, in terms of both the wider political economy and the immediate issues at stake. Most importantly, Scott argues that no situation of domination is ever static; external changes and the negotiations involved in any social interaction alter both official and hidden transcripts.

Both men and women can refer to the official transcripts of masculinity to legitimize their control of others, while subordinates respond by creating variant masculinities and other gendered identities. McElhinny (Chapter 9 in this volume) shows how male *and* female police officers use the images and professional tools of a hegemonic masculinity to empower themselves. And other examples of women associating themselves with masculinized power are numerous: the Queen and Princess Anne command regiments of the British army; political leaders everywhere (including women) don flak jackets to associate themselves with military might; many men and some women simply 'power dress'.

By comparison, the hidden transcripts of subordinates are poorly documented. Women accidentally-on-purpose burn toast to express their displeasure with their spouses; or they have headaches to resist sexual demands. More dramatically, they may chose to engage in sexual liaisons which may diminish publicly men's masculine credentials (cf. Lindisfarne, Chapter 4 in this volume; Foxhall, Chapter 7).

Subordinate men too engage in gendered behaviours which restore self-esteem: thus, Shire, like Forrest (Chapter 5 in this volume) and Back (Chapter 10), describes another macho style – that adopted by Shona men living in towns, who with flip-flops and a pair of jeans were like kings (cf. Moodie 1988). Elsewhere, as we have noted above, the military may dominate young men's experience and define acceptable sexualities. President Clinton's ambition to allow gays into the US armed forces has been strongly resisted. 'Homosexuality as contagion is the model here, though the anxiety it causes the toughest marines makes you realize just how fragile the institution of heterosexuality must be'; yet for the gay man sitting in a gay bar near a military base, 'it is as easy to have sex with a marine as it is to get bashed by one for being a fag' (Moore 1993:15). In the *Barrack-room Ballads* Kipling also offers many striking examples of the interplay of hegemonic masculinities and subordinate variants.

O it's Tommy this, an' Tommy that, an' 'Tommy, go away';
But it's 'Thank you, Mister Atkins,' when the band begins to play – . . .
For it's Tommy this an' Tommy that, an' 'Chuck him out, the brute!'
But it's 'Saviour of 'is country' when the guns begin to shoot;
An' it's Tommy this, an' Tommy that, an' anything you please;
An' Tommy ain't a bloomin' fool – you bet that Tommy sees!

(1990: 322)

If hidden transcripts validate integrity and reputation (Scott 1990: 7), this raises further important questions about how human worth and dignity are related to gendered identities. Or more fundamentally, with Strathern (1987), we must ask how are difference and inequality gendered, and how then do we account for unequal experiences of violence and the frequent association of violence with men. Strathern argues that every action is inherently forceful because it is inherently transformative (see below). As a general position, this makes sense, but it cannot account for the ways force is defined, enacted and experienced by others. Rather, as our discussion of the macho man and numerous examples from our ethnographies show, the puzzle lies in how local definitions and judgements about violence are linked to local attributions of masculinity.

Moore (forthcoming) argues from ethnographic examples that gendered violence is a consequence of people's inability to control their presentation of themselves or how they are represented by others. Such a general argument, like Arendt's conviction that 'violence appears when power is in jeopardy' (quoted in Morgan 1989: 84), account for differential experiences of gendered violence only when four other conditions are met. First, the interaction must be framed in terms of a direct (relational) discourse of male/female difference (cf. McElhinny, Chapter 9 in this volume); second, the discourse must strongly masculinize a hierarchical idea of power; third, physical violence, as opposed to other reactions, must be plausible and/or acceptable; and fourth, a (violent) action must be interpreted, by some people at least, as illicit or unacceptable.

With these premises in mind, consider Moore's example of men who

> cannot control their lovers as they would wish, they cannot control other men's access to these women, and therefore they cannot control the definition of their own masculinity because they cannot control the definition of or the social practices surrounding the femininity of their lovers. The only women they can control are their wives, and it is they who confirm their husband's masculinity, by their proper adoption of the opposite feminine subject position, and so their husbands hit them.
>
> (forthcoming)

As we discuss below, Strathern (1988) considers that cross-gendered inter-action can momentarily make partial identities appear coherent and whole (cf. below). Just as strong drink can 'put hair on a chest', so too can violence sometimes be seen to enhance masculinity: the man who beats his wife (Loizos, Chapter 3 in this volume), or the groom who deflowers his virgin bride (Lindisfarne, Chapter 4), may – for that moment at least – feel himself to be a 'real man'.

That impotence leads to violence is familiar, but the further steps to understanding what Morgan has called 'ejaculatory politics' (1989: 84) are instructive. By identifying the particular idioms whereby masculinity is associated with power, the ways violence may be gendered and sexualized (in wife-battering as opposed to marital rape or queer-bashing, for instance) can be explored. So too we can consider the parallels between interpersonal violence, the impersonal violence of terrorism and warfare, and that of gendered states. Thus, we may ask what the relation was between the rhetoric of male heroism, the feminization of the state as both sister and whore, and the reintroduction of Koranic punishments for fornication and adultery during the early days of the Islamic revolution in Iran (cf. Thaiss 1978; Najmabadi 1991). Such complex questions require subtle answers. To study structures of inequality which include both hegemonic and subordinate masculinities, it is helpful to reconsider anthropological approaches to gender and to place men's studies in this context.

STUDYING MEN: OLD ANTHROPOLOGY BUT NEW MEN'S STUDIES?

Malinowski, one of the 'founding fathers' of social anthropology, defined anthropology as 'the study of men embracing woman' (cited in Moore 1988: 1). Taken at face value, this observation is apposite. Mainstream anthropology has tended to consider women only in the situations in which they are literally embraced by men. As Moore has pointed out, studies of kinship and marriage have been central to definitions of the discipline and have ensured the inclusion of women in ethnographies, albeit as mothers and wives rather than as social agents in themselves (1988: 1; cf. Ortner and Whitehead 1981: 10). Men, on the other hand, have been described as social actors in all manner of different locations and positions, yet their gendered identities have usually been taken completely for granted.

Gilmore, whose *Manhood in the Making* (1990) is one of the few cross-cultural studies of masculinity, anachronistically cites Shapiro's criticism that in anthropologies of gender,

> the focus is on women; the social and cultural dimensions of maleness are often dealt with implicitly rather than explicitly. Much of the recent cross-cultural research is not only about women, but by women, and in some sense, for women.
>
> (Shapiro 1979: 269, quoted in Gilmore 1990: 1)

Gilmore attempts to make good this imbalance by providing a cross-cultural survey of how 'people in different cultures conceive and experience manhood . . . as the approved ways of being an adult male in any given society' (1990: 1). Yet Gilmore's project is fundamentally flawed by the very presumptions we seek to challenge here. He assumes that maleness is unitary, grounded in evolution and innate psychological and biological dispositions, and categorically opposed to that which is female. Moreover, he does not enquire how apparently unitary 'persons' are constituted and assumes that there is, in any setting, a single way of 'being a man'. Gilmore's focus is on versions of hegemonic masculinity and he tacitly accepts the mystifications these entail: that the abstraction 'masculinity' is something generic and ubiquitous if not universal and that 'men' exist as a natural, unmediated category. In effect, Gilmore is a positivist; for him, both masculinity and men are 'real', 'out there' and amenable to 'scientific' study (cf. Hart's comments, Chapter 2 in this volume).

Most tellingly, and in spite of the illogic involved, Gilmore dismisses confounding ethnography 'where manhood is of minimal interest to men or where the subject is entirely elided as a symbolic category among members of both sexes' as 'exceptional' or 'anomalous' (1990: 4). We suggest that it is just such cases which should arouse anthropological interest. Indeed, it is by attending to ethnographic details and cultural forms which may at first appear exceptional, ambiguous or anomalous that new areas for enquiry arise.

Malinowski's designation of anthropology as the study of 'men embracing women' has other resonances for *Dislocating Masculinity*. We argue that the scrutiny of men, as men, must also embrace prior studies of women and femaleness and locate discussions of masculinity in the history of gender studies. The appropriation of this earlier work under the rubric of men's studies has been discussed by Canaan and Griffin (1990). With them, we would urge a critical awareness of such retrogressive tendencies in the new studies of men;[3] equally, when work in gender studies is ignored, it is fair to wonder if unscholarly interests are being served.

With the emergence of the women's movement in the late 1960s and early 1970s an anthropology of women also began. An initial aim was to analyse the place of women in the ethnographic literature. Several sources of male bias were identified, among them the way male and female anthropologists incorporated Eurocentric ideas of male dominance into their fieldwork, with a consequent emphasis on the beliefs and activities of men in the community under study. As with the early women's movement generally, the 'problem' was to put women back into the picture. The aim was to ask questions and describe the world from a woman's viewpoint and, in the case of applied anthropology, to find strategies whereby women could articulate and remedy their subordinate position *vis-à-vis* men (cf. Rogers 1980). However, the categories 'women' and 'men' were not only accepted as universals, but defined the new area of study.

This first wave of 'feminist anthropology' provided the impetus for a wide variety of detailed ethnographies whose focus was on women. Many of these uncritically used notions such as 'women's status', 'role' or 'position' *vis-à-vis* men to document hitherto undescribed lives. More challenging works described the marginal character of discussions of women in earlier ethnographic accounts (cf. Goodale 1971; Singer 1973; Weiner 1976). They, and others such as Strathern (1972), were part of a new generation of ethnographies which asked basic questions about the *relationship* between women and men. This was a critical step. Even at this early stage, feminist anthropologists were moving away from the static dichotomies associated with the apparently 'natural' categories, 'men' and 'women'.

The analytical notions which had perhaps the greatest influence on early women's studies in anthropology were closely related to other contemporary theoretical interests in psychoanalysis, structuralism and Marxist or Weberian social theory. Rosaldo and Lamphere's (1974) edited volume *Women, Culture and Society* introduced four influential papers – by Sacks, Ortner, Rosaldo and Chodorow – which set the scene for an anthropology of gender. Each of these papers had a formative influence, inspiring ethnographies and extending theoretical debate. A second edited volume, Reiter's (1975) *Toward an Anthropology of Women*, was a further important source of ethnographic studies of women; it included an ovarian paper by Rubin which anticipated many current themes in gender studies. As we describe below, the arguments put forward by these five writers continue to reverberate today and have recently reappeared, anachronistically and in simplified forms, in the context of men's studies.

The male writers who have contributed to the men's studies canon seem to agree in one avowed aim – to redefine masculinity, whether in academic, popular or therapy-oriented terms. To be fair, the burgeoning literature on men and masculinity derives less from anthropology than from sociology and psychology. However, whatever their point of departure, many of these writers are extremely naive anthropologically, while others have taken up theoretical positions which ignore important recent work on gender. As we shall see, the men's studies literature and its concern with the so-called 'crisis in masculinity' does not yet provide much help on theoretical issues, but is perhaps in itself a promising area for ethnographic investigation.

MOTIVATED MASCULINITIES?

Many writing in men's studies claim to share a common goal with feminist scholars. Thus, Brod, an important figure in men's studies in North America, has paid effusive lip service to feminism. However, as Hanmer (1990) points out, Brod's actual citations of feminist work are few and self-serving. The extent to which he has failed to take account of the methodological and epistemological issues raised by various feminisms is apparent in his statement that,

> In inverse fashion to the struggle in women's studies to establish the *objectivity* of women's experiences and thereby validate the legitimacy of women's experiences *as women*, much of men's studies struggles to establish the *subjectivity* of men's experiences and thereby validate the legitimacy of men's experiences *as men*.
>
> (1987: 6)

It need hardly be pointed out that even in the early 1970s, when the emphasis was on defining a female Self and consciousness-raising, women's studies was never only about women. Feminists have always been concerned with fundamental issues relating to questions of power, yet Brod's aim emphasizes the personal at the expense of the political, and his unmarked use of the subjective/objective dichotomy reproduces the positivist dualisms (such as passive/active, body/mind and reason/emotion) which are deeply implicated in gendered inequalities in the west. He seems to be unaware that anthropologists have convincingly described the conceptual difficulties in generalizing from the western dichotomies (MacCormack and Strathern 1980) or how they are problematized in current work in feminist theory (see below).

Such 'common-sense' dichotomies, derived from western psychoanalytic and structuralist assumptions about 'nature' and 'culture', were, however, initially borrowed uncritically by anthropologists. In 1974, Ortner revealed some of the political implications of such dualisms. Her analysis, a direct extension of Lévi-Straussian structuralism, focused on procreation to locate women within the nature/culture dichotomy. Women were identified with 'nature' and consigned to the 'cultural' control of men. By investigating the asymmetry of these dichotomies, Ortner drew attention to the 'naturalization' of dominance. Since then, anthropological studies of gender have moved on; as we shall see, much writing in the genre of men's studies has not.

On another tack, Brod announces that he 'would like to begin a sketch of a distinctive men's studies socialist feminist analysis of capitalist masculinity' (1987: 13). Again, his very statement reveals the anachronism of his position. In anthropological studies of gender, Sacks' return to Engel's *The Origin of the Family, Private Property and the State* (1974) marked the beginning of sophisticated materialist analyses. In this work, the origins of sexual asymmetry, patriarchy and the objectification of women were associated with the emergence of social hierarchies based on the control of private property (cf. Etienne and Leacock 1980). Subsequent neo-Marxian and socialist feminist studies have ranged from those about domestic labour (cf. Molyneux 1979) through production and reproduction (cf. Edholm *et al.* 1977; Young *et al.* 1981) to gendered aspects of the international economy (cf. Elson and Pearson 1981; Mies *et al.* 1988). Writing in 1987, Brod's conflation of the many different stances within socialist feminism simply is not credible.

So, what exactly is distinctive about Brod's approach? Two things stand out. First, he is asking questions as a male, a fact which he celebrates. Secondly, he implies that only what he terms 'New Men's Studies' can offer a necessary corrective to the 'female bias' in work on feminist-inspired topics, such as violence, parenting, health and sexuality. However, we might be forgiven for wondering about the nature of this 'corrective' when Brod, writing about male violence, emphasizes militarism rather than rape or battery; or when he discusses the subject of pornography, we hear virtually nothing about the multiple forms of violence this entails: Dworkin's work (1981) is not mentioned, yet we learn of pornography's toll on men. For Brod, redressing the female bias in gender studies requires a new discipline. He writes, 'Only men's studies can provide the requisite systematically focused study of masculinities' (Brod 1987: 275). In effect, Brod is arguing that 'it takes one to know one'. We would ask how such privileged exclusion can be justified as social science.

Ortner's (1974) use of the nature/culture dichotomy in anthropology prefigured a number of later developments within feminism, such as the move to reclaim and revalue the essential 'feminine'. The latter involves a shift from the politics of equality to a variant of the politics of difference which focused on women's 'irrationalism' and 'naturalness'. Within men's studies (and in popular books such as that by Bly), there has been a similar move to reclaim the 'natural', from which, it is argued, men have excluded themselves.

Seidler, a sociologist and prolific contributor to the debates in men's studies in Britain, is far more sensitive to the issues of power than is Brod. Seidler (1991a) has described the objectives of the men's groups of the 1970s as being less concerned with validating the legitimacy of men's experiences than with addressing gendered inequalities by finding new, 'non-sexist' models of behaviour. Certainly, there can be no doubt about the relief some men feel at now being able to participate in feminist debates (cf. Hearn 1992).

Seidler elsewhere (e.g. 1991b) draws on feminist work to situate the nature/culture dichotomy within the rationalist tradition of the Enlightenment and argues that masculinity came to be associated with reason and the mastery of both the 'natural' and the emotional. Yet, rather than dispense with these dichotomies as fundamentally flawed, Seidler, like Brod, seeks to redeploy them in reverse. Thus men are urged to engage with their emotions and somatic selves and to come to terms with their feelings and desires. There is, sadly, a misplaced optimism in Seidler's position: he seems to presume that by revaluing the personal, political change will follow.

The nature/culture dichotomy which Ortner used to explain the subordination of women was complemented by Rosaldo's discussion of another dichotomy, that between the private or domestic and public domains (1974). Women were located in domestic settings, while the association with men and public culture was also seen to define 'society' generally as masculine. This presumed division became influential in studies which sought to compare men's and women's differential scope for controlling resources. Rosaldo's work was an important stimulus for further ethnographic studies because it required that all social arenas be investigated for their political entailments. From her work, and that of others (e.g. Nelson 1974), came the insight that informal political and economic processes can remain invisible in accounts which examine the public or formal sites of resource allocation.

The narrow association of women with domestic and men with public spheres was soon discarded by anthropologists because of its misleading simplifications about the nature of gendered power and the household as gendered space (cf. Harris 1981; La Fontaine 1981). However, the private/public dichotomy, like that of nature/culture, has recently been reinstated *in reverse* within men's studies. For instance, there are now many accounts which conflate 'the domestic' with men's involvement in parenting (see, for example, the section on 'Men in Domestic Settings' in Kimmel's edited volume, *Changing Men*, 1987). These fail to explore the interesting questions which are raised by locating men from the perspective of the household (Foxhall, Chapter 7 in this volume), considering the specific masculinities which are discursively aligned with domestic domains (Loizos, Chapter 3 in this volume; Shire, Chapter 8), or examining how masculinities change over the life course of an individual (a topic treated in various ways by all our ethnographies).

But perhaps the reduction of 'the domestic' to parenting is not accidental. In the men's studies literature, there is some discussion of gay men as parents, most of which is heterosexist in its assumptions. More often, however, reproduction is presented as a curiously sexless activity. This literature tends to take for granted the association between active (hetero-sexuality (versus celibacy), potency (versus impotence) and virility (versus sterility); here as in popular formulations, a macho man is also one with a high sperm count (cf. Highfield 1992)! So, for example, Brod criticizes studies of parenting for not examining how men's public roles affect their private fathering activities (1987: 42), but his emphasis hides other considerations. As Segal puts it, men have been allowed to 'retain power in the public sphere while having access to the satisfactions (often without the frustrations) of family life' (1990: 1; cf. 46–9).

The experiential and psychological aspects of male parenthood loom large in popular and academic discussions of masculinity. It is notable that feminist rhetoric is used to secure 'fair play' for men while patently disregarding wider questions of power. Brod calls attention to the female biases in research on reproductive health, but he fails to mention other relevant issues: for example, the fact that various attempts at developing a 'male pill' were arrested at early stages when men began to display symptoms, such as depression or loss of libido, which are accepted as 'normal' for female users of oral contraceptives. Or, in a similar vein, 'Motivations of abortion clinic waiting room males: "bottled-up" roles and unmet needs' by Shostak (1987) presents a 'male partner's bill of rights' based on *Ms* magazine's (1984) 'pregnant woman's bill of rights'. Yet, unsurprisingly, Shostak fails to report on the 'expectant fathers' who have no contact with the abortion clinic and perhaps deny all responsibility for the pregnancy in the first place. However, the domain of pregnancy and birth, already controlled and made an object of specialist knowledge by male-dominated obstetrics (Martin 1987), is another recent enthusiasm among 'new men' and in the men's studies literature. As Stolcke has remarked, it may be a case of 'new reproductive technologies, same old fatherhood' (1986).

In the men's studies literature, the interest in male parenting is paralleled by a focus on the acquisition of 'sex roles'. Again, the theories which find favour are those which were prominent in the early days of women's studies. Chodorow's neo-Freudian work (1974) on the origins of female subordination depends on a universalized assumption that female and male children experience fundamentally different relations of mothering, related to the psychological dispositions of women as carers and men as controllers. As Kandiyoti writes,[4]

Object-relations theories express a serious preoccupation with the pre-Oedipal process of separation of the psychically undifferentiated child from the primary caretaker, who is usually the mother. They argue that gender differences are created relationally in the process of this separation. This opens up the possibility of discussing how gender differences are produced in different relational contexts and are thus amenable to transformation and historical change. However, the question of difference *within* the same gender category is dismissed as less problematic than those *between* gender categories (see, for example, Chodorow 1978: 4). One cannot escape the conclusion that differences based on class, race, sexual preferences and so on are somehow less constitutive of the human subject than gender difference and are somehow 'added on' to the psychological bedrock represented by the latter. So despite the implicit recognition that different organizations of the family and society should yield different patternings of the psyche, the fear of falling into 'sociologism' prevents most theorists from stating more the *potential* of their theory to integrate the social.

For these reasons Chodorow's approach has been widely criticized within anthropology as reductionist and Eurocentric. It posits fixed notions of identity and, more crucially, it cannot account for what has been called 'structural disadvantage' (cf. Kandiyoti, Chapter 12 in this volume). However, it has gained considerable currency in the popular literature. Chodorow has the distinction of being cited as one of the major feminist sources in men's studies in the USA (Brod 1987: 13) and has been cited in Britain by Seidler (1987), among others, while the anthropologists Herdt (1981, 1984), Brandes (1980) and Gilmore (1990) adopt neo-Freudian approaches to explain the development of masculine identities.

The recent US literature on men by men also draws on social and developmental psychology. The emphasis is placed on men as individuals, on their 'roles' and on 'male identity'. Rather than subjecting the notion of 'sex roles' to the thoroughgoing critique current social theory would demand, the quest, as Pleck puts it, seems to be for 'new paradigms in the study of sex roles that are more relevant to the need of contemporary society' (1987: 38). Reformulations of role theory, far from undermining hegemonic forms of masculinity, merely recast them in another guise. The expansive literature on therapy is instrumental in this process, presenting the 'wounded male' who needs to be 'healed' and bemoaning the 'hazards' of male privilege. Indeed, interest seems to be less in men's studies than in 'new men'.

In his later work, Seidler (1991b) argues for the urgent need to consider issues of agency. His critique of the dominant paradigms within men's studies reveals their repeated failure to engage with questions raised by feminists. Like Seidler, others in Britain, such as Hearn and Morgan (1990a) and Porter (1992), also make deliberate efforts to include feminist precedents – and feminist voices – in their overview of possible directions for men's studies. And, as we have seen, Connell (1987) and Brittan (1989) have offered critical insights and made substantive contributions to the sociology of masculinity.

Yet these studies too fail to raise some of the most basic questions anthropologists would ask about masculinity.

In appropriating the personal, there has been a tendency to forget the political and ignore the vested interest many men have in resisting change. It is ominous that in much of the men's studies literature the category 'men' continues to be treated in an essentialist manner. Consider, for example, Kimmel writing of 'non-sexist sex': 'safer-sex programmes encourage men to stop having sex like men . . . [others] are men who, like all real men, have taken risks . . . sex is about danger, risk and excitement' (1990: 107–8). Note how Kimmel both celebrates that spurious category, 'real men', and insinuates a version of macho masculinity into his outrageous statement. Kimmel's presentation of a hegemonic masculinity in a scholarly guise should be a matter of concern. Elsewhere he has written,

> Inspired by the academic breakthroughs of women's studies, men's studies addresses similar questions to the study of men and masculinity. Men's studies seeks neither to replace or supplant women's studies; quite the contrary. Men's studies seeks to *buttress*, to *augment* women's studies, to *complete* the radically redrawn portrait of gender that women's studies has begun.
>
> (1987: 10, our emphasis)

It is impossible to resist asking: what portrait of gender is men's studies creating? As Canaan and Griffin make clear, the issues at stake in the development of men's studies as a discipline go beyond the question of theory to address those of academic privilege. Kimmel's telling choice of metaphors supports their contention that men's studies may be 'part of the problem rather than part of the solution' (1990: 214).

GENDERING THE BODY

The pervasive use of paired oppositions within the anthropology of women of the 1970s derived in large part from the influence of structuralism. Such usage privileged idealized versions of gendered difference and implied that 'men' and 'women' are natural objects rather than cultural constructions. Even more fundamentally, it begged awkward questions about the presumed dichotomy 'male' and 'female'. An alternative perspective seems far more appropriate: that biology itself is a cultural construction and that the link between a sexed body and a gendered individual is not necessary but contingent.

Rubin's (1975) contribution to the nascent anthropology of gender attempted to dislodge the 'naturalized' biological notions embedded in western discourses on sexual difference. In a devastating critique of psychoanalysis and structuralism – two major theoretical strands running through mainstream anthropology – Rubin demonstrated their congruence as 'in one sense the most sophisticated ideologies of sexism around' (1975: 200). Focusing on what she termed the 'sex–gender system', Rubin brought the term 'gender' into contemporary use, arguing that,

> gender is a socially imposed division of the sexes [which transforms] males and females into 'men' and 'women', each an incomplete half which can only find wholeness when united with each other . . . from the standpoint of nature, men and women are closer to each other than either to it or to anything else. The idea that men and women are two mutually exclusive categories must arise out of something other than a nonexistent 'natural' opposition. Far from this being an expression of natural differences, exclusive gender identity is the suppression of natural similarities.
>
> (1975: 80)

The theoretical eclecticism of Rubin's important early article anticipated many of the questions raised by recent work in the anthropology of gender (such as Strathern 1988) and the wider debates surrounding postmodernism. But Rubin was, in a sense, writing before her time.

In the decade after Rubin's comments, constructionist theories of gender found favour with anthropologists. Once gender came to signify the socially 'constructed' parts played by men and women, another version of the nature/culture dichotomy took centre stage, yet its antecedents were already well rehearsed. Ideas about the socialization of the individual had been prominent in the psychological and sociological literature since the 1930s, and equally, cross-cultural applications of such universalist theories have had a long history in anthropology and, even now, retain their hold on men's studies.

In both socialization and constructionist theories, there is a paradox. While the social construction of gender categories is carefully described in terms of particularities, the very notion of 'gender categories' usually presupposes an incontrovertible gender dichotomy, which in turn rests on notions of essential biological difference. So, we are left with the cultural construct 'gender' and the notion of biological 'sex'. Thus, while the nature/culture dichotomy has been shown to be culturally specific, the dichotomy itself has, in effect, merely been restated in a different form. Cultural and historical specificity has been laid on to presupposed biological universals – male and female bodies.

There are five basic problems with the constructionist position. The first is that these arguments leave us with the dichotomous categories 'men' and 'women'. Secondly, they assume that there are unitary, but unformed, individuals. Once children are given a gender label as either 'male' or 'female', it is presumed that this monolithic identity adheres throughout their lives. In such arguments, people are socialized into sex/gender roles and they play them more or less well thereafter. Thirdly, though the constructionist position explicitly seeks to distance itself from considering the sexing of the body (on the grounds that this will inevitably lapse into a form of biological essentialism), this discourages investigations of how the body itself is socially constructed. Fourthly, by locating gender constructs in terms of the unitary person, constructionism affirms deeply embedded western biases in favour of the individual and the 'commodity logic' that implies: that in some contexts people people are understood and treated as if they are things (cf. Strathern 1988; and see below). Fifthly, relations between men and women are seen in terms of the interaction of fixed, polarized entities. This obscures the extent to which attributes associated with men and women in any particular setting overlap and are mutually constructed.

Many of the more important recent anthropological studies of gender are constructionist in their emphases, and several of the five basic issues mentioned above are never seriously addressed. 'Sex', in the physiological sense, is distinguished from 'gender', which is seen as cultural and learned in a specific setting. However, to cast the construction of 'sex' and 'gender' in these terms is, as Gatens notes, both confused and confusing. Gatens challenges the constructionist position and its association with the politics of gender equality, and shows that 'the apparent simplicity of the ahistorical and theoretically naive solution' (1983: 144) of constructionism is a further variant of western dualisms.

In some cases the constructionism is crude, as when Shore distinguishes: (1) 'reproductive sexuality', which he limits to the 'biological and reproductive aspects of sexual dimorphism', from (2) 'psychological sexuality', by which he means the 'psychological and subjective aspects of sexual identity', and (3) the domain of 'gender', which includes the whole range of cultural experience (1981: 194). In other cases the constructionism is less apparent. The following comment by Geertz is challenging and it is not immediately evident that his use of the word '*inter*sexuality' (that is, implicitly between *two* sexes) subverts his intention:

> Gender in human beings is not a purely dichotomous variable. It is not an evenly continuous one either, of course, or our love life would be even more complicated than it already is. [This raises] certain problems for common sense, for the network of practical and moral conceptions woven about those supposedly most rooted of root realities: maleness and femaleness. Intersexuality is more than an empirical surprise; it is a cultural challenge. . . . If received ideas of 'the normal and natural' are to be kept intact, something must be said about [the] rather spectacular disaccordances with them.
>
> (1983: 81)

So pervasive is the dichotomy between 'male' and 'female' in western discourse that anthropological attempts to describe the complexities of certain gendered behaviours have foundered on measures which re-create the dichotomy in an intermediate form. Thus, for example, the proposal by Wikan (1977) that Omani transvestites be regarded as a 'third', intermediate, gender occludes many of the most interesting issues (cf. Cornwall, Chapter 6 in this volume).

As Kaplan and Rogers (1990) note, there is today much evidence of how biological research has focused on sexual diamorphism *in response to* the cultural importance of this dichotomy. New research points away from the polarization of 'male' and 'female' whether in terms of anatomy, hormonal physiology or sexual attraction. As Cornwall reports (Chapter 6 in this volume), Kessler and McKenna's study (1978) suggests the extent to which western distinctions privilege the presence of male genitalia in categorizing the two 'sexes' on which two 'genders' are culturally elaborated. The definition of what is 'male' by the possession or absence of the penis is, they argue, no cultural universal. However, in the west the rhetoric of hegemonic masculinity, and its association with male privilege, often makes the link appear direct (that is, referential); cf. Sanders' excellent study (1991) of a similar process revealed in the gendering of hermaphrodites by medieval Islamic jurists. As Cornwall's work (Chapter 6) illustrates, the possession of an (anatomical) penis may only be contingently linked with attributions of maleness. Not only 'being a man' but 'being male' can be interpreted differently in different situations.

Though Foucault's theories are in essence constructionalist – he describes the different ways in which gender is attributed to human beings in specific historical and cultural contexts – he makes clear in *Discipline and Punish* (1977) that the body is not a biological given. For Foucault, bodies are the sites of resistance and of power over others. He notes that the inscription of power on bodies is a direct, material process which functions through the disciplinary procedures and self-regulation of everyday life: work and rest, diet, dress and sexual mores. Such processes make bodies into *particular* kinds of body. They are rendered social through ethnic or other markers, physiological through surface and metabolic transformations, and psychical through moral dispositions and experiences of pain and pleasure. There are no neutral or 'natural' anatomical bodies. Rather, historical and cultural specificity is *incarnated* through individual, embodied agents who construct social narratives by acting on and reacting to others. In Stoller's words, 'anatomy is not really destiny; destiny comes from what people make of anatomy' (1976: 293). And of course anatomy tells us little about sexual practice; and it tells us less about desire or the ways sexual fantasies or cultural styles may be construed within a single setting or cross-culturally.

We argue that there is no 'natural', nor necessary, connection between men and masculinity. However, this does not mean that this relationship is completely arbitrary. In any particular context, cultural idioms and history define the categories through which gender is embodied. As Grosz has written,

Masculine and feminine are necessarily related to the structure of lived experience and meaning of *bodies*. As Gatens argues in her critique of the sex/gender distinction (1983), masculinity and femininity mean *different things* according to whether they are lived out in and experienced by male or female bodies. Gender is an effect of the body's social morphology. What is mapped onto the body is not unaffected by the body onto which it is projected.

(Grosz 1990: 73–4; cf. Butler 1990)

Conversely, the body itself may be affected by what is mapped on it: thus, for instance, the ascription of masculine traits to female sexed bodies may have a variety of implications. However, these implications cannot be assumed. It is wiser to consider gendered styles and manners, desire and sexual behaviour as separate issues. Then what becomes instructive is the way different kinds of body are valued: as Forrest's 'muscle queens' (Chapter 5 in this volume) and Shire's account of young boys' operations on their penises (Chapter 8) show, different styles of maleness can be *made* through deliberately altering the body. And, as Kandiyoti discusses with respect to the fireman of Ottoman Istanbul (Chapter 12 in this volume), a particular masculine style may be admired in quite different ways by younger or older men or by women. And we must also remember that masculinities are *performed* or *enacted* in specific settings: in the gymnasia of ancient Greece (Foxhall, Chapter 7 in this volume), or contemporary gyms (Forrest, Chapter 5), playing scoccer at a mission school (Kanitkar, Chapter 11) or playing basketball at a youth club in south London (Back, Chapter 10).

There are two important points here: first, sex cannot be accorded any direct (referential) character; and, second, though in any particular setting there would seem to be a contingent (indexical) relationship between the gendering of individuals and the sexing of bodies, this relationship is in no sense fixed. In short, we would emphasize the importance of Gatens' insistence on taking a critical view of *the alleged neutrality of the body*, 'the postulated arbitrary connection between femininity and the female body, masculinity and the male body' (1983: 144). Compare Zita (1992) on 'male lesbians' with Clements' remarks on the butch's masculinity 'which within a lesbian relationship is actually contextualized and resignified in a butch identity by the fact that this particular "masculinity" is *juxtaposed against a culturally intelligible female body*. The lesbian butch's sexual identity represents not just a superimposed masculine identity or merely a de-contextualized female body but the destabilization of both terms as they come into erotic interplay' (1993: 26).

In *The Gender of the Gift* (1988) Strathern offers a theory of embodiment which unseats conventional definitional certainties and tackles the problem of how gendered difference is produced and experienced in social transactions and discourse. Not only does she offer many new insights into how such processes may occur, but she reinforces ethnographically the feminist philosophers' insistence that there can be no simple correspondence between sexed bodies and male and female perspectives. We discuss some of Strathern's arguments in greater detail below. However, the breadth and coherence of her position is such that her arguments must be understood within the wider context of postmodernism.

POSTMODERNISM AND THE POLITICS OF GENDER

By exposing the partial perspective of every commentator, postmodernist writing unseats both the certainties of feminism as a political project and the notional objectivity, and authority, of the anthropological observer.

The move to recognize the existence of multiple perspectives and their political and material implications resonated with feminist critiques of male bias within western social and natural science.[5] More recently, however, the politics of difference within feminism have led to the rejection of the category 'women' as untenably essentialist, and feminist political positions have tended to come unstuck (cf. McElhinny, Chapter 9 in this volume).

For anthropology, recent postmodernist critiques have also had far-reaching and often uncomfortable consequences. They have forced anthropologists to re-examine their basic premises, to focus on the experience of the ethnographer and the implications of descriptions of the 'other' in ethnographic writing. This has raised a number of awkward political questions. Ethnography has served the interests of colonialism and created unequal 'others'. The language which anthropologists have used to construct their 'other worlds' has lent a distinctive western flavour to their accounts. It has also imposed anthropologists' 'ways of reasoning' and created a standard against which others have often been judged and found lacking.[6]

A further, and more unsettling, thrust of the postmodernist challenge has been to dismantle the certainties upon which western theory has rested. Notions of Truth, Reason and, indeed, Philosophy (Rorty 1979) have been shown to be products of a particular phase in western thought. Lyotard, a principal commentator on what he terms *The Postmodern Condition* (1984), describes large-scale theories which purport to provide general explanations of social relations as 'grand narratives of legitimation'. Such theories, he argues, have been put forward as if they existed outside the specific historical and social contexts in which they were formulated. They purport to generate 'truths' about the human condition, but in fact they fail to embrace the complexity of local conditions.

Lyotard's argument echoes recent challenges which have been posed within feminism. Earlier feminism had a very singular and exclusive focus on the oppression of women by men. The white, middle-class voices which were raised in protest spoke for 'everywoman'. This effectively silenced marginal and/or dissenting voices, denying different sexual orientations and identities as well as the experience of other forms of oppression.[7] As with anthropology, early feminist writings were criticized for replicating colonial discourses. There has been a move from a singular notion of 'feminism' to an understanding that we need to talk of multiple, situated 'feminisms' (deLauretis 1986).

This shift has led to an appreciation of identities as multiple, contested, and at times contradictory.

Postmodernism has the effect of making all explanations relative. Everything becomes a matter of perspective; and perspectives change with scale and context (Strathern 1991). Thus, theories which rely on notions such as 'culture', 'class', 'race' and 'gender' become problematic because they depend on ascribing essences, or essential attributes, to members of the categories they create. Category creation itself is an act of power.

We have seen how oppositions like 'men' and 'women' are such essentialist categories, while assertions of gender difference tie us to particular political positions (di Stefano 1990). Butler (1990), taking a radical stance on this issue, argues that the very notions of 'men' and 'women', as one of many oppressive binaries, are regulative ideals which produce inequalities. She argues, following Foucault, that we must transcend the notion of a gender difference itself. Butler contends,

> Gender ought not to be construed as a stable identity or locus of agency from which various acts follow; rather, gender is an identity tenuously constituted in time, instituted in an exterior space through *a stylised repetition of acts*.
>
> (1990: 140)

However, Butler is neither very curious about the possible cross-cultural applications of her proposal, nor greatly concerned about the *processes* whereby hegemonic masculinities such as we have described naturalize inequality.

TAKING APART MASCULINITY

Foucault's situational understanding of power, coupled with Scott's methods for exploring resistance, open up new possibilities for understanding of masculinities. Strathern's radical critique of western analyses of gender in *The Gender of the Gift* (1988) dislocates further the male bias and Eurocentrisms which are inevitably present in anthropological discussions.

For Strathern, gender is an open-ended category, one based on Wittgenstein's idea of 'family resemblances'. Gender is understood as the 'categorization of persons, artifacts, events [and] sequences ... which draw upon sexual imagery [and] make concrete people's ideas about the nature of social relationships' (1988: ix). While it seems that the use of sexual imagery is common to human beings everywhere, as we have seen, neither the character of such images nor their relation to social experience are fixed or universal. Within any local setting, sexual images are only one among many sets of metaphors of identity and their use is both unpredictable *a priori* and ever-changing from the point of view of those who use them.

Strathern's argument focuses on how gender difference itself is constructed by considering local discourses of agency, causation, personhood and identity. From this perspective, 'idealized masculinity is not necessarily just about men; it is not necessarily just about relations between the sexes either' (Strathern 1988: 65). Rather, it is part of a system for producing difference.

Strathern argues that a corollary of the historical ambition of anthropologists to study bounded coummunities is their focus on the bounded person who is socialized to play particular 'roles' in adulthood. Strathern offers a far more interesting approach. She argues that agents are differently constructed in different cultural settings and uses Marriott's notion of the 'dividual' to ask new questions about how human beings are gendered.

> To exist, dividual persons absorb heterogeneous material influences. They must also give out from themselves particles of their own coded substances – essences, residues, or other active influences – that may then reproduce in others something of the nature of the persons in whom they have originated.
> (Marriott 1976: 111, quoted in Strathern 1988: 348)

How are people understood to be internally differentiated? What are the qualities which may be attached to, or incorporated by, persons and which may be exchanged with others? How do people dispose of parts of themselves in relation to other people?

The idea of 'dividual' people treats human beings as having permeable, changing boundaries and experiencing constant movement between different aspects of social life. Strathern argues that gender is one way such movement, and the plural, divisible and ever-changing elements on which it depends, is conceptualized. In so doing, she points to a far more subtle idea of personhood than most western theories allow and provides a way of thinking about difference which does not immediately collapse into dualism. She argues, 'Being "male" or being "female" emerges as a holistic unitary state only in particular circumstances . . . each male or female form may be regarded as containing within it a suppressed, composite identity' (1988: 14–15). There are many ways in which persons experience themselves and others as 'dividuals', but these remain largely unmarked because of the western emphasis on the unitary person and propensity for 'commodity logic'.

Strathern argues that it is commodity logic which disposes us to be fascinated by the attributes of things and to locate possession, ownership, control and ideas of power in a one-to-one relation between discrete attributes and the unitary individual (1988: 338).[8] In terms of the relation between attributes and persons, we are sometimes explicitly aware of the extent to which people become part-objects in social exchanges. The anthropological literature on brideprice and dowries, or on institutions such as slavery, addresses such questions directly. However, commodification is only one logic of partibility and exchange.

To take a few simple examples, consider the 'dividuals' described in the lyrics of the following popular songs. The title 'My heart belongs to Daddy' is an example of commodity logic and a predilection for construing possession through metonymy, while 'Take another little piece of my heart, baby' depends on a notion of partibility. Other song titles suggest quite other ways personhood can be experienced and transformed through interactions with others: thus, 'I've left my heart in San Francisco', 'I've got you under my skin' and 'I'm gonna wash that man right out of my hair'. However, the emphasis on bounded individuals is so strong that the alternative images of personhood such lyrics imply are usually ignored.

Of course some radical images of gendering are meant not to be ignored: as in 'Man enough to be a woman'! Among these examples perhaps the most interesting are the following soul titles. 'Your love has made me a man' carries western notions of love as a thing to be possessed and exchanged, but the *mechanics* of the transformative properties of love invite new questions about partibility and agency. In the title, 'That man has made a woman out of me', the man who makes a woman – *who is a producer of gendered difference* – does so in terms of particular idioms, which also define his masculinity *and* the inferior masculinities of men who are unable to effect such an apparently magical feat.

Strathern offers insights into just such transformative aspects of gendering and uses the notion of 'impingement' to discuss the effects people may have on each other. This broad notion has much to recommend it: it is descriptive and, unlike 'power', is automatically associated neither with men nor with social dominance. Moreover, it can be used to describe aspects of any social transaction; it is a subtle way of talking about social efficacy. Strathern focuses on agency and on the revelation of potentials, enablement and knowledges. Her use of the idea of the divisible person and her related theory of interaction are compelling: they raise many new questions which can be asked ethnographically.

By emphasizing local understandings of gendered essences and the partible bits of people (scents, tastes, touch, thoughts, emotions; substances such as breast-milk and semen; and psychic, somatic and material conditions of well-being and misfortune) which may transform and be transformed through interaction, Strathern addresses directly questions of the *production* of representations of gendered difference (cf. Braidotti 1992: 187ff.). This opens up an investigation of 'the respective powers or influence that each sex possesses' (Strathern 1988: 68). Three brief examples from our ethnographies illustrate cases which can usefully be described in terms of impingement and the mutual construction of gendered identities. Thus, Shire (Chapter 8 in this volume) describes how boys fear they may grow breasts if they spend too much time in the female terrain of the kitchen, and he explains why men 'can't go to the moon'. The female sex-workers in Alicante consider that by helping men to lose their virginity in 'an appropriate manner', it is they who teach men 'to be men' (Hart, Chapter 2 in this volume). Elsewhere, as Lindisfarne describes (Chapter 4 in this volume), the idea of a female virgin's defloration by penetrative sex is so crucial to 'being a man' that the illusion of virginity is often maintained by trickery.

Impingement is a useful idea because it does not prejudge relations of power in any particular case. However, questions of hegemonic masculinity and masculized power cannot simply be dismissed. As Overing (1986) and others have written, westerners find it virtually impossible not to regard the sexes in a permanent relation of asymmetry. Combined with perceptions of coercion and collective action, gender asymmetry can create a potent image of domination (Strathern 1988: 330). However, such an image is less compelling if it is located in the political economy which produces it. Moreover, assumptions of difference or symmetry are never simple: an overt ideology of inequality between the sexes, or between class or racial groups, will necessarily conceal the combination of their labours. In such cases, structures of mutual dependence are likely to be at odds with hegemonic ideals. The stereotypes of subordinates as dangerous or loathsome – as in the case of the alleged chaotic and voracious sexuality of Middle Eastern women (Lindisfarne, Chapter 4 in this volume) or in the 'fear and desire' couplet associated with racism (Back, Chapter 10 in this volume) – help to naturalize 'inferiority' and may in part be internalized by the subordinates themselves.

Yet the opposite can also hold true: from images of gender equality, concepts of inequality can be fashioned (Strathern 1988: 143), as in the case of institutions which distinguish people as 'separate but equal': compare, for example, Forrest's discussion of the gay community (Chapter 5 in this volume) with Kandiyoti's description of aspects of sexual segregation in the Middle East (Chapter 12 in this volume).

Strathern uses the notion of 'replication' to talk about the collective character of relationships among people of the same sex. In experiences of replication, she insists that the excluded sex is always there by implication. Thus, if activities are locally interpreted as the arena of one sex, the other sex is there as cause. Otherwise, it is present in artifacts (as Shire shows in terms of weaponry and paraphernalia, Chapter 8 in this volume) or even in those parts of the body which embody the other sex (Strathern 1988: 121), as in the case of the *travestis* (Cornwall, Chapter 6 in this volume), or which only exist to be transformed by the other sex, as is the case of the virgin's hymen (Lindisfarne, Chapter 4).

In short, gendered identities are necessarily constructed with reference to others who are represented as different and/or dominated. Equally clearly, agents do not create asymmetry, but enact it by adopting relative, momentary and provisional positions (Strathern 1988: 333–4). But, if this is the case, how then can we understand those situations which are experienced and described in terms of domination?[9]

As we have mentioned above, Strathern argues that every action is inherently forceful – an act of domination (1988: 327). We know too that the meaning of specific interactions must be located in the interpretations of the actors, subjects and their audiences. We have argued that hegemonic ideologies frame experiences of subordination, but they do not completely define them. Rather, gendered difference and inequality are negotiated and recreated *more or less* in repeated interactions, but no interaction is identical.

Investigations which focus on embodied interaction and impingement can also allow for explanations in terms of negotiation of interpretations. And it is also possible to investigate how the accumulation of experience can introduce new social forms and meanings into apparently conventional situations: hegemonic ideologies and their subordinate variants change over time. We return to our conviction that ethnographic descriptions of masculinity need to be located squarely with respect to contested inter-pretations of power.

LOCATING MASCULINITIES

The relativism of postmodern thinking, which precludes the possibility of a centred position from which to articulate moral judgements, can be as apolitical as early feminism was politically extreme in its ideas of male domination. For anthropologists and others whose aim is to describe the complexity of people's everyday lives, the contemporary problem is to discover a convincing theoretical basis for addressing the relation between the two positions.

In one sense, this is easy, because the contrast between the two positions has been overdrawn, not least because their respective proponents have often themselves seemed disembodied and their social backgrounds and political interests ignored. Thus, contrary to what McNay, writing on Foucault, suggests,[10] the problem is not about establishing 'basic norms, which serve as a safeguard against the abuse of power and the domination of weaker individuals'(1992: 8). Rather, the problem lies in not being sufficiently alert to the fact that ethical positions are *always* enunciated by individuals with particular social identities and material interests. And it is about being willing to engage with the consequent political entailments.

As we have suggested, the political questions about representation – who speaks for whom in what contexts – have been central to recent debates in both feminism and anthropology. In this respect, it is crucial to be aware that difference 'is not simply difference as distinction but rather that difference is infused with hierarchies of power' (MacKey 1991: 2). MacKey's 'revised politics of location' offers a way out of the ethnical impasse of post-modernism. Following Mohanty, a first step is for each individual to define 'the historical, geographic, cultural, psychic and imaginative boundaries which provide the ground for political definition and self-definition' (Mohanty 1987: 31, cited in MacKey 1991: 6). The second is to become critically aware of the relation between experience, identity and political perspective (MacKey 1991: 12). Clearly, this relation is redrawn and emerges afresh through every social interaction. Such an awareness allows each person to explore complex, overlapping, and intersecting encounters and relations of difference, and 'it avoids and transcends the easy and destructive polarization of victims and perpetrators' (MacKey 1991: 14). MacKey ends her excellent paper by asking 'whether or not some of these insights can be applied directly to anthropology' (1991: 15). Our answer is 'yes', and we would argue that it is directly relevant to the study of masculinity.

Three further steps are needed to link a feminist politics of location and anthropological studies of masculinity (cf. Lindisfarne-Tapper 1991). First, it is important to accept the postmodern challenge and relinquish any remaining pretext to objectivity and its attendant, and static, essentialisms.

Secondly, if the distinguishing feature of anthropological method is participant observation, then this must play an *explicit* part in the formation of a political voice. If we think of our everyday lives as a kind of fieldwork experience, the lesson is clear. Just as all anthropologists are gendered in the field, so too are they politicized: who talks to the anthropologist, and whose points of view does the anthropologist learn to share? Through the process of fieldwork itself, gendered political identities from 'home' are relocated through interaction in the field. And, after fieldwork, that process of politic- ization continues. We contend that by attending to this process, a responsible anthropological voice is created. Of course, it is a subjective, personal voice, but it is a voice through which individual anthropologists can describe the intersection of their past positions as gendered political agents, their gendered socialization in the field, and the ways they reposition themselves in later academic and other debates.

The third and most problematic step is producing knowledge about others. If anthropologists dare to speak personally, and thus automatically to speak for others whose points of view they have in part assimilated, it is crucial to ask who will listen and why. A critical understanding of the relation between the anthropologist's shifting gendered political identity and those of the audience is essential.

One aim of this volume is to disrupt hegemonic notions of gendered difference which are used in ways which disempower. People's everyday experiences of inequality, and differential access to resources, can be located politically without reintroducing ideas of essentialized, gendered 'whole persons'. Individuals embody many different subjectivities. Though hege- monic discourses of masculinity may suppress, they never totally censor, contradictory subjectivities. In focusing on the subordinate variants of hegemonic masculinities, we challenge the authority of hegemonic for- mations. Thus, we argue that a postmodern position – that there can be no single account of social life, only a multiplicity of interested perspectives – does not preclude moral judgements. We do not hope to provide definite answers to questions of gendering (there can be none), but to raise further questions and suggest new strategies for locating masculinities.

NOTES

1 As Braidotti, among others, has argued, Foucault's social philosophy as a whole is dominated by

> sexual-specific premises . . . which posit the primacy of masculine sexuality as a site of social and political power . . . [in his later work, he assigns] the sexes to precise roles, poles and functions, to the detriment of the feminine.
>
> (1990: 42)

See also Braidotti 1992; McNay 1992.

2 Scott's aim is to explore the character of resistance in extreme social settings: slave societies and concentration camps among others, though he acknowledges that

> the literature on gender-based domination and on working-class culture and ideology has proven insightful at many points. They share enough similarites to the cases I rely most heavily on to be suggestive. At the same time the differences limit the analogies that can be drawn.
>
> (1990: 22)

Scott seems to discount gender because of mistaken premises. First, he treats gender as if it has to do with women only, and, secondly, as if women's subordination is defined by experiences which are 'personal and intimate' (1990: 22). A third mistake seems to stem from his concern that women's lives are not sufficiently separate from those of men to allow them to develop forms of resistance, and, finally, he argues that it is too difficult to identify structures of resistance in situations where civil and political rights blur the picture (1990: 22). Scott's own reluctance to engage with questions of gender does not preclude others taking his argument in that direction.

3 There have, of course, been notable exceptions: see, for example, Brandes 1980; Herdt 1981, 1984; Herzfeld 1985; Loizos and Papataxiarchis 1991; and the excellent bibliography in Gilmore 1990.

4 The passages from Kandiyoti which we quote here, we have with her permission, pirated from her Chapter 12 in this volume. While Lacanian theories have had a considerable impact particularly among French feminists, they have received little attention in the men's studies canon (cf. Seidler 1991b). Again, in Kandiyoti's words,

> The Lacanian approach claims to provide an account of the constitution of the human subject and uses the Oedipal conflict and castration complex as a metaphor for the child's entry into human culture. This approach ultimately makes a preoccupation with concrete mothers and fathers seem rather trivial and irrelevant. Yet, even though all subjects are constituted through sexual difference, gender remains both totally fundamental and totally elusive (see, for example, Mitchell and Rose 1982: 2). Accounts of how exactly subjects are formed through their sexuality differ, while feminist positions on Lacan have ranged from endorsement to outright rejection. Whatever the position adopted,

to the extent that Lacan posits a historically invariant concept of human nature, he invites charges of essentialism.

5 See, for example Harding and Hintikka 1983; di Stefano 1990. Recent work in feminist theory has explored in detail some of the entailments of a radical postmodernist stance: see, for example, Butler 1990; Fraser and Nicholson 1988; Hodge 1989; Mascia-Lees *et al.* 1989; Nicholson 1990; Scott 1989; Weedon 1987.

6 On the implications of postmodernism for anthropology, see Clifford and Marcus 1986; Fardon 1990; Strathern 1992. Many anthropologists and others have written about anthropology's association with colonialism: see, for example, Asad 1975; Said 1978. On epistemologies, see, for example, Salmond 1982; Wolfram 1982; Hacking 1983.

7 See, for example, hooks 1982; Moraga and Anzaldua 1981; Mohanty 1991. Feminism has also been associated with colonialism: see Spivak 1981; Mohanty 1987b. Ramazanoğlu (1989) provides a useful introduction to the issues involved.

8 Strathern is happy to import Marriott's notion of the 'dividual' from India into her discussion of Melanesia. It is notable that Beteille has remarked that a notion of biological substantialism is not peculiar to traditional Hindu culture, but is even more in tune with modern capitalism (1990: 498, 450).

9 Strathern's move from the general notion of impingement to domination is a more difficult and problematic part of her argument. She writes that men have the advantage over women because 'a man sees his acts replicated and multiplied in the acts of like others': but then the consequences of this 'apparent' male domination of women must be tackled (1988: 327). It may well be that in Melanesia such domination does not stand for anything but repeated 'small personal encounters' through which a man manifests his strength by demonstrating a woman's weakness (1988: 327–8). However, if male dependence on a female 'other' is a 'precondition for acts of male excess' (1988: 336), much more needs to be said about the rhetoric of such excesses, their incidence and the compliance, or resistance, of women and other men who are thus forced into subordinate positions. Given the great detail of her work, it is somewhat paradoxical that one of the difficulties with Strathern's immensely innovative and instructive analysis of gender is that she leaves too little space for discussions of the negotiation of interpretations and explanations of historical change.

10 Thus, in *Foucault and Feminism* (1992) McNay writes of the problems of reconciling postmodernism with an ethnical position, noting that Foucault refused 'to outline the normative assumptions upon which [emancipatory social] change should be based' (1992: 8). But she herself seems to imply that such norms would be enunciated by individuals who were somehow free of particular social identities and interests.

Chapter 2

Missing masculinity?
Prostitutes' clients in Alicante, Spain

Angie Hart

In this paper I explore the meanings that different actors, in a particular ethnographic setting, attach to the notion of an individual who is at once a man and a prostitute's client. I consider the interdependency of the two terms, and how their relationship often verges on the parasitic, while each simultaneously pushes the boundaries of meaning of the other. This contested space for meaning relates to the potency of both concepts. Historically in western thought, the hegemony of discourses of men/'maleness' and of men/'clientness' are such that they are both often taken for granted and treated as synonymous rather than being openly articulated as men/maleness and men/clientness.

Maleness often hijacks personhood, thereby precluding the latter as a shared space for women and children. With clientness, the reverse process occurs. Textual and popular discourses of prostitution are generally negative discourses; not surprisingly, they are mostly discourses about women prostitutes. Precisely because of the hegemony of male/maleness discourses, (male) clientness is often given a privileged back seat, leaving women prostitutes up front with only the faintest whiff of an idea that clients exist as well.

Slowly, this situation is beginning to change. The occasional feminist voice speaks out, exposing clients (for example, McCleod 1982), or deconstructing 'masculinity', as in this volume. However, the general outlook is bleak. Anthropological and sociological studies of 'masculinity' bring the concept of 'maleness' to the fore; the paradox is that male discourses occupy a privileged status and 'masculinity' studies go some way towards reinforcing this. Some of them are critical, but many are not. And most texts on prostitution, when they mention clients, present them *en masse*, precluding a contextualized analysis of who these men are and where their responsibilities lie.

My chapter aims to redress this situation and examine men and/as clients in one particular setting. It points to the plurality of discourses regarding the notions 'man' and 'client'. Male selves are messier than many studies of 'masculinity' would like to acknowledge, and so too are client selves, often stereotyped and essentialized in texts on prostitution. There are, of course, no observable hegemonic discourses in this ethnographic setting. Patterns do emerge, but they are at once informed by powerful counter-patterns – hence discourses conflict.

THE ETHNOGRAPHIC CONTEXT

My ethnographic material was collected during 1990 and 1991 in a central neighbourhood in Alicante, a port on the east coast of Spain. Historically the area had been Alicante's main heterosexual prostitution site, although at the time of the fieldwork the numbers of male clients and female prostitutes going there were on the decline. The identity of the neighbourhood continued to be linked with people who, for parts of their lives, assumed the role of, and were categorized in, countless popular and professional discourses as marginal persons: clients of prostitutes, prostitutes, alcoholics, drug addicts and dealers, criminals, black Africans and gypsies among them.

Some of these people lived and worked in the area, whilst others came during the day to frequent the many bars or to hang around in the streets. Alicante's plain-clothes drug squad had a strong presence on foot in the neighbourhood, as did the local police, who regularly patrolled the area by car. Although soliciting, running a brothel and living off immoral earnings are technically illegal in Spain, the police turned a blind eye to all of these activities. Prostitution in the neighbourhood was characterized by a low level of education amongst the clients and workers, poor health and living conditions, low attendance at STD clinics, unsafe sex and infrequent condom usage, alcoholism and drug use. Although Spain is now a democratic country, most of the clients and prostitutes had spent thirty-six years of their lives under a dictatorship. Prostitution as an institution had undergone significant changes within their lifetimes, with the influence of the church decreasing and the tolerance of sexual expression increasing. This complex historical background cannot be explored in this chapter, but its salience must be emphasized (Capel Martinez 1986).

Male clients were mostly over the age of 45 and many were pensioners. The ages of the prostitutes working in the neighbourhood ranged from 30 to 62. Low prices attracted men from low socioeconomic groups, living in a variety of household arrangements, generally outside the neighbourhood. Some clients lived alone, others with a female partner (mostly within a marriage), whilst a number of widowed clients lived with family members. Most of the clientele were regulars. There was no coherent pattern to the frequency of their visits and many regulars had a sexual relationship with more than one prostitute.

I came to know clients and prostitutes through my collaboration with a Catholic charity centre in the neighbourhood run by Cáritas, the main Christian aid organization in Spain. After working from this centre for a few months, I was in a position to undertake 'participant observation' on the streets and in the bars.

MISSING MASCULINITY?

Anthropologists of Spain have produced a considerable literature concerning local conceptions of what it means to be a man. Most of this literature has concentrated on Andalusia and has been written by male anthropologists: see, for example, Brandes 1980; Driessen 1983: Gilmore 1987b; Gilmore and Gilmore 1979; Marvin 1984; Murphy 1983.

While they use the terms 'masculinity', 'maleness' and 'men', none of these authors critically examines these terms and all appear to have been writing in ignorance of intellectual debates about 'masculinity' that began in the 1970s and were grounded in feminist theory (e.g. Dubbert 1979; Friedman and Sarah 1982; Jackson 1990). Grappling with discussions of 'masculinity' by ethnographers of Spain renders the reader exasperated and bewildered, for they muddle up indigenous uses of the related terms *macho*, *machista*, *hombre*, *hombria* and *masculino* (for a critique, see Corbin and Corbin 1987: 167; de Piña Cabral 1989: 402). There are of course some regional differences in the use of lexical terms about men. However, if ethnographers are to discuss Spanish concepts using English words, some clarification is necessary.

Elsewhere, in sociology, some authors have attempted to ground their analyses in a rigorous consideration of this fundamental terminology (Brittan 1989; Chapman and Rutherford 1988; Segal 1990). That much of this writing is largely theoretical and could greatly benefit from anthropological input is a tragic irony. Anthropologists are beginning to realize only now that anthropology has a great deal to say about 'masculinity'. But can we absorb the wealth of literature on 'masculinity' and add something meaningful to it? Or is it too late? At a semantic level, I think that it *is* too late: throughout this chapter I avoid using the buzz-word 'masculinity' because it has been scarred with too many meanings to be of analytical use in a short paper. However, at a more general level it is *not* too late: indeed, anthropologists should have a lot to say about men. I explore the notion of 'being a man' through an examination of particular discourses of clientness, yet even the phrase 'being a man' has some unhelpful connotations. If we concentrate on 'being a man', we may become side-tracked into considering only ideals of male behaviour. Here 'being a man' is to be taken in terms of the Spanish *ser hombre*, to mean 'being a man' in a general sense, rather than in terms of ideals. In the neighbourhood there were many different ways of being a man, not just in relation to achieved status.

One of the most recent anthropological volumes dealing with what it takes to be a man is Gilmore's *Manhood in the Making* (1990). His quest is to find out how different cultures 'conceive and experience manhood, which I will define here simply as the approved way of being an adult male in a given society' (1990: 1). Gilmore travels on an ethnographic space and time machine from India to Ethiopia, Spain to Sri Lanka, in pursuit of his ideal men. Whilst commending Gilmore for undertaking such a hazardous and difficult mission, I am uneasy about the manner in which he accepts ethnographic accounts as 'the truth', as media for the voices of 'the people' of whichever particular culture he happens to be passing through. I also take issue with the manner in which he uncritically writes of what 'the people of *x* think about men', with little or no distinction between who these particular people are. Gilmore's mission led him in pursuit of harmonic integration. I suggest that no such telos exists, that Gilmore was chasing an illusion. Societies are messy; people are often contradictory and fragmented. Hegemonic discourses are teased and contested by wilful counter-discourses.

A further problem with Gilmore's work and with that of other ethnographers writing on 'manhood' concerns their focus on those aspects of 'manhood' that are supposedly perceived by 'the culture' to be positive and acceptable. This is an important point with regard to the politics of gender relations. If we are to concentrate on the positive and acceptable, there is little room even for indigenous criticisms of male behaviours. Such indigenous criticisms are often likely to be found in women's and children's discourses, and authors' ignorance of such counter-patterns continues the tendency in anthropology of privileging male experiences. Furthermore, authors who have concentrated on 'ideal images of manhood' have not acknowledged the manner in which such discourses of male selves have often, in a complex way, subsumed a discussion of female selves. Thus 'ideals' of manhood somehow become ideals of personhood – and nobody appears to have noticed.

I suggested above that the term 'masculinity' has suffered from overkill in Anglo-American sociological literature. In Spanish sociological literature, on the other hand, the term *masculinidad* has not been hijacked by 'progressive' gender theorists. Consequently the two terms cannot be directly translated; the one does not share the intellectual genealogy of the other. Furthermore, in the area where I conducted research, actors did not use the word *masculinidad*. It is a formal word, one that informants in Alicante would have been unfamiliar with. For me, it has specifically Anglo-American connotations, and has no place in this chapter.

In my fieldsite, informants used many different words to talk about men. In general they used the word *hombre* (man) and other 'synonyms' such as *tio* (bloke), *varón* (man/bloke) or, somewhat tongue in cheek, *chico* (boy/lad). *Macho* referred to an instinctive, animal aspect of male sexuality, rather than to the contrived image of strength to which it refers in British English. However, just as frequently, synonyms of 'person' were used to talk specifically about men. Moreover, notions of maleness were frequently tied up with notions of clientness. Before I consider their relationship, I locate the shaping of discourses of clientness in the relevant literature on prostitution.

GROSS GENERALIZATIONS?

Anglo-American sociologists writing on 'masculinity' insist on dragging 'men', warts and all, onto centre stage. Meanwhile, in studies of prostitution, the male central actors lurk timidly in the wings. Most Spanish and Anglo-American works – including popular film and fiction, theological 'family' guidance texts and 'deviance' studies, charity reports, and academic sociological studies – concentrate resolutely on female prostitutes, and refer to male clients rarely, and mainly to illustrate a point about a woman prostitute. Even when they do mention clients, their impressions of clients generally come from having spoken to prostitutes in one-off interviews. Some authors rely on stereotypical notions of clients recorded in earlier works by similarly uninformed authors, thereby reinforcing earlier stereotypes and misconceptions. Much of this literature has had considerable influence on health policy and social policy, and has contributed to a stereotyped image of clients among laypeople and professionals alike.

'Clients' are assumed by much of the literature to be an unproblematic category. Throughout the Spanish and Anglo-American literature on prostitution, the term 'prostitute's client' is generally taken to refer to an adult male. Conversely, the idea that clients are men is somehow 'built into' the popular 'common-sense' notion of a prostitute's client. But not all men are 'literally' clients; they do not all pay women for sex. Statistical studies suggest that, in countries where client–prostitute relations obviously exist, men who are clients only ever constitute a certain percentage of a given population.

Answers to questions such as 'Are all men clients?' depend on where one looks for meaning. Often authors submerge them into the whole of which they are undoubtedly a part, and discussions of clients thus becomes a kind of metonymnic discourse on men. Anglo-American authors often write as though they were speaking of all the men in the world, totally ignoring cultural differences. Spanish authors then use the work of Anglo-American writers and apply it to Spain with no discussion of how Spanish experiences might be different (e.g. Acosta Patiño 1979). There is, then, little recognition of social, political, economic and historical factors affecting a Spanish man's 'clientness'. He is everyman.

Certain Spanish authors of theological and medical texts appeal to the 'fact' that men have greater sex drives than women, thereby explaining men's greater need for sex and hence their visits to prostitutes (e.g. Cañas 1974). Other authors, while not accepting that men have greater sex drives than woman, nevertheless believe that there is 'something' in men that 'drives' them to prostitutes. In this regard, many feminist and traditional Catholic theologian writers certainly agree that prostitution is bad for society. Some feminists may point to men's conditioning by society (e.g. *Vindicación Feminista* 1979), whilst theologians may be at a loss to point to precisely what it is in men that 'makes' them do this. However, both camps, feminists and theologians, seem to feel that there is something in all men that produces clients.

Feminists relying on a theoretical framework based on the notion of patriarchy may well see either all men as prostitutes' clients or prostitutes' clients as somehow standing for/being symbolic of men in general. Those who see all men as clients do so because they see any woman who marries as an inevitable prostitute who exchanges sexual services for material gain (e.g. Jeffreys 1984). However, because those who see the institution of marriage in terms of client–prostitute relationships concentrate on women, it is difficult to say how they perceive men as clients. Thus although these feminist writers must, on some level, 'see' men in marriage as clients, they do not discuss husband–wife relationships in terms of client–prostitute relationships.

Such arguments, feminist and theological, concerning the omnipotence (for whatever reason) of men as clients, are reductive and allow no theoretical space for the notions of agency and change. They preclude a political consideration of the ways in which particular individuals affect the lives of others.

Another prominent discourse articulated by many writers on the subject is psychologically based, stressing that clients are very definitely not ordinary men. There is something particular about them that is most often expressed in negative terms. For example, Cañas (1974: 8) sees clients as shy, neurotic, unbalanced or sexually and emotionally hypodeveloped. One dominant discourse goes so far as to say that they are psychologically abnormal (e.g. Jiménez de Asúa 1929). This mental condition may range from mild shyness to dramatic perversions or the inability to have a relationship with a woman that successfully unites physical and spiritual 'love'. Others suggest that there is something compulsive about the behaviour of a client. He goes to a prostitute because he is addicted; he is not a free man. Another textual discourse to be found in the Spanish and Anglo-American literature that seeks to explain why certain men go to female prostitutes looks to the basic physical abnormalities of prostitutes' clients. They are old and infirm, severely disabled, or simply hideously unattractive. They exist in contradiction to an abstract body definable as 'normal' men (e.g. Draper Miralles 1982). Such authors stress the comfort that 'abnormal men' find in prostitution.

DOUBLE PERSONALITIES

Prostitution has always been a tricky subject for feminists, with most of them seeing prostitutes as victims and clients as the guilty party. However, in common with most authors on prostitution, feminists concentrate their discussions on prostitutes rather than on clients. A few, though, do have a little to say about clients, and one prominent discourse is that of clients represented as hypocritical men – even with split personalities. These hypocrites then collaborate with a hypocritical society that upholds virginity, and subsequent marriage and motherhood, as ideals for women (e.g. Falcón 1967: 57). What such feminists seem to be saying is not that clients are abnormal men, but rather that they are typical actors in a collaborative double act between 'society' (which is also made up of women – a fact often overlooked) in general and men in particular.

A contemporary Spanish sociologist of deviancy, Lamo de Espinosa, writes sympathetically of men's dilemma that 'forces' them to take on this double role in life:

> A man who does not have legitimate access to a woman finds himself in a dilemma. A man who does not 'do it' [*ejercer*] is not a man, and yet at the same time he cannot 'do it' legitimately . . . the strength of culture is so strong that actors comply with both demands by looking for an alternative conduct that resolves the dilemma, albeit by way of fluctuating behaviour.
>   (1989: 148) (All translations are my own.)

Lamo de Espinosa seems to be referring to unmarried clients, rather than married ones. He offers no reasons as to why married clients should go to prostitutes. This is unusual, because most commentators concentrate on married clients. Theories concerning why men go to prostitutes have often discussed how lack of communication between husbands and wives lead to this (Draper Miralles 1982; Falcón 1967). However, they are less concerned with why single men, or men in other types of relationship, go to prostitutes.

Extrapolating textual discourses of clientness here may give the reader the misguided impression that such texts have considered clients at length. Discussions of clients generally appear only as counter-patterns, in brief discussions of male responsibility. Depending on the context, clients' actions are either condemned or excused, but then *all* authors I have come across in relation to prostitution return to the 'main' issue: whether to condemn or to excuse prostitutes.

THE ETHNOGRAPHIC CONTEXT

Discourses of clientness were given much more of a free rein in my fieldsite than in the literature on prostitution. In Alicante, the phrases I translate as 'prostitute's client' (see below) were generally taken to refer to adult males. However, men who had sexual relations with prostitutes rarely referred to themselves as 'client', although they were inclined to talk about other men as such. I quickly realized that clients responded to me better if I did not call them clients. Using this term often caused offence, and some men would deny that they were clients, even if it was obvious that they paid for sex with a prostitute.

Thus I referred to them as men (*hombres*) or friends (*amigos*). In general, they referred to themselves as people (*gente*) or, less frequently (when they wanted to directly emphasize a gender difference), as men (*hombres/varones*) or blokes (*tios*). Note the difference in terminology in the following generalizations from two regular clients, both of whom had a low socioeconomic status, were able-bodied and were married.

> Jaime, 80 years old: 'I've been to prostitutes all my life. A man likes a change and needs a lot of sex. Women don't need so much.'
> Juan, 65 years old: 'People like me need to go to prostitutes, we need a lot of sex.'

When specifically discussing their positive relationships with particular prostitutes, a recurrent pattern was for regular clients to articulate these relationships as a discourse of friendship. Clients referred to themselves and to prostitutes with whom they enjoyed good relations as friends (*amigos*). Victor, a retired, able-bodied man in his seventies, described his relationship with a prostitute in her twenties as a familial relationship. He referred to himself as uncle and to the prostitute as his niece. This couple was referred to in these terms by many neighbourhood people.

A significant pattern with regard to women prostitute informants in the neighbourhood was their use of the word *clientes* to refer to male clients when they were talking about them in a formal manner. However, the term that most prostitutes used for clients, certainly when talking to them, was *amigos*.

Particular clients were further distinguished. For example, Encarna, a 46-year-old single prostitute, often referred to one of her (supposedly unmarried) clients as her boyfriend/fiancé (*novio*). They appeared to have a very close relationship, and he called her his close friend (*amiga intima*), although, significantly, not his girlfriend. Other prostitutes sometimes called clients *novio* as a term of affection, or at other times as an ironic slant on their relationship. A number of prostitutes called elderly clients 'grandads' (*abuelos* or, more friendly or patronizing, *abuelitos*). However, unless they were displaying anger towards them, these terms were not used in front of such men.

When a clear euphemistic choice of vocabulary was deemed appropriate, as in the case of the nuns discussing clients with prostitutes, the term 'men' (*hombres/varones*) was often employed. Prostitutes also used the term if a man's client status was unclear. Informants with negative opinions of clients referred to them euphemistically as 'men who go with these women' (*hombres que van con estas mujeres*).

There was also another type of 'client' who did not generally go with prostitutes, but who simply stood and stared at them. These men were known by prostitutes as '*mirones*' or '*curiosos*' (literally 'watchers/voyeurs' or curious people). If they ever had sex with prostitutes, they usually paid very little, and were generally held in contempt by prostitutes and some other men. Men never referred to themselves as *mirones* within my hearing, although one did inform me, laughing, after I asked if he was a '*curioso*':

'[The prostitutes] call me a *mirón*, not a *curioso*.' 'Is there a difference?' I asked. 'No' he replied, 'I don't think so'. Antonia, the prostitute with whom I was talking, agreed (also laughing) that there was not.

Whenever I spoke to *mirones*, they stressed their lack of ability to pay. One pensioner informed me that his wife took charge of their money, he was given only 'pocket money'; hence he had to save up to go with a prostitute. Coming to look was better than nothing, and it passed the time.

DISSECTING CLIENTS: HIERARCHIES OF 'MANHOOD'/PERSONHOOD

An important idea often articulated to me in the field was that the type of *client* a man was said something about the type of a *man/person* he was. This is something barely discussed in the literature on prostitution. As outlined above, such texts treat clients as a mass of cardboard cut-outs and therefore are not sensitive to the way in which men within the category of client are perceived differently in different contexts. In the neighbourhood, ideas about what sort of men individuals were were tied up not so much with the kind of sex that they wanted, but rather with the status of the prostitutes with whom they were seen to have sex (cf. Cornwall, Chapter 6 in this volume). This was also connected with local conceptions of the clients' own status.

High-status clients

Certain men who came to socialize in the neighbourhood were considered by themselves and by others to have a high status. These were generally men who owned a car, had what was considered to be a decent job (as a mechanic, for example), and who had – or could successfully convince people that they had – a large, comfortable flat or two. Wealthy northern European men who had settled in the area also had high status, whereas poorer North Africans did not.

These particular men often insisted that they did not go with the neighbourhood prostitutes, but that they went to clubs, where there were 'decent' prostitutes. A retired Dutchman in his early sixties, who had settled in Spain with his wife, explained:

I never go to prostitutes in Alicante because everyone knows me here, I work here . . . I go to Benidorm, but don't tell anybody. In Alicante I just chat to prostitutes. The prostitutes in this neighbourhood are tramps. They are very low. I like to go to clubs where I am made to feel good.

This man was obviously trying to impress me, the anthropologist, although it is interesting that he did not try to deny going to prostitutes. This illustrates how going to prostitutes was not usually seen to be a problem. The issue was the particular type of prostitute with which this man was associated. In this particular instance, I knew the man to be lying. He did go with one of the neighbourhood prostitutes – I had regularly seen him paying to go into the brothel. He lied presumably because he did not want me to think that a 'high-status' man such as himself went with 'low' prostitutes.

Another client, Joaquín, was a divorced plumber in his forties who also had considerable status in the neighbourhood. He told me that although he went with one of the neighbourhood prostitutes, he would not want anybody there to know about it. She came to his house in another part of town.

> I'm telling you because I don't mind telling you, but I don't want you to tell other people we know mutually, that I've told you I go with Antonia . . . . If I go with a woman, I don't need to go and do it in the neighbourhood and let tongues wag. I prefer to do things privately. People love to talk although it doesn't bother me, I've got my business and am doing well. But I've got my status to think about and I don't want tongues wagging about me.

Thus for a man/client to define himself as or be defined as one with high status, he had to be at the very least a 'high-class' man/client. I expect that many people in the neighbourhood were aware, or at least suspected, that Joaquín went to prostitutes. However, the very fact that Antonia went to him (that is, to his house) put him above the other clients in his own eyes as well as in the eyes of other clients and prostitutes.

This was quite typical of such socioeconomically advantaged clients, although it was not invariably the case. Another 'high-status' client, Arturo, a local man who owned a bar and a bakery, insisted that prostitutes went to his house. He frequently boasted to me about his 'education', 'profession' and 'wealth'. However, Arturo did not enjoy consistent high status in the eyes of prostitutes, clients and other neighbourhood people because he was an alcoholic who was frequently seen inebriated in the neighbourhood. Whilst he was able to persuade two prostitutes to have sex with him in his own home, he was often laughed at and taken advantage of financially by prostitutes when he was drunk. One day he came into the bar. Lolita, one of the prostitutes who had sex with him at his house, ordered a drink and sandwiches for herself, me and two prostitutes. She helped herself to the money for these items from Arturo's pocket without his knowledge. Finally, 'high-class' clients could not persuade all prostitutes to go to their houses for sex. Rita and Maria, the oldest and most affluent prostitutes in the neighbourhood, rarely went to clients' homes. If they did, it was because they were particularly good friends with the client, or received high remuneration.

Low-status clients

Clients in the neighbourhood were often described as low-class people by informants in a variety of contexts outside it. Men who expressed negative views on clients in the neighbourhood had no difficulty in distancing themselves from them. Those who did not go with neighbourhood prostitutes often made derogatory remarks about men who did, although they were generally focused on the prostitutes' status rather than that of the clients.

One evening in a neighbourhood bar, I was introduced to a lawyer in his early thirties. My friend Maria (also a lawyer) introduced me to him as an anthropologist studying prostitution in the neighbourhood:

> He said, laughing, 'How hilarious. They really are a freak show, aren't they? The greatest one in Alicante. I know a lot about this. It's incredible how any-one would go with those fucked women [*tiradas*]. They're old and ugly . . .'. Maria asked me who the clients were. He answered 'Old idiots'. He then immediately returned to giving us the benefits of his 'insights'. 'Most of the prostitutes, 90 per cent of the ones in Alicante, are drug addicts.'

I did not know whether this man was a prostitute's client in another context. What he had in common with other informants (with the exception of certain prostitutes) was his interest in dismissing clients and concentrating on a discussion of prostitutes. On another occasion, a client of a high-class brothel remarked:

> Prostitution in the neighbourhood and the other street place makes me very sad . . . . They're fucked, not hygienic, will do anything they're asked . . . . And the clients need them because they're just like the prostitutes. In a normal place nobody would think of sleeping with a woman like that, someone who's been with Moors, Moroccans, ill people, and so on. It's the cheapest, the dirtiest, the lowest in every sense.

Once again, the male clients were not given centre stage. Indeed in this and in the former statements from men, clients as men were not specifically mentioned. Rather they became 'old idiots' (not idiot men), 'anyone' (not any man), 'nobody' (not no man), and 'somebody' (not some man).

When acting as a group, neighbourhood prostitutes generally assigned the lowest status of client to the *mirón*, with his lack of worth as a man judged by his *lack* of a relationship with a prostitute. To them, he often represented a kind of personification of impotence (economic, sexual and social). One day I was standing around with a group of prostitutes. A *mirón* came up to listen, and the two prostitutes whom I was with became very angry. One screamed at him: 'Piss off, stop getting free excitement. Stop giving yourself a wank for free. You should pay for it *like any decent man*' (her emphasis).

This attitude to *mirones* was not always consistent. Sometimes, when there were few conversation partners in circulation, and a prostitute was alone, she might concede to converse with a *mirón*. I witnessed a number of such conversations. The man's status of *mirón* was temporarily suspended and they had animated conversations. During one such conversation, Rita and Lolita expressed sympathy when the pensioner *mirón* told us that he was very poor. However, the same man could be communicated with in terms of his negative *mirón* status on other occasions depending on the mood of a prostitute and/or whether or not she was in the company of colleagues and/or other clients.

MARITAL POTENCY

Married clients who went to prostitutes never directly expressed to me any feelings of guilt, nor articulated substantial moral qualms about their actions. A general pattern was that they either hid their married status from me, or, once their married status was discovered by me or disclosed by them, justified their reasons for going to prostitutes. Miguel, a 59-year-old plumber, revealed:

> Trouble is my body asks me to come here and have sex. I need it a lot. If I didn't get it I'd feel physically ill, I'd go mad and would hardly be able to see straight.

His justifications for going to prostitutes imply that he was addicted to going to them. If he had stopped, he would have had withdrawal symptoms, rather like those a drug addict might have if s/he could not get her/his 'fix'. And yet, he also acknowledged that he went voluntarily: 'I only do it because I can afford it. If my wife or children wanted for anything I'd buy it them rather than go to a prostitute.' This client suggested that he was psychologically addicted to prostitutes *as long as he could afford to be*. In some senses his abdication of responsibility for his actions concurs with those textual discourses, discussed earlier in this chapter, that see clients as psychologically ill. However, his psychological illness conveniently allowed him to acknowledge his responsibilities as a husband and father first.

Clients' justifications most frequently took the form of appeals to their need for sex and/or sexual problems in their marriage. A significant number of clients informed me that they were 'impotent'. However, sexual problems in their marriage were always blamed on their wives. Such 'problems' included wives allegedly not wanting or needing sex, or being old, ill or menopausal.

A minority of married clients expressed concern about the potential effects on their marriages of their liaisons with prostitutes. For example, one client told me that he was worried about AIDS because of his wife. A small number of clients also expressed concern that their wives might divorce them if they discovered that they went to prostitutes. Jaime, a salesman in his fifties, told me:

> My wife thinks I'm in Albacete. My wife doesn't know I go to prostitutes. If she found out or if any of my four kids found out, I'd die. I love my wife more than anybody else in the world. I just come to prostitutes because my body asks for it. I'm happily married.

The general visible lack of a consideration of responsibility on the part of married clients illustrates some of the ideas expressed in feminist texts, discussed earlier in this chapter. Those that did reveal slight moral qualms were able to fall back on the potent discourse that it is natural for men to need sex, thus responsibility is not an issue (for a discussion of clients' responsibility in relation to HIV transmission, see Hart 1992). However, it is clear that their actions were not tolerated (even by themselves) and encouraged in any simple way. The very fact that some clients did not want to reveal to people in the neighbourhood, often including the anthropologist, that they were married suggests that their liaisons with prostitutes were not unproblematic. This was perhaps a status protection mechanism, because clients knew that their worth in a number of contexts as a client/man/person was calculated on the basis of whether or not they were married.

The perceived double personality/hypocrisy of clients caused tension between some of them and prostitutes when they were outside the neighbourhood. Most clients and many prostitutes were anxious to separate their identities inside and outside the neighbourhood. Some prostitutes complained that clients ignored them outside the neighbourhood if the clients were with their families. However, if the prostitutes were with their families, the clients might, out of spite, greet them. Hypocrisy on the part of clients (especially married ones) was a frequent topic of conversation amongst neighbourhood people. Actors notably missing from such conversations were clients. The manner in which 'they' came to prostitutes, but outside joined in the public's condemnation of them, seemed to be particularly annoying. However, a number of prostitutes also remarked to me that they themselves condemned prostitutes when they were not in the neighbourhood. Yet many prostitutes (often the same ones who expressed anger at 'clients'' hypocrisy) enjoyed a rather different relationship with unmarried clients, many of whom were retired and had considerable free time outside the neighbourhood. For example, Venturo, an elderly widowed client who lived with his son and his family, was friendly with Antonia. He walked around town with her, they went shopping together, and she phoned him at home. Some unmarried clients accompanied prostitutes on neighbourhood excursions. Though men were often concerned about what their families might think, they did not have wives to consider.

Some prostitutes knew how to manipulate the shock value of a client's marital status if they wanted to make a non-prostitute think negatively about 'clients'. The nuns in the Cáritas centre seemed particularly sporting targets in this regard. The older ones especially were suitably impressed and horrified by the knowledge that 'most' clients were married. They did not seem to understand why men with wives went to prostitutes. One 59-year-old nun asserted: 'Their wives should have sex with them even if they don't want to. Just to keep the marriage together.' It was not only nuns who articulated such beliefs about sex and marriage. For example, a divorced client in his forties denied that married men went to prostitutes:

> These women have got too many problems: diseases, they're drug addicts, thieves. Nobody wants that, except men who can't get any other woman. But for somebody who wants status and a family it's no good. . . . If a wife knows her husband wants things it's only logical that she gives them to him . . . . Men who go to prostitutes go to fulfil biological necessities because they haven't got a wife.

In both of the above excerpts from fieldnotes, both nun and client informants fell back on apportioning blame to wives rather than to husbands. It was assumed that marriage was a sexual contract, and that wives should keep their side of the bargain. The husbands' side of the bargain was not discussed. However, one might assume that, in accordance with hegemonic neighbourhood discourses on marital relations, it was implicitly accepted to be economic provision for their families.

I spent some of my fieldwork time with two male volunteers who helped at the Cáritas centre in the neighbourhood. One was an unmarried bank clerk in his late twenties; the other was a widower in his seventies who ran his own finance business. Although both were devout Catholics, their personal opinions differed somewhat on this subject. Jaime – the younger, unmarried informant – seemed somewhat confused:

> True that men need sex. Prostitution is necessary but lots of men who come here are married, got wives and everything . . . I don't think it's good for single men to go to prostitutes either, although I know it's a physiological need. I can understand it more in a single man than a married one, but it's still not good.

Antonio, the widower, appeared to be considerably firmer in his beliefs, although he revealed them only when pressed by me.

> I definitely do not accept men going to prostitutes. I am totally against it, they are vice-ridden people [*gente viciosa*]. My religion doesn't accept them. . . . It's a sin, you can't play with a woman's body and, moreover, pay her for it. It's not at all honourable [*nada honoroso*]. . . . If a Catholic sells himself to buy a woman he's not very Catholic at that moment. He loses control, goes out of his mind [*perde razón*].

Antonio, then, appeared to subscribe to the view that prostitutes' clients – if they were Catholic – were unbalanced and had 'gone off the rails'. His interpretation was that clients were not normal. They were mad 'at that moment' when they were clients. However, he appeared to be saying that this was only a temporary state. Once a client 'came back to his senses', he could presumably be a good Catholic man again. His views endorsed textual discourses of clientness that emphasize abdication of responsibility, discussed earlier in this chapter.

GROSS GENERALIZATIONS REVISITED

As discussed above, the notion 'client' was frequently an unstable category and was often deconstructed by different informants. However, there were many occasions when the reverse was the case, and clients were discussed as a coherent group. This coherent group was often articulated as being more than the sum of its parts. Thus the notion that clients and men were one and the same thing was often articulated to me in the field. Indeed, while indexing my notes it was often difficult to know where to put things – in the category 'men' or the category 'clients'. Clients and prostitutes alike often spoke as if the two terms were synonymous. Some clients had ways of defining what they as clients were by appealing to what men were. Their ideas coincided with discourses prevalent in some of the literature on prostitution. For example, many clients spoke as though all men were potential clients by appealing to the 'fundamental' male sex drive to justify their clientness: 'Men are different to women, they need more sex' was a typical comment from a variety of clients. This group persona appealed to by many clients comes back to the issue of responsibility. It may be seen as a kind of diffusion of responsibility, or at least as a mechanism for sharing it. However, some clients appeared to be so confident of the male natural instinct to have sex (with a prostitute) that it is fair to say that responsibility was never revealed by them to be an issue. I would also suggest that this was probably not something that many of them thought about.

It was significant that although many clients appealed to the symbiotic relationship between man and client, they rarely manifested physically as a (male) group. Most of them circulated alone; one group of men (some of whom were clients) who played cards together in the bar on a regular basis was an exception to this pattern. This was quite different to other prostitution areas that I visited. I accompanied two neighbourhood prostitutes on a working holiday to a street-prostitution area in Valencia, where I observed the considerable social contact of clients with other clients. The clubs that I visited revealed a similar pattern. Men often frequented them in groups. The lack of a coherent, physical, client-group identity in the neighbourhood appeared to be a recent phenomenon and was said by a number of elderly clients (who had known the 'good old days') to be a sign of the decay of prostitution in the neighbourhood. The fragmented nature of the client group can be contrasted with the frequent presentation of the prostitutes' group identity.

Discourses of clientness that emerged from prostitutes often constructed clients as a uniform group, despite their patchy presence in the neigh-bourhood, and despite concurrent local discourses that fragmented them. Sometimes prostitutes expressed ideas about how the male sex drive makes men become clients; a popular expression was 'Most men come because they need to.' Antonia, a 40-year-old prostitute, said, 'Men definitely have more of a sexual appetite than women.'

Prostitutes often expressed opinions about what certain academic feminists might call patriarchy. They did this by stating that all men are prostitutes' clients; they are prostitutes' clients because that is the manner in which men choose to oppress women. Fundamentally they all hate women and so they come to humiliate prostitutes in order to punish women. Somehow, 'client-ness' is the manner in which this desire manifests itself. Sometimes prostitutes seemed distressed by the notion that men try to get whatever they can out of women. One day, Rita was in a terrible state:

> I can hardly face my clients today. I hate them all and I vow I'll get back at men if it's the last thing I do. What I want to do before I retire is lead men on, making out I'd go with them for free. But then, at the last minute, turn away and say 'Do you really think I'd go with you sons of bitches [*hijos de putas*, literally sons of whores!] for nothing?'. They're enough to make you hate them. All they do is take advantage.

On another occasion I was discussing a client with the same prostitute. He was very abusive to her and we agreed that he was 'a horrible egotistical bastard'. Rita continued in a very angry tone:

> All men are, I hate them all. They're worthless and so I just use them for what I can get. That's why I never have sex with men for free, I want to get as much out of them as I can, rather than the other way round.

Although the prostitutes often saw clients in terms of men oppressing women, some of them – exemplified by Rita's comment above – ironically saw their own roles in prostitution as empowering. Thus in a roundabout way, client–prostitute relations were constructed as the only non-exploitative man–woman relationship. In this context, the discourse of clientness was one that empowered women.

Some prostitutes often used examples of certain clients' behaviour to illustrate negative ideas about men in general. These were frequently expressed through folk statistics. While in a group of prostitutes discussing clients, one 64-year-old woman, Maria, stated:

> Ninety per cent of men are animals. They don't mind who they fuck as long as it's a woman. And they might be nice to you outside [on the street], but once inside [the brothel] they abuse you. They all want you to suck their pricks and they never want to suck your pussy . . . educated men are the exception to this. They know how to treat a woman well and are more sincere. Most men don't care who they fuck, most of them would even fuck drug addicts.

Maria's statement was immediately challenged by two colleagues (both of whom, on other occasions, had expressed opinions similar to Maria's). Rita said: 'This is what they pay for, it's obvious. If they pay for something they obviously want to get the maximum: maximum service, maximum time.' It was only when she was challenged that Maria attempted to back up her argument by talking about men who belonged to the non-client category.

> I've lived with four men and they were all the same. They said nice things to you, said they loved you, were really loving, but then they would fuck any other woman around. I had to keep changing because each one was a deceiver [*enganador*] and I wanted to find one that wasn't. If I had my time again I would never have a relationship with a man, never.

It seemed that prostitutes were trying to work out what connection there was between the two concepts of clients and men. Was 'client' simply a sub-category of the generic term 'man', or was there more to the taxonomy than this? Of course their views on this depended on the particular idea of men or of clients that they chose to articulate at the time. Sometimes prostitutes suggested that they knew all about men because they had relationships with clients; they knew men better than anybody else. Indeed, some expressed the idea that it was they who taught men to be 'men' through losing their virginity for them in an 'appropriate' manner (cf. Lindisfarne, Chapter 4 in this volume). Of course it should be remembered that many prostitutes had relationships with men in their 'private' lives, not only in their work. In many cases this understandably produced tension; the public and the private were not as easily delineated by prostitutes in the neighbourhood as reported in some studies of prostitution.

WHERE NOW?

Many of the discourses that are recurrent in textual accounts of clientness emerged in neighbourhood discourses constructed by clients, prostitutes and other neighbourhood people. Some were seen as mentally ill, some as disabled; some were excused because of their natural sex drive, some were seen as addicted to sex; most married clients were seen to lead 'double lives'. One hegemonic discourse concerned ideas about the natural male sex drive.

With the growing deconstruction of this discourse, some feminist authors have called on clients to take responsibility for their actions. In the neighbourhood, although prostitutes sometimes discussed issues of responsibility in relation to clients, they rarely did so when clients were present.

Another pattern which emerged was that male informants (clients and non-clients) avoided facing up to the issue of responsibility. When my questions homed in on this, men frequently blamed the actions of clients on women, or steered the conversation back to women. Thus wives were blamed for a lack of sex within marriage, and prostitutes were blamed for prostitution. This complements a historical tradition with regard to textual discourses of prostitution; women are put centre-stage.

However, beyond the issues of responsibility, local discourses of deconstructed clients contrast sharply with discourses prevalent in textual accounts.

Locally clients became human beings; they were often not seen as a cohesive group, and their identities were not uniformly negative as is suggested in most of the literature. They were seen as men/people/clients. Some enjoyed friendships with prostitutes, some were liked and respected in the neighbourhood at certain times, others were not. Some could afford to buy sex, others contented themselves with looking. To examine 'male clients' as a faceless group is too simplistic. All had other identities and responsiblities and were judged according to variety of standards of behaviour.

In terms of men's studies, I have highlighted some of the dangers of concentrating on ideal types and have chosen to consider variant discourses on men in a particular setting. Placing the notion of being a man/person/client in an adequate historical, political, cultural and sociological context is complex, yet I trust that I have shown the value of working towards this end.

NOTES

I would like to thank Andrea Cornwall, Judith Ennew, Alison Field, Nancy Lindisfarne and Peter Rivière for their helpful comments on early drafts of this paper; and the Economic and Social Research Council for financially supporting this research.

Chapter 3

A broken mirror
Masculine sexuality in Greek ethnography

Peter Loizos

David Gilmore, an anthropologist who has written on Mediterranean culture, recently published one of the few comparative studies of masculinity. He suggests that in many cultures manhood involves three major demands – to procreate, to protect and to provision. His argument is about systemic necessities, and how these shape the challenges which mould both individual males and men-in-groups. Gilmore concludes that: 'Manhood is the social barrier that societies must erect against entropy, human enemies, the process of nature, time and all the human weaknesses that endanger group life' (1990: 226).

In this chapter, gender ideas are approached rather closer to the ground, in specific discourses, contexts and institutional domains, and without any assumptions of functional necessities. I am not happy with statements about 'masculinity' in Greek culture as substantive generalizations, even though it is easy to concede that some clustering of related concepts exists when terms like *andras* (a man, a husband), *pateras* (a father) and *pallikari* (an upstanding unmarried youth) are employed throughout Greece.

Greece as a state is highly centralized, with the Ministry of Education imposing one kind of uniformity and the mass media contributing skeins of contrasting and contradictory uniformities. 'Greek culture' is, therefore, an idea of some specific and limited value. Greece is characterized by distinctive regions, contrasting production regimes and differing rates of social change; these features are cross-cut by cities, classes, the church and the army, each a producer of contrasting discourses and assertions about gender.

I wish to explore a handful of linked themes which suggest a sense of the varied contexts in which masculinities can be understood. These include marriage, procreation and householding as hegemonic gender values; the ways that different types of post-marital residence seem to relate to different emphases in maleness and femaleness; sexuality, and expressions of personhood which are not part of the conjugal householding package; celibacy as a domain for difference; male friendship and its contextual variations; and lastly, local ideas of an independent, autonomous masculinity, and contrasting ideas of a domesticated maleness.

My own field data were collected from 1968 onwards. I was guided by Durkheimian assumptions and had undoubtedly assumed that maleness and femaleness would be the subjects of widespread cultural consensus and standardization. While this framework may have been valid for some preliterate cultures, I now feel that it cannot accommodate the organization of gender concepts in complex states in which region, class and institutional differences are important.

New fieldwork should explore the full range of gender identities in a discrete research area. However, here, I am only able to proceed by juxtaposing fragments of material from various Greek ethnographies. I do not recommend this approach – I simply offer a suggestive *bricolage faute de mieux*. This volume proposes a theoretical emphasis in which male identities are asserted in specific acts or contexts. The editors argue that masculinity is not a stable essence, present throughout a lifetime or a stage of life, but a series of negotiated identities, acts of will, assertions, performances, fragments of a person who at other times and in other contexts may have other gender attributes. I am largely sympathetic with these emphases, but suggest at the end of this chapter that they leave us with a fresh set of difficulties.

RESIDENCE RULES AND GENDERED CONTEXTS

The ethnography of Greece has with a few exceptions concentrated largely on marriage, procreation and householding (usually as an integrated package), and this has marginalized much else. One aim of this chapter is to redress the balance somewhat. In study after study we are told that full adult status for both men and women requires an indissoluble marriage, blessed with children. In order to carry this off, a household must be set up and maintained. The tasks of husband and wife are only at an end when they have seen all the children of their marriage themselves married off, and when a number of grandchildren have been produced. In some communities these grandchildren are named after their varied grandparents and are held to be in some sense continuations of them, both through the general kinship medium of 'shared blood' and through the more specific fact of the re-creation of a dead ancestor in a living descendant. At specific stages in the development cycle, the expectations for men and women are specific, and different, as Campbell noted when he wrote that 'This opposition of the sexes provides the frame for contrasted ideal types of social personality for men and women at each of the three stages of adult life' (1964: 278).

Campbell's emphasis on the importance of position in the developmental cycle – the young unmarried, the married and mature, and the elderly being the three distinctive stages – should have been a very important entry-point into the analysis of gender concepts, but it has not had a sufficiently strong impact on subsequent thinking (Loizos and Papataxiarchis 1991: 3–25). Approaches which favour an emphasis on continuous negotiation and renegotiation are only now beginning. The mature married householders have made the ethnographic running, to the neglect of the other two age categories.

In modern Greece, young unmarried males have been, until the last twenty years, usually expected to control their sexuality as best they could; young unmarried women were not thought to experience the need for sexual expression in the same way as men (Hirschon 1978), and part of the adult parental 'game' was controlling the access of young men to young women. Early marriage was something the economically viable could bestow on their children as a gift, and the poor had to wait and to save. Divorce was a tragedy and a scandal, and in any case very hard to obtain from the church.

The relational character of maleness and femaleness seems to have a somewhat different character in each of three post-marital residence configurations, which I shall sketch in now, and return to later. The most marked picture of dominant, controlling males and subordinated women was described for pastoral communities, for some fishing communities, and associated with agnatic kinship (Campbell 1964; Herzfeld 1985; Friedl 1962; du Boulay 1974). A woman moved to her husband's group at marriage and, as a junior person, entered the household which might have included her senior affines. Where there was marked agnation, the discourses tended to bond male corporations – brothers, fathers, cousins – and to overvalue men, as opposed to women. Campbell's account of the Sarakatsani contains many of these elements, even though the kinship system, as he presented it, was formally bilateral. In his chapter on 'Honour and Shame', he describes how sexuality is seen as sinful, polluting, secret and shameful, and how women are held to be the 'weak vessels' in all matters sexual.

In some agricultural communities there was a more even-handed pattern of gender relations. Kinship might be more bilateral in emphasis, post-marital residence was often neo-local, and relations between husband and wife suggested ideas of complementarity, balance, perhaps a tug-of-war, but one between opponents of equal size (Loizos 1975a, 1975b).

A third type of complex has been described in which the kinship system emphasizes lines of women, there is uxorilocal post-marital residence, and neighbours tend to be matrikin (Dubisch 1976, 1986; Kenna 1976; Bernard 1976; Vernier 1984; Beopoulou 1987; Papataxiarchis 1988). These communities have been described by Papataxiarchis as 'matrifocal' in precisely the way such a term has been used to describe Caribbean households, with the exception that marriages are always formalized – consensual unions are not tolerated. There are few signs of 'male domination' in these communities. It is the woman of the house who offers the visitor hospitality, and discourses within the household do not systematically downgrade or undervalue women. Indeed the moral community can be understood as composed of competing matriarchs sitting in judgement over each other's daughters and granddaughters, while assessing the adequacy or inadequacy of the in-married husbands.

One of the funnier moments in Papataxiarchis' ethnography involved the attempt by some local men to open a night-club within the space of the village, in which women from outside might have danced – and more – for the entertainment of local men. This attempt was seen off by the community's women in short order. In my own fieldwork, I can still remember the sheepish embarrassment of one of the supposedly tougher and more confident men of the village, when his wife said to me in front of him: 'Mr Peter, you won't believe this, but my husband actually goes to Nicosia and wastes good money on the tarts in the bouzouki-joints. Now, what does an educated man like you think about *that*?'.

I was to hear from other village men about powerful political figures and merchants who as a gesture of friendship to their friends and clients 'closed the cabaret for the evening'. This meant that they paid the owner of a night-club to keep the general public out, and allow only the host's personal friends in, while paying in advance for expensive prostitutes to entertain them sexually. For some village men, this represented an impressive act of generosity, but there were other men in the village, and virtually all the women, who would not have been impressed. It is this pluralism which is at the heart of my disagreements with Gilmore.

I have reached my main theme, sexuality, and have already pointed to one of the significant differences: in many communities, there seems to be a fairly concerted effort to 'capture' sexuality for the household, for procreation and, obviously, for heterosexuality. That, at least, is the official version, but all kinds of other things can and do go on and they are phenomenologically, and in human terms, just as important as the official discourses. Here, I shall have to skip about a bit ethnographically.

MEN AND THEIR SEXUALITIES

Campbell writes of how the northern Greek, patrilocal shepherds he studied used the standard Greek word *pallikari* to mean a young adult, but still unmarried, man. Consider some of the rich description provided:

> Women walk behind their men when they are together in public and show them respect. In church the women huddle at the back or line the left-hand wall. Women agree that they are inferior to men in every way, and they continually bemoan their fate that they were not born into the other sex ... This opposition of the sexes provides the frame for contrasted ideal types of social personality for men and women at each of the three stages of adult life. For the unmarried but adult shepherds, the boys [*ta paidia*], the *pallikaria*, physical perfection is an important ideal attribute. A youth ought to be tall, slim, agile and tough. Ideally, at least, a *pallikari* is never short in stature. A certain regularity and openness of feature is desirable but without any hint of effeminate fineness ...

But moral qualities are also demanded of the young shepherd, especially courage and strength of purpose. If in addition to these qualities he also possesses the necessary physical attributes, a young Sarakatsanos can fairly claim to be *levendis kai pallikari*. The first of these terms is perhaps the more composite, describing a youth who is handsome, manly, narrow-hipped, and nimble; such a youth will distinguish himself at a wedding by his upright carriage, restrained manner towards his elders, and his agility in the dance. *Pallikari* is rather the hero warrior with physical strength and assertive courage who is prepared to die, if necessary, for the honour of his family or his country. Caution must always be foreign to his nature . . .

Such young men, Demetrios added, since they do not know women, are *pastriki*,that is, clean and pure. Male virginity is the ideal. And continence is thought to confer a certain invulnerability on those who face dangers, especially the danger of bullets in war or brigandage. Of sex relations in marriage, Aristoteles, a young man of 28, who in every way conforms in conduct and person to the ideal *pallikari*, was able to say before other men that he was ashamed to think of them. Sex, sin, and death are related; similarly virginity, continence, and life. The Sarakatsani anticipate marriage with joy, but also with regret. The founding of a family is wholly good, yet marriage, sex relations, and children, inevitably foreshadow death. The *pallikari*, not the head of family, is the ideal of manhood.

(Campbell 1964: 278–80; words in the Greek alphabet have been transliterated)

Campbell also gave highly pertinent material about attitudes to male homo-sexuality and made clear both the generally negative character attributed to it, and the ambiguity that only the passive partner was stigmatized. However, that was an account of shepherds in northern Greece in the early 1950s.

Elsewhere things are or have become somewhat different. Papataxiarchis notes that one of the commonest terms of address between young rural men in Lesbos (and my own Cypriot village in the late 1960s and early 1970s conforms with this) was the term *malaka*, which means masturbator.[1] It can be said insultingly, but it is very often to be heard affectionately. The suggestion here is that young men see themselves facing a common predica-ment, with a common low-cost solution. Dr Sheena Crawford, when teasing young men in the Cypriot village of Kalavassos about the ironies of a world in which brothers insist on their sisters remaining virgins while attempting unsuccessfully to seduce other men's sisters, was told: 'Fortunately, God gave us hands.' The implication, the gesture, implied 'self-expression'.[2]

At this point it is worth mentioning three aspects of sexuality as seen from the point of view of the Greek army. First, the regulations in the Greek army permitted periods of leave for 'natural reasons of bodily health'. This was understood to mean heterosexual contacts which, until the last twenty years, usually involved prostitutes since young Greek males typically do not get engaged until after completing military service. The modern army is no longer seeking to operate with the ideal of the virginal, continent *pallikari*, familiar from the epics, and from the Sarakatsani. Secondly, part of the induction process into the Greek army involves a physical inspection to ascertain that a man is not homosexual. All modern armies carry out physical inspections, and whatever the military and medical rationales for these, they can be interpreted (following Goffman 1961) as one useful degradation ritual which gets the conscript off balance and suggests that he is subject to the total power of the institution, down to and including control and surveillance of his body and its functions. But the concern with sexual preferences is quite explicit in the Greek case.[3] And since part of the army's mission is to turn 'boys' into 'men', when conscripts do not perform well, their instructors humiliate them with remarks about how they resemble women.[4] A tacit censorship has operated with respect to homosexuality in western European armies, and still operates in the British armed services.[5] In this respect the Greek case is not unusual.

Lastly, during the reign of the Greek military Junta, 1967–74, there was a considerable fuss made by the regime on the subject of homosexuality in classical Greece. Its existence in classical times was explicitly denied by the state, and all references to its legitimacy then were censored from newspapers and other publications which could be controlled. Colonel Ioannis Ladas in 1968, while Secretary-General at the Ministry of Public Order (*sic*), physically assaulted a journalist and his editor on the weekly *Eikones* because they had produced an article on homosexuality which noted that many distinguished men in ancient Greece had had this orientation. Clogg (1972: 41) suggests that this incident did not destroy Ladas' career, but simply led to him being placed under the closer surveillance of one of the regime's triumvirs, Pattakos.[6] The official construction of Greek conservative, nationalist, military masculinity was, it appears from this, neither chaste nor virginal, but very squarely heterosexual.

HOMOSEXUALITIES

There is much more to understanding masculinities than the army attitudes or regulations. It is widely remarked, by Campbell and others, that the word *poushtis* in demotic Greek signifies a man who receives another man sexually, who solicits to be penetrated, or accepts and enjoys it. This role is strongly stigmatized and *poushtis* is a common term of abuse, much harder to use affectionately than *malaka*.

A man who takes what is termed the 'active' role, that of penetrating the *poushtis*, may sometimes be referred to by the rarely used word *kolombaras*, 'arse-taker', but he is not singled out and stigmatized. His activities seem to be ignored and 'unstressed' in linguistic terms. This is difficult ground, and my information is thin. I do not suggest that such a practice is widely approved or publicly admissible, but rather that it has a twilight status. In some parts of Greece, a man who acts as the active partner in homosexual intercourse can still retain his sense of self-respect as conventionally male, according to my informants.

My reading of this is that *men fuck* (*i andres gamoun*) and that this is a masculine and *dominant* thing to do, and that whomsoever or whatever is so used is the subordinated and therefore inferior party. In discourses about homosexuality there are also hints that it is a 'bad habit' which was somehow acquired during the Ottoman period from the Turks.[7]

A digression on violation

Penetration can be as much about power, then, as intimacy. Let me give a brief illustration from my own field data. The leader of the Greek nationalist anti-British underground in my village rejoiced in the nickname 'Yeros', the Old Man. Two of his younger adjutants later, after independence, stopped following his political lead, and were known to support a different leader from his own favourite. This was related to tensions at the national level, which were only with difficulty contained in the village. Someone said something witty about this and it was repeated for days afterwards in the coffee-shops: 'The Old Man should have fucked his two lads, and *then* they would have listened to him.'

At first I thought this was some veiled hint about the Old Man having homosexual preferences, but men explained patiently that this was not the point at all: men have sex with (*gamoun*) their wives, and wives obey them. So, had he treated them like wives, he would not have had disciplinary problems. In their own words my informants were implying that Yeros would have been a super-male, which has echoes of Lacan's notion of the 'Phallocrat'. It appears from this that to discipline is to feminize; to have penetrative sex with someone is to discipline him, and thus to feminize him.

Here, I must again return to contemporary British society, to preserve a reasonable relationship between Greek ethnography and my maternal culture. Under the sub-heading 'Prisoner's inquest told of sex attack', there was a report of the suicide of an 18-year-old man at Feltham Remand Centre, a 'Young Offenders' institution currently notorious in Britain because of the frequent suicides there:

> On the evening before he died Mr Waite was sexually assaulted with a snooker cue and was forced to give two inmates his watch and trainers. A Feltham inmate told the court that it was common for other inmates to insert objects into the anus of a new prisoner, 'It is all part of the welcoming committee. Each wing has somebody who thinks they run it and they do all sorts of things.'
>
> (*Independent*, 10 March 1992)

A society which cannot stop things like this happening in its prisons has no grounds for smugness about its civilized institutions. But the other matter to be noted in the context of this chapter is that such assaults are described as 'sexual'. They are degrading and humiliating and involve the use of force; it would be slightly less confusing, perhaps, if they were called something else. The incident does, however, suggest a similar equation of penetration with power.

There was a belief among some village men in Cyprus that a woman would always find the first man to take her virginity irresistible and, significantly, able to command her for the rest of her life, even if she married another man. Small wonder, then, that the men wanted to marry virgins, and small wonder, too, that I heard men discussing striking their wives occasionally, as if it were a routine matter of imposing a husband's authority, and nothing remarkable.

On one occasion, such a discussion concerned whether or not it was reasonable for a man who came home late to wake up his sleeping wife and insist on having sex with her whether she wanted to or not. Opinions differed. One man felt it was somewhat unreasonable, and if the woman was not willing, she had a right to be allowed to sleep. Another man said, with a laugh, that, if he found himself in this situation and his wife refused, he would be inclined to fetch her a couple of blows (*na tis doko ena-thkio mbattsous*). 'But not heavy ones', he added, and he laughed, and the other two men laughed.

In the context of interpersonal relations, to be a dominant man can imply the use of force to subdue or discipline someone else, and neither the other person's gender, nor the physical weapon (a penis, a fist) need be distinguished.[8]

Definitions that control and diminish

I was made personally aware of various lines of demarcation for masculinities during my fieldwork. First, there was the question of the long sideburns which I have worn since the middle 1950s. They gradually stopped signifying rock-and-roll rebellion and became part of my persona. But to my male village friends and relatives they were problematic:

'Peter, when you shave, just raise your sideburns an inch or so!', said a couple of close friends over drinks one evening.
'Why?'
'*Mirizoun poushlikia* (they imply you are passively homosexual).'
'But I'm not.'
'Then don't go around looking as if you are. People are malevolent.'[9]

Then there was the whispered explanation for how one of the rich but uneducated men in another village had made his fortune as a salesman. The man who had given him his start was a 'known' homosexual, and the villager when young had been good-looking: 'So possibly the wholesaler fucked him.' The suggestion of economic patronage power leading to sexual exploitation was not particularly homophobic, because several merchants in the region were said to have used their position as employers of female labour to attempt seductions. It can be inferred, as in the case of the EOKA leader and his unruly adjutants, that the village salesman as subordinated party was seen as feminized.

Although villagers have well-defined notions of non-sexual love (*agapi*) between men, village definitions of homosexuality reduce it to very specific sexual practices. Moreover, they allow no space for companionate relationships or friendships of any morally elevated order, if there is a current of sexuality within them. To put this another way, there is a huge conceptual space – a negative polarity – between friendship between men and sexuality between men. I heard nothing to suggest that people saw areas of ambiguity, or offered elusive interpretations of when a handclasp, an embrace, an arm around the shoulders should be interpreted as 'sexual' and when 'merely' as a gesture of asexual friendship.

These attitudes are a far cry from Plato's Symposium. If there were an ecology of social relations, then village views on homosexuality would celebrate a loss of variation, an overvaluing of a few high-yielding strains of manhood and a reduction of everything to very clear-cut definitions.

PHALLIC POWER AND ITS LIMITATIONS

I have been talking of phallic sexuality as a practice and metaphor of domination. The use of sexuality by men as a weapon in a kind of *Kulturkampf* is reported by Sofka Zinovieff (1991), who studied the phenomenon known in Greece as 'spear-fishing' (*kamaki*). This is the male pursuit of tourist women for sexual conquest, the business of which is elaborately socially organized. First, the men tend to be lower-class; secondly, they often hunt in pairs; and thirdly, *kamaki* is a competitive game being played among men and to impress men. To illustrate some of the more poignant but aggressive features, some now-departed tourist has written a love letter to Andreas, who has little to do over the winter but sit with other men in the coffee-shop. He may read the letter out to a chorus of comments, but his final act is one of rejection: to dismiss the woman by tearing up the letter with a suitably derogatory gesture.

Zinovieff suggests that in these encounters and their sequels, not only is a particular woman conquered and later, symbolically, humiliated in absentia, but there is also a sense of peripheral Greece getting its own back at the expense of wealthy and powerful northern Europe. The thought which does not apparently occur to the spear-fishermen is that they may be the hunted just as much as they are the hunters; sought by 'getaway people' for 'a holiday fling'.[10]

It has to be said that spear-fishing preoccupies only a minority of the eligible men in the town Zinovieff describes. It is considered disreputable by local women, and men known to indulge lose out in the marriage market, for they will not be readily accepted as grooms. So, we once again have the evidence of several different constructions of acceptable masculinities within the same ethnographic community.

In rural Cyprus, I noted in 1968 ambiguities and ambivalences about how far a mature man needed to express himself through sexual conquest or sexual encounter. One informant, a prominent communist leader, told me with some pride that he had been married for more than twenty years and during that time he had never had sex with a woman other than his wife. 'And not for lack of opportunities', he said, 'opportunities' meaning travel outside the village, and particularly foreign travel. In a similar way to that taken by the Greek army regulation which allows men leave from the army 'for reasons of health', certain young married men in the village treated themselves to a prostitute if their foreign travel required them to 'cross water'.

Conversations in the coffee-shop included such questions to the traveller as, 'Did she put her legs in the air?', and when in a spirit of teasing enquiry I asked if being married to an attractive young wife ought not to have precluded the 'need' for such escapades, the riposte, issued with a smirk or a stare, would be, 'What? Must we eat louvia-beans every day?'. And when I suggested that wives might be encouraged to 'put their legs in the air', I was told that local women did not behave like that, nor would their husbands want them to! For some married men, it was not necessary even to cross water – the twenty-six miles to Nicosia gave them the licence they needed.

To return to the communist who had remained faithful: he was among the more respected and physically tough men of the village. He had carried a pistol, frequenting gambling cliques and bars when young. But he explained to me that his communism included a belief in the equality of men and women, and if he were to have had an extra-marital liaison, it would have meant he granted his wife the right to do the same, 'And you know I couldn't accept that; it is my duty as a husband to satisfy her', he said with a large grin. Clearly this adherence to a principle was important to him, because during a row with another man, who had (although married) been attempting to seduce an unmarried girl, my informant got angry and shouted out in public, 'Do you suppose just because I do not chase after the daughters of Alpha or Vita, my cock doesn't stand up?'. My informant was proud to be a sexually active man, but felt he was no less a man for confining his sexuality to his wife. Indeed, in his own eyes, he was more of a man (*parapano antras*).[11]

MONASTIC CELIBACY

Having looked at several varieties of male sexuality, it is perhaps time to remind ourselves that Greece has had the Orthodox church at its cultural centre for two thousand years, and that this church, in its early, formative period, took the position that the higher form of spiritual life for Christians was not the married, procreative state, but celibacy. There is an immediate sociological paradox to be noted, since the communities of monks and nuns, however economically self-sustaining they may be, are dependent for their biological continuity on the very activities of the secular, married laity which they hold theologically to be inferior. To put it simply: monasteries and convents cannot legitimately reproduce their memberships physically, only spiritually. So, spirituality in this world is inevitably a condition dependent upon the very flesh it seeks to transcend.

Marina Iossifides (1991), in her account of Greek nuns, has shown how they resolve this paradox by various methods: one is to create rules which separate food preparation from any taint of sexuality, so that bread must be made by a woman who no longer menstruates; another is to consume food which is plain, and to the accompaniment of readings from the scriptures; and a third is by declarations of their wish to leave this life sooner rather than later, in order to be united with Christ. Where the secular laity seek long life and many children, the nuns enter the convent through a tonsure ceremony which symbolically breaks their relationship with the world of their biological kin, and they learn to decry the value of earthly life in favour of life everlasting.

A number of anthropological studies of Orthodox male monasticism are currently under way, and it is too early to report on their findings on the theme of masculinities. But it is a definitional truism that Orthodox monasticism involves a celibate masculinity in which sexuality is highly controlled and a community of spiritual brothers is created under the authority of a spiritual father. There are many interesting questions, including the extent to which there is a clear and contrasting boundary between the world of secular householding, biological procreation, and the desire for long life in a healthy body, and how far doctrines of world and bodily renunciation lead to a system of values which parallels the account of nuns just discussed. Because there are marked differences in how men and women relate to the secular world, it is unlikely that monks in their interpretation of their lives as masculine beings will simply prove to be the mirror images of nuns, and on Mount Athos, to take a single example only, there is a range of monasteries representing varieties of Orthodoxy. In some, the physical regime for the subjugation of the body is much stricter, and the degree of opposition to the secular world much sharper. So we may expect to find that even among monks, masculinities are plural rather than singular, divergent rather than convergent.

OF 'FREE SPIRITS' AND 'DOMESTICATED MEN'

The theme I finish on is that of two opposed ways of being masculine, drawing on Akis Papataxiarchis' Lesbos data, Herzfeld's Cretan material and my own Cypriot fieldwork. Papataxiarchis noted that Lesbos villages have matrifocal kinship as the organizing principle of neighbourhoods and the house is a female domain; a woman's status, power, property are located in her house and householding. Men appear in these houses only by virtue of their relationship to women, and they are not particularly at home in them.

Where casual observers and early feminists perceived Greek men in coffee-shops as enjoying some kind of patriarchal privilege, it is clear in Lesbos (and in Argaki, Cyprus) that men are in the coffee-shops because they would be out of place in their wives' houses, except to eat and sleep, and sometimes to entertain. Men are to be thought of as *extruded* into a public male space, in which they find little else to do except perform, compete and act as spectators, judges, critics and chorus to those who strive to stand out (Herzfeld 1985).

Papataxiarchis sees the coffee-shop as a 'domain' (Collier and Yanagisako 1987), and I follow him, noting that it is a more informally and weakly instituted domain than those created by the church and the military. In the coffee-shop domain, we can see a form of masculinity being enacted by those I shall term 'men of spirit', in which those who play the game at all seek to stand out, to dominate, to excel, by drinking deeply and paying handsomely, by dancing with style and distinction, and by gambling. In their discourses on being male, they emphasize the notion of the autonomous man, who does not spend his spirit in calculation. He may be married, or he may have chosen to remain unmarried, but if married, he is certainly not *domesticated* (cf. Kandiyoti, Chapter 12 in this volume). Papataxiarchis describes how these men can also imagine a life in which men and women can enjoy each other's company without the fetters of marriage, householding and procreation. They can imagine themselves as free spirits. They could cheerfully 'live in sin' with a woman of equally free spirit. Such women are not normally to be found in any Greek village known to me. If they ever exist outside of male imaginations – another debating point – they tend to migrate to the towns and live in the fringe world of night-clubs, performers and entertainers of various kinds.[12]

It was such free-spirited men who, as I reported earlier, tried unsuccessfully to bring a night-club to the village. It is also this style of man who tends to have a male 'friend of the heart', a very special and greatly valued male friend, who is not a kinsman, and with whom a man should spend his leisure hours, drinking with him every evening if possible.

The other kind of man, whom I term 'domesticated men', do not imitate the 'men of spirit' in these matters. They cannot stay at home, but their participation in coffee-shop and tavern is a much more measured affair. They do not emphasize their autonomy, but stress their constrained condition as responsible householders with obligations to support women and children. In Cyprus, they might describe themselves as *pantremenoi anthropoi*, married male persons, to emphasize their lack of freedom and the relative sobriety (in both senses) of their spirits.[13]

The two versions of masculinity in Lesbos are more or less reproduced in the Cyprus village I studied. At the time of my fieldwork, I tended to see them as psychological types, rather than alternative styles of masculinity, and I have never managed to give a sociological explanation for why some men went one way and some another – another debating point, perhaps. Herzfeld's Cretan material describes the 'real men', the ones who steal each other's sheep, carry guns, and conduct feuds, as if they were simply the pinnacle of male aspirations in the community. But he has given us, I suspect, a single point of view.

I would not be at all surprised if the men who do not steal sheep, who either drop out of shepherding after being leaned upon by the harder men and go into agriculture (an activity dismissed by the shepherds as 'effeminate'), have a well-articulated discourse in which other concepts are foregrounded. The quality known as *anthropia* – that is, feeling for one's fellow-humans – might be emphasized instead of being good at being a man, *kal' antras*; as might respect for the person and property of others, rather than the virtues of violence and theft. The word *politismenos*, civilized, might even be used. It is notable that Herzfeld cites examples of fathers being ambivalent towards their son's sheep-stealing, whereas mothers can sometimes be decidedly hostile, refusing to eat stolen meat and ordering it to be removed from the house (1985: 168–9). This implies that there is neither a simple value consensus nor, perhaps, an unchallenged hierarchy of achievements.

CONCLUSION

In this chapter I have raided Greek ethnography opportunistically, highlighting a range of cultural practices and contrasts. The idea has been to suggest that not only is there no single sense of masculinity in that abstraction called 'Greek culture', but that from one local context, institution, domain or discourse to another we can easily find contrasting ways of being masculine. Obviously, this is all relational, and we have had to think in passing about constructions of femaleness as well. I think the implications of this approach are quite far-reaching: they take us away from any kind of whole-system modelling of society, culture, or general ideology of the Bloch and Parry (1982) variety, which is analytically stimulating, but which, in an ethnographic field as varied and dynamic as that of contemporary Greece, suggests many pitfalls.

How far can one abstract a 'gender ideology' from such complexities? One of the best known papers on gender in the Christian Mediterranean is Brandes' (1981) fascinating paper about masculinity in Andalusia, in which men appear to be fearful of and hostile to women, and to believe that sexual intercourse is likely to drain and destroy them. The information seems very striking, almost surprising, when you read it as an account of a stable, comprehensive, across-the-board view of 'how men see women'.

But in a later paper, Brandes (1992) describes the fieldwork in Andalusia. It turns out that he spent his first months making contacts and fieldwork friendships by going almost every day to an all-male bar. Only later did this situation stop, and Brandes started to see men in contexts where women were also present, and indeed, to have much conversation with women. How far did those early bar-room conversations produce a peculiarly intense and specialized masculine discourse about women, which he reported in his 1981 paper?

Brandes' decision to write about that fieldwork in the way he has done suggests he has had significant 'second thoughts' about the original article. If the arguments of my chapter and this volume are accepted, then it would be a mistake to allow Brandes' earlier paper to have the last word on how men think about women in Andalusia (cf. Hart, Chapter 2 in this volume), and, at very least, his later paper needs to be read as a modifier.

Consider as a thought experiment the kinds of discourse about the other sex you would expect to get in a refuge for battered women, a brothel after it had closed, a Jesuit seminary before the Second Vatican Council, an army barracks in contemporary Greece or Britain, or the all-male bars in many cities where middle-aged bachelor men hang out, men who have long since given up trying to get a wife since they lack the economic drawing power and sobriety to make them attractive.[14] In this last context we might hear discourses of compensatory male independence and the overvaluation of male gender in the teeth of systematic rejections. In none of these cases should we assume that this was the *only* way of thinking or speaking about the other sex which would come to the speaker's lips: other contexts, other listeners – other discourses.

It is methodologically unsafe to add up lots of contexts in which gender ideas are expressed, and construct out of these a 'Greek view of masculinity' or 'a Greek style of being male'. I regard those particular distorting mirrors as finally broken and I do not see that they can be put back together again. The challenge for the immediate future is to make reliable statements which are not about unique constellations of action and discourse and are therefore more sociologically profound than intelligent journalism. At the moment, most of us can do nothing more aggregative than point to ranges of difference, and occasionally regroup a small number of such characterizations as a 'logic', as Collier and Rosaldo (1981) suggest. If this activity is more descriptive and more minimalist than the whole-system theorizing which previously prevailed, it is also more modest and more accurate.

NOTES

I am grateful to participants in seminars at the School of Oriental and African Studies, University of London; Department of Byzantine and Modern Greek Studies, King's College, London; Department of Anthropology, Durham University; and the Institute of Anthropology, Oxford, for their comments, and to the editors of this volume for their more detailed suggestions. Yiannis Papadakis also made some helpful comments. The errors and omissions are, of course, my own.

1   My own childhood in south London and adulthood in north London bring to mind numerous memories of young working-class boys and men calling each other 'wanker', masturbator. It is used as a term of scorn at soccer matches to imply that players are performing in a lacklustre fashion, because, by implication, they have spent their energies masturbating. It can be used affectionately between friends, as a 'rough' greeting, much as men friends in the Cypriot village I studied curse each other vividly.

2   Campbell attended a seminar where I read a version of this paper, and gave me to understand that his account of sexuality was indeed concerned with official values. I am less reticent here but will undoubtedly incur criticism from those Greeks who would have preferred me to follow Campbell's example.

3   Akis Papataxiarchis, personal communication.

4   Yiannis Papadakis, personal communication.

5   The *Independent* (11 June 1991), under the sub-heading 'Victims of sexual prejudice in uniform', reported that between 1987 and 1990, 34 men and women were dismissed with disgrace after court martial, some being given prison sentences of one to two years. A further 272 men and women were 'administratively discharged' because they were homosexuals. Their discharge papers were marked 'services no longer required'.

6   The tendency of modern authoritarian-nationalist regimes to be hostile to homosexuality is noteworthy, Mussolini's Italy and Castro's Cuba being two examples which come readily to mind. Perhaps it is the 'strength' of the nation, conceived of as a heterosexually macho strength, of men as inseminators, warriors and patriarchs, which is at issue? But here the authoritarians seem unable to group the notion of homosexual warriors. According to the *Oxford Classical Dictionary*, Pelopidas, leader of a band of 300 warriors – the defenders of Thebes – had them organized as pairs of lovers.

7   I am grateful to Yiannis Papadakis for this point.

8   This was brought home to me when an otherwise thoughtful and progressive communist described the humiliation of a man in a coffee-shop brawl. The man had challenged a couple of tough brothers, who had set about him, and started to beat him to the point that he lost control of his bowels. My informant laughed at the memory of his enemy's humiliation in a way which equated him with a baby, or a very old, infirm person.

9   My masculine status in the village was problematic. When I first arrived in 1966 for a brief holiday, I was married and was joined by my wife. When I returned to the village for fieldwork in 1968, I came alone, and explained when questioned that I was divorced. 'Who was to blame?' (*poios ftai?*), I was invariably asked. I would answer, 'Neither of us. We separated in a friendly fashion. Our characters did not agree.' This was treated with scepticism as it was not grounds for divorce in village eyes. Divorce was unusual – I did not record more than five informal separations in more than seven hundred marriages. After a few months in the village, I was asked in an all-male drinking group how I could manage 'without a wife/woman'. I agreed that as a formerly married man it was 'difficult'. In no time at all several of my close relatives and their friends had bundled me into a car and we were driving towards Nicosia. The formal object of the evening was to make sure that I should not have to remain sexually frustrated any longer, but the other agenda was to prove to the rest of the village that my divorce had not come about through my lack of libido.

10 The recent British film *Shirley Valentine* played with the theme of a gently

predatory Greek male exploiting a succession of tourist women (cf. Bowman 1989).

11 I must find space for the following point about male potency and its wider significance. I was comprehensively interviewing 200 male 'household heads' (a term which had not struck me as problematic in 1968). At one phase of the interview I was asking them about the number of children they had. As part of my enquiries, I asked if their wives had ever miscarried, which seemed a common occurrence. The village idiom for talking about miscarriage is to say that a child 'fell' (from the womb). I asked one of my friends, a barrel-like fellow rejoicing in the nickname 'Wild Man' for his potential fierceness, if his wife had ever had a child who 'fell'. He replied, smiting his chest and grinning hugely, 'When *I* put 'em in, they *don't* fall out!'.

12 In due course, Diane Mueller, now carrying out field research in Athens, will have something to tell us about that world.

13 When I say they cannot stay at home, I mean it. A piece of 'personal ethnography' here: in London, at certain times when the Cypriot community was in a state of political ferment, I would be telephoned by members of numerous cultural groups seeking to recruit activists. In order to have a reasonable excuse to decline, I would deliberately mention my young family and pressing work burdens, and finish off by saying I had become *anthropos tou spitiou*, which is best rendered 'a man who stays at home'. My interlocutors never failed to tell me, 'No – you haven't', since the phrase carries a negative connotation. Men should be out, in public, having opinions, taking part.

14 I have in mind bars in Finsbury Park and Camden Town, districts of London with significant numbers of Irish working-class men, who have one of the latest ages of marriage and highest proportions of bachelors in Europe.

Chapter 4

Variant masculinities, variant virginities
Rethinking 'honour and shame'

Nancy Lindisfarne

Anthropological descriptions have often emphasized idealized, hegemonic versions of gendered identities and ignored the shifting reality of people's experience as gendered beings. Such an emphasis is particularly evident in the literature on honour and shame. An ideal of female virginity and versions of hegemonic masculinity have been much discussed: the radical differentiation of men and women has been taken for granted and there has been a focus on local idioms which naturalize the privileges of socially dominant men. I suggest that it is now time to move on: that it is more instructive, and less circular, to treat gender as a contested discourse. When gender is problematized, it becomes possible to ask how people make gender known to themselves and how gendered identities may be reified to express apparently absolute differences between men and women while simultaneously defining inequalities *within* these categories.

The ethnographic literature of the Mediterranean and Middle East is rich and contains some fine descriptions of hegemonic masculinities (see, for example, Herzfeld 1985). This literature offers the possibility of reanalysis: how are different versions of masculinity related to each other in any particular setting? And how are attributions of masculinity themselves constructed? Fiction can be an even richer source of ideas about the ways difference and inequality are defined and enacted through sexual images. In this chapter, the ethnography I present is a deliberate collage. My aim is to raise new questions concerning, first, the extent to which abstract notions of female virginity and chastity construct idealized, hegemonic versions of masculinity and femininity; and second, the plurality of gendered identities which emerge in practice.

In the anthropological literature, 'honour and shame' has been treated as a loose category around which comparative descriptions can be organized. As Davis has written,

> Among systems of prestige and control . . . honour systems are distinct [in that] they generally have as one of their components the control by men of women's sexuality, and the resulting combination of sex and self importance makes a unique contribution to the human comedy in life.
>
> (1969: 69)

Glosses on systems of honour and shame are disarmingly consistent in their focus on competitions between dominant men and the passive subordination of women. The flavour of conventional analyses is well conveyed in David Gilmore's account:

> Sexuality is a form of social power ... women themselves are often nonproductive materially – ideally they are 'excluded' from nondomestic work. ... Rather, they carry an immaterial or conceptual resource, their chastity, arbitrarily elevated to central position as an exchange value ... female modesty is metamorphosed, almost in the manner of a fetish, into a pseudocommodity, or more accurately, a capital good ... the masculine experience of sexuality becomes broadened conceptually to encompass a triad involving two men or groups of men and a woman, who is reduced to an intermediating object. Female sexuality becomes objectified, not only a libidinal goal in itself, but a contentious and arbitrating social index for masculine reputation.
>
> (1987a: 4–5)

In a related passage, Gilmore writes that 'the correlative emphasis on female chastity and the desirability of premarital virginity remains strong throughout the region despite modernization' (1987a: 3), yet the considerable variation (past and present) throughout the region throws doubt on the status of his generalization (cf. Wikan 1984).

Gilmore has described a dominant folk model which couples a rhetoric of gender with what, following Scott (1990), might be called a 'euphemism of power'. In this way Gilmore illustrates how local idioms of honour and shame *and* anthropological analyses can underwrite forms of patriarchy. His focus is on men's activities and on ideals expressed by dominant men (cf. Lever 1986). Yet, by his own account, the dynamics of the system depend on the *relation* between men and women. Moreover, Gilmore's description is at a level of abstraction which simplifies and lends a spurious coherence to a much messier social reality. One consequence of this descriptive tidying is the way 'men' and 'women' are presented as radically different; there is the implication that these gendered identities are biologically given and remain constant throughout the life of an individual. And, because gender is presented as unitary, it seems unproblematic that gendered difference is located in a quasi-physical attribute – female chastity or modesty, the virgin's unbroken hymen – which is then treated as a thing and ranked and valued along with other commodities.[1]

ATTRIBUTES AND THINGS: A VIRGIN'S HYMEN

Malti-Douglas, in her excellent book on gendered discourse in Arabo-Islamic writing, illustrates how a gendered attribute (such as a virgin's hymen) can be used to define all dimensions of personhood. Malti-Douglas examines the rich medieval corpus of anecdotal prose, the *adab* literature, in which 'woman' becomes a character type whose voice, wit and survival depend on her duplicity, her physicality and the manipulation of her body. Thus, in one oft-told story, a slave girl being offered for sale to a caliph is asked, 'Are you a virgin or what?'. She replies, 'Or what, O caliph'. He laughs and buys her (1991: 36). In a second story,

> two slave girls were shown to a man, one a virgin and one who had been deflowered. He inclined to the virgin, so the deflowered one said, 'Why do you desire her since there is only one day between her and me?' But the virgin replied, 'And surely a day with thy Lord is as a thousand years of your counting.' The two pleased him so he bought them. In a variant ending, the man buys only the virgin.
>
> (1991: 36)

Many ethnographies of the Mediterranean and Middle East report on an obsession with female virginity which amounts to a kind of fetishism. Such a fixation with dismembered body parts, Strathern suggests, may be intimately related to ideologies of private property (1988: 133ff., 338, 373). Certainly, virginity is often commodified: the hymen is a store of value which may be disposed of and exchanged. For instance, in Zakariyya Tamer's short story, 'The Eastern Wedding', 'the price of the young girl is agreed on, so much per kilo, and she is taken to the marketplace and weighed in' (Tamer 1978: 71–9, quoted in Malti-Douglas 1991: 142). Such calculations are by no means only fictional exaggerations: marriage payments may be calculated in terms of both the cost of a woman's upbringing and her purported virginity (cf. Tapper 1991: 142ff.).

Treated from this perspective, there are many questions to be asked about parts or aspects of human beings which can be objectified, owned and alienated, sold or exchanged. What are the sources of value and how do they produce gendered difference? What is the commodity logic which allows men to see women as other men's property and renders women part-objects through brideprices? Thus, in the stories retold by Malti-Douglas, how are buyers and sellers, as well as the women for sale, gendered by such transactions? Or if, as I will argue, protection and predation, responsible and competitive behavour are intimately related aspects of dominant versions of masculinity, then how do men protect women? How is male agency under-stood and how does it impinge on which parts of those who are being 'protected'? In short, how are the metaphors of property and protection constituted, experienced and sustained in everyday life? Put more generally, how do fetishism and commodification intersect to construe masculinity and femininity in systems which make use of idioms of honour and shame?

The categorical images of competitive men and passive women that we are presented with in the summary accounts of honour and shame are often contradicted in more extended ethnographic descriptions. Other indigenous notions of honour associate men with conciliatory, cooperative behaviour and allow women agency in certain contexts as wives and mothers, on the one hand, and as devilish creatures of voracious sexuality, on the other (cf. Pitt-Rivers 1965, 1977). As Davis notes, it seems likely that these apparent contradictions are, in large part, the product of analyses which neglect 'the practical consequences for an individual of having more or less honour' and the ways in which 'honour is awarded, or manipulated' (Davis 1969: 69). When attention is paid to everyday negotiations involving both men and women, a range of variant masculinities and femininities emerges.

COMPETITIONS AND THE CONTROL OF PEOPLE

In any setting, notions of honour and shame are not separate from the political economy; rather they are a mode of interpretation through which inequalities are created and sustained. Thus, the rhetoric of hegemonic masculinity depends heavily on stereotypes of women: as weak, emotional, both needing support and potentially treacherous. Female virginity and chastity are both prized and precarious. In practice, the protection of and predation on *men* as well as women can be justified in terms of values derived from the ideology of honour and shame.

Take, for example, the Durrani Pashtuns of Afghanistan. Among the Durrani, versions of hegemonic masculinity are expressed through a range of idioms which may be translated in terms of a notion of 'honour'. These idioms celebrate maleness in terms of both physical strength and moral strength of character, rationality and responsibility; honourable men are those who are physically attractive, 'far sighted', 'mature' and 'deep' (Tapper 1991: 208ff.). Such men are likely to be those who most effectively monitor virginity and control the sexual behaviour of 'their own' women; they are also likely to act as oppressors of other men and usurpers of 'other men's' women (1991: 239).

Men prey on other men, most often using the idiom of a woman's reputed behaviour to explain and justify their actions. Men who demonstrate weakness, by failing to control either women's behaviour or their own independence in the arrangement and completion of marriages, lose credibility and find themselves on a downward spiral. They become extremely vulnerable to further exploitation. Thus, a man may be labelled 'dishonourable', or femininized as 'soft' or 'weak', when a daughter elopes and 'is stolen' by another man; when he is forced to arrange a marriage for a daughter against his wishes; when he is cuckolded; and even when others, acting on gossip about women's behaviour, take advantage of his precarious control of household resources in sheep or land.

In effect, women's actions, the choices they make with respect to their sexuality and the consequences of those choices are treated as an index of a man's success or failure to provide economically and compete politically.

Moreover, in spite of the severe sanctions associated with women's sexual misbehaviour, these are not uniformly applied. Not only does female prostitution exist within the community (Tapper 1991: 236ff.), but men are sometimes judged foolish when, in conformity with idealized notions of honour, they over-react (*sic!*) by killing a woman in circumstances when they can literally ill afford to do so (Tapper 1991: 225; cf. Gilsenan 1976). Among men, degrees of affluence, political credibility and control of other people coincide. Conversely, women often have more personal autonomy (but little else) when the men of the household with which they are associated are poor and vulnerable to the machinations of other men.

Some men are more able or willing than others to conform to the ideals of hegemonic masculinity. Subordinate variants also form a continuum which depends on interpretation. Men do not act without a cogent explanation of their motives, and an account of their expectations and various gains. However, they will be believed only if there is no doubt that they are operating from strength, not weakness. What is interesting is the extent to which some men can exercise choice and take advantage of positions of relative dominance, while others opt out or fail to assert their control over resources of all kinds, including (in hegemonic discourses) a woman's virginity, sexuality and fertility.

There is a considerable discrepancy between, on the one hand, men's and women's public agreement with the dominant ideology of gender and, on the other, the great range of their actions. In competitions for 'honour' many nuanced masculinities are created, yet because the interpretations of dominant men often frame discourses on gender, an illusion of hegemonic masculinity, the related ideal of female chastity and the gender hierarchy between men and women remain intact. It is arguable that this is a measure of the fiercely competitive environment in which the Durrani live. Men's everyday lives are riven politically. Their commonality (and privileges) *as men* depend almost entirely on the rhetoric of honour and shame and the collective disparagement of women. In short, the ideal of male domination is sustained in reiterated statements which put a rhetorical gloss on the cumulative, but diverse and often ambiguous, episodes during which individual men and women interact unequally. A patriarchal ideology may be embodied in the lives of socially dominant men, but this does not mean that all men are successful patriarchs, or that all women are passive, virginal or chaste.

SUBVERSIVE WOMEN AND SUBORDINATE MASCULINITIES

The idioms of honour and shame construct various masculinities in terms of the control of women's sexual behaviour. These idioms can be used to differentiate men from each other and to describe a man in terms of different masculine identities in different contexts. Yusuf Idris' short story 'The shame' (1978) illustrates how the abstract value of a woman's chastity may be interpreted in practice and how various masculinities are created through such interpretations. The story is written from the point of view of male protagonists whose perceptions are fused with those of their male author.

'The shame' explores the masculinities revealed in the relationship between a woman's guardian and the man accused of seducing her. Farag, the brother, uses bravado to hide his fear of responsibility for his vivacious sister Fatma, who 'even aroused the dormant virility in little boys' (p. 158).

Fatma's imputed lover Gharib, a rake and bully, is secretly intimidated by Fatma's beauty, propriety and fear of being compromised by sexual innuendo – the 'shame' of the story's title. None the less, the villagers fabricate a relationship between them. Farag's duty is to kill his sister and her lover: 'but, before he made himself guilty of their blood, their own guilt must be proved' (p. 165). In this, the village women were bolder than the men, forcing a physical examination of Fatma's hymen, while simultaneously heaping curses on her putative lover Gharib (pp. 166, 167). Two women examine the girl, one an experienced 'dresser of brides' whose home is said to be the site of clandestine meetings of men and women and who, villagers fear, might lie about what she discovers, the other a much respected Christian woman whose honesty is not in question. Meanwhile, the brother, Farag, 'were he not a man, . . . could have been taken for a grief-stricken widow bemoaning a dead husband' (*sic*, p. 168).

Fatma's innocence is proved, yet Farag beats her mercilessly: 'he felt bound to perform some spectacular act by which to reply to the people's gossip'. In his turn, Gharib's father abuses his son and threatens to drown him, yet the father is 'secretly proud to have sired a seducer no woman could resist, and that his son was accused of rape' (p. 174). Both Fatma and Gharib are severely chastened by the episode and well-meaning friends suggest they should marry to save face all round. In the end Fatma, who had, in spite of her innocence, lost 'that thing that gave her purity' (*sic*, p. 176), returns to her ravishing ways with new-found defiance, while Gharib remains the unreconstructed rake.

The story derives its narrative impetus from notions of hegemonic masculinity, but it actually describes various and nuanced interpretations of honour. Thus, the cause of men's violence toward women (and men) are twofold: a man's commitment to ideals of honour as judged by neighbours and others, and his dishonour, which lies not only in the actions of women but in those of men who have challenged his authority as a surrogate father, brother and neighbour and rendered him socially impotent. Local attributions of dishonour suggest ways in which the rhetoric of honour also inscribes ideas of the unique, bounded and coherent person. The notion of 'dishonour' is one way of describing the discrepancies between presentations of masculinity before different audiences, while violence may be a means through which the illusion of wholeness is reasserted.

In this story and others (e.g. Tamer 1985), it is the voices of superiors, men who control resources, that are most audible. But they are not the only ones. Dominant or hegemonic versions of masculinity (or femininity) do not exist in isolation; rather they define a range of appropriate behaviours. What is crucial is that the limits of control are not fixed, but are repeatedly negotiated in everyday interactions. And it is through such negotiations that subordinates can modify and transform dominant idioms and structures.

A VIRGIN, OR WHAT?

Contextualized interpretations of female virginity and chastity play a central role in the construction of particular versions of masculinity. This relation can be compared cross-culturally and historically and would ideally also include a consideration of related themes: among them, notions of male virginity and chastity, as well as the ways in which myths of seduction and betrayal construct a Don Juan archetype of masculinity (cf. Miller 1990).[2]

To return specifically to female virginity: in upper Egypt and the Sudan people explain pharaonic circumcision and the infibulation of girls of 7 and 8 as preventing 'any suspicion on the bridegroom's part that the bride is not a virgin' (Eickelman 1989: 193). However, as Boddy's work attests, virgins are made, not born. A divorced or widowed woman 'may undergo reinfibulation in anticipation of remarriage, thus renewing, like the recently delivered mother, her "virginal" status' (Boddy 1982: 687). Boddy argues that both operations are less about the control of female sexuality than about its socialization. She writes,

> Through occlusion of the vaginal orifice, her womb, both literally and figuratively, becomes a social space: enclosed, impervious, virtually impenetrable. Her social virginity . . . must periodically be reestablished at those points in her life (after childbirth and before remarriage) when her fertility once again is rendered potent.
>
> (1982: 696)

Though a man's increased sexual pleasure is sometimes offered as an explanation for the operation, Boddy dismisses this argument as implausible:

> it may take as long as two years of continuous effort before penetration can occur. For a man it is a point of honor to have a child born within a year of his marriage, and often, the midwife is summoned in secret, under cover of darkness, to assist the young couple by surgically enlarging the bride's genital orifice.
>
> (1982: 686; cf. Boddy 1989: 53–4)

Virginity in this case is in no sense 'natural' but is created by an elaborate operation insisted upon and performed by women. Nor is sexual intercourse necessarily an unmediated act between bride and groom. Moreover, virility is reckoned less in terms of male sexuality than in those of fertility:

that is, what men share is the right to allocate and benefit from a woman's reproductive potential, but it is women, whose femininity is enhanced by infibulation, who carry the burden of producing a masculinity focused on fatherhood (1982: 687–8).[3]

In the rhetoric of honour and shame, the hymen is often commodified and female virginity presented as an all-or-nothing attribute. Yet nowhere in practice do things seem to be so simple . It is Boddy who is exceptional when she describes the local understandings of an alternation between discrete gendered identities and the transformative power of gendered interaction.[4]

Certainly 'virginity' as it is associated with pharaonic circumcision and infibulation is a specific notion which differs from 'virginity' as it is understood elsewhere in the Mediterranean and Middle East. However, the important question is this: how are images of an 'infinitely renewable virgin' (Carter 1991:153)[5] related to particular versions of an idealized male sexuality? Not only is the seduction of a virgin a widespread idiom which conveys a notion of essentialized, almost heroic virility, but the repetition of such an act sometimes defines the very essence of maleness. For instance, Boudhiba writes of visions of paradise as an 'infinite orgasm' where men experience eternal erections and have repeated intercourse with *houris* who, after each penetration, become virginal again (Boudhiba 1985, cited in Delaney 1991: 319–20). The practice of hymen repair, like that of reinfibulation, raises questions about the relation between notions of virginity and the masculinities they construct.

Writing of lower-class Neapolitans, Goddard begs the question which should be asked wherever there is a sexual double standard: why bother with virginity, particularly when it is often a charade? Goddard criticizes the literature on honour and shame for its functionalist circularity, male bias and focus on normative aspects of the honour code in small-scale communities (1987: 168, 171–3). She rightly argues that the honour code must be understood in terms of its implications for women and the extent to which they are 'consenting and active participants in [the] manipulation of honour' (p. 179). However, it is not enough to explain the double standard in terms of women being 'seen as the boundary markers and the carriers of group identity' (p. 180). Rather, it seems likely that more basic processes of gendering are at stake.

Goddard writes that virginity 'is a crucial element in the relationships of men and women' (p. 175): 'men want or even expect to marry virgins'; a woman's sullied reputation diminishes her chances of marriage, while after marriage a woman's fidelity is assumed (pp. 176–7). Meanwhile, 'it is expected of a "normal", "healthy" man that he will take every opportunity for sex that presents itself and his self-image will be thereby enhanced', while women who 'themselves control their sexuality and decide whether or not to dispose of their virginity' (p. 176) realize their 'potential corruption' if they transgress (p. 177). None the less, sexual experimentation both within and outside the institution of 'a house engagement' is not uncommon and women, who themselves dream of white weddings, are often pregnant when they marry the man who was their first lover (pp. 175–6). Failing such a marriage, women have only two options: the streets, or hymen repair, which, in a large city like Naples, is a relatively anonymous, inexpensive and simple operation (pp. 175–7).

Hymen repair is by no means unique to Naples, or without historical precedents (cf. Weideger 1986: 148). In the central Middle East young, unmarried women may now even have the operation performed before they go out with each new boyfriend! And, when the state of a woman's hymen may be investigated by either her own or a prospective groom's family, some Middle Eastern women, during premarital sexual encounters, will insist on anal, rather than vaginal, intercourse to avoid trouble and shame.

Herzfeld has also pointed to the puzzles surrounding virginity. He notes that among Cretans, 'sex before marriage is tolerated for women, and reference to chastity has a rhetorical value' (cited in Loizos and Papataxiarchis 1991: 230, n.22). Herzfeld's explanation of the apparent paradox of the idealized virginal woman and everyday sexual licence is that women *creatively deform* their submission [to male dominance]'(1991: 80–1); cf. Kandiyoti's idea of 'bargaining with patriarchy' (Chapter 12 in this volume). Herzfeld is probably right, but he does not go far enough. His argument does not explain why demonstrations that a bride is *virgo intacta* are widespread, nor does it allow for a discussion of the ways in which stereotypes of women structure inequalities between men. Surely, the unasked questions are why female virginity is an important ideal in the first place, and why it must be sustained by hypocrisy and practised subversion. A Spanish saying runs, 'If all Spanish women are virtuous and chaste and all Spanish men are great seducers and lovers, someone has to be lying.' Or, as an Iranian friend put it, why does every middle-class marriage begin with a lie to which both bride and groom subscribe: that the bride is a virgin on her wedding night?

THE RHETORIC AND PRACTICE OF WEDDING-NIGHT DEFLORATION

The celebrations which follow the bloodied proof of a bride's virginity are extensively documented in the ethnographic literature. Yet as we have seen, female virginity cannot be treated as a uniform cultural trait. However, within any one setting, the rituals associated with a bride's defloration radically differentiate men from women (as part of a dominant discourse on gender) and also define a range of other gendered identities (which are normally muted by local and anthropological emphases on hegemonic masculinity).

The ethnography of wedding-night defloration provides a striking example of the force of Strathern's argument about 'dividual' persons whose identities depend on exchanging parts of themselves with other persons (cf. Strathern

1988: 14ff, 348ff.; cf. Cornwall and Lindisfarne, Chapter 1 in this volume). Thus, the unambiguously 'female' and 'male' identities of bride and groom depend on intercourse and the exchange and transformation of essences and separable bits: semen, the penetrated hymen and hymenal blood among them. Momentarily, an archetypal masculinity and femininity are created and revealed through interaction. Through the sex act, gendered identities and an act of domination are temporarily, but literally, embodied. And the marital state also anticipates further exchanges and transformations: among them, marital intercourse and the creation of the ungendered child in the female womb. However, in the return to everyday life, new, ambiguous identities emerge. Clichés of feminized masculinities and masculinized femininities abound: among them hen-pecked husbands, cuckolds whose wives have given them 'horns', termagant matrons and 'big balled women' (Brandes 1981: 229, 231; cf. Blok 1981: 429).

Following Strathern, we can begin to ask questions about the ways in which ideas of gender difference are produced by 'dividual' persons. Just as the bride and groom acquire fleeting but unambiguous gender identities through consummation, so too do the generic categories 'men' and 'women' receive confirmation through the defloration of a bride. Consider how the Algerian men Ghalem describes are, *qua* men, united through the orgasmic quality of the public rituals associated with consummation:

> the excitement of the group grew; the women were waiting impatiently for the consummation of the deflowering ritual. On the men's side of the house the anticipation was less visible, but it stirred up the desires and imagination, and their memories of pleasure of the heart and body . . . [The groom] drank his tea gravely, hoping to overcome his anxiety. He was intimidated by this very young girl; she did not appeal to him; her body was not open to life, but he had to make a woman of her and quickly, since they were waiting outside. . . . The ears glued to the door outside heard the young woman's cries. . . . On the men's side a few good riflemen fired the wedding volley. The joy was at its zenith, the party reached paroxysm. [The groom], hugged and congratuated by the friends around him, had only one desire, to get out, to get out quickly. [His friends'] bodies stiffened with desire, and then, relieved by that strange and secret complicity of men, proud of their virility and in that moment deeply bound together.
>
> (1984: 34–5)

Ghalem's description of the wedding night raises questions about desire which have hardly been addressed in the literature on honour and shame. How is it constituted – as an emotion or force, a need, in terms of satisfaction – and where is it located? How are romance and the active sexuality of men and women understood and in what ways can jinn spirits, devils, the evil eye and love potions activate and transform them? Are there other aspects of sexuality which might qualify desire? For instance, the vagina, hymen and womb, like the penis, often seem to have an active quality, a quality perhaps most fearsomely expressed in the images of Aisha Kandisha, a terrifying hag with pendulous breasts and toothed vagina. How might we understand the polluting effects of semen and hymenal and menstrual blood, as well as the blood of childbirth? Notions of contamination, transmitted through genital contact, ingestion or material objects, certainly hinge on tacit premises about 'dividual' persons and the exchange of essences. In short, it seems certain that the construction of gendered identities is far more complex in practice than the idealized images of penetrative sex, or their lewd counterparts, imply.

Westermarck's extended description of ceremonies of the 'bride's drawers' (1914: 228ff., 266ff.) in Morocco offers ethnographic examples of the variant masculinities and femininities which are a product of an idealized notion of bridal virginity. Thus, he notes the groom does not necessarily manage intercourse on the wedding night and the ceremony takes place only after hymenal blood has appeared (pp. 229, 271). A masculinity which trades on images of male potency must be altered by such a delay and, in turn, define subordinate masculinities. Westermarck does not discuss such delays further, yet his account of consummations treated as *le droit de seigneur* or performed by a paid proxy (1914: 271–2; cf. Giovannini 1987: 66) suggests the range of possibilities which may be practised.

In some places manual defloration rather than *lege artis* relieves the groom of worries about his potency, but in general, impotence seems to be hedged round with taboos. Some of these are local: thus, popular accounts of 'wedding-night murders' in Turkey suggest that brides may be killed merely for being the inadvertent witnesses of their husbands' impotence.[6] In the ethnographic literature, impotence is a topic often mentioned only in passing:[7] thus, we learn little of the consequences for a groom who fails to deflower his bride because he is too old, fat, or terrified. And what of those who are helped by a friend or proxy, a midwife, their mothers and sometimes even by their mothers-in-law? One poignant image is of a young boy who cries out in an Afghan ballad:

Je ne suis qu'un petit garçon, père;
Pourquoi me maries tu?
Ma femme ne me connaît pas;
Elle se fait des rêves d'une mari.
Hai! Hai! Le matin j'ai si froid.[8]

A striking and terrible image comes from Michel Khleifi's superb feature film, *A Wedding in Galilee*. The groom's impotence is a metaphor for the helplessness of the Palestinians in the face of their Israeli oppressors; as the wedding guests pound obscenely on the door, the young bride deflowers herself with a knife and defiantly displays her own hymenal blood.

Clearly, public recognition of a man's capacity for penetrative sex with his virgin bride often defines an adult masculinity and associates this kind of sexuality with economic privilege and control over others. However, in spite of the importance of this moment, it is interesting that Westermarck, like most other ethnographers, jumps from the spectre of impotence to the problem of the non-virgin bride. Both bride and groom may have a vested interest in covering up not only male impotence but also the bride's prior unchastity. As Westermarck notes in passing, a man will hesitate to accuse his bride of unchasteness because he thus admits that he himself has slept with a 'bitch' (1914: 236, 254, 270). Unfortunately, he does not explore further the perception of interests which may lead to a cover-up, but he does offer some clues to the fabrication of hegemonic masculinity.

Hymen repair is a strategy for preserving the illusion of virginity, and there are others. Westermarck writes,

> it may also happen that the bride's parents, in order to avoid a scandal, bribe the bridegroom to conceal the fact ... in which case the blood of a fowl or pigeon is used as a substitute for the lacking signs of virginity.
> (1914: 229; cf. 240, 243, 246)

It is worth considering not only the sheer logistics of the chicken-blood solution, but also the subordinate masculinities which it constructs. In what ways does the groom's ignorance of, or acquiescence to, such a strategem qualify his relations with his new in-laws and his bride? And are they all implicated in a cover-up *vis-à-vis* their neighbours? And there may be quite other dynamics when virginity is irrelevant or faked in wedding-night encounters. The issue to be documented ethnographically is who is using the rhetoric and rituals of virginity in political contests with whom. Thus, Loizos tells of a Cypriot couple who took great glee in telling him how, in the 1940s, they had conspired together to empty a bladder of chicken blood on the marriage bed and avoid parental knowledge and disapproval of their pre-marital encounters. Then it was shameful for a bride to be pregnant at her wedding, while her groom would be mocked as a donkey because of his uncontrolled sexuality.[9] Or the trickery may only concern the bride and groom: Rifaat's short story 'Honour' (1990) tells of a non-virgin bride who deeply dislikes her new husband. The woman pays a midwife to help her put ground glass in her vagina to make herself bleed and to cause her groom excruciating pain.

Indeed, virginity as it is revealed by, and reveals, virility may be ritually marked in circumstances which completely belie it or make its proof impossible. Jamous (1981) and Combs-Schilling (1989), both writing of Morocco, argue that the use of henna in wedding ceremonies actually precludes the need for dissimulation. They argue that henna symbolizes blood and

> blood spilling rather than sexual intercourse consummates ... first marriage ceremonies ... sexual intercourse may or may not have happened

before that night and may or may not happen on that night. Yet as long as the male spills blood and it is publicly exhibited, . . . the young man becomes a man and the young woman a woman, each acquiring the rights and duties associated with the new status.

(Combs-Schilling 1989: 197)

While such an argument mistakenly renders all 'young men' and 'men' the same, there can be no doubt that such circularities protect hegemonic ideals. And there are others: thus, among some Moroccans, it is common for a man to have intercourse with his fiancée before the final wedding ceremonies have taken place. Thereafter, 'the absence of the marks of virginity in a bride is interpreted as an indication that the bridegroom has previously had inter- course with her . . . [and] it may happen that she is already with child or even a mother at the wedding' (Westermarck 1914: 243, 248–9; cf. Tapper 1991: 77–8).

Rhetorically, the virgin's unbroken hymen is an attribute which stands for a unitary individual, and at that moment when chastity is proven, it defines that individual's gender as entirely and unambiguously female. Hymenal penetration also creates an unambiguously gendered male: it is the means by which a man makes known his virility to himself and others. Finally, hymenal penetration effects a radical transformation: the womb thus acted upon is transformed and can be made to realize its fertile potential and, by extension, that of the man.[10]

DIVISIBLE PEOPLE, GENDERED IDENTITIES AND HEGEMONIC IDEALS

Defloration by penetrative sex seems an essential component of the hegemonic masculinities of the Mediterranean and Middle East. Indeed, female virginity as an idealized notion is so important that it is often reified through deliberate trickery. Where there is such a focus on virginity, impotence and delayed consummation, as well as drugged brides (Dorsky 1986: 124–5), wedding- night rape (Hegland 1992; Westermarck 1914: 265) and the absence of proof of a bride's virginity, all become pressing if censored concerns. In short, we will greatly mislead ourselves if we consider that the display of bloodied linen, the cries of joy (by all but the bride), the gunshots and waving flags have to do only with the abstractions we translate as 'honour' and 'shame'.

Rhetorically, notions of virility which depend on the defloration of a virgin bride amount to a wholesale, and circular, affirmation of male superiority and control over women: 'The concepts of honour and virginity locate the prestige of a man between the legs of a woman' (Mernissi 1982:183). Both the groom and other male wedding guests celebrate their empowerment as actors and audience, and before an audience of women. Of course, the rhetoric of this empowerment is varied and specific: thus, in Morocco, male potency is ritually linked with the social power of the aristocracy and that of the Sultan (Westermarck 1914: 233; cf. Jamous 1981: 265ff.; Combs-Schilling 1989: 190ff.). But disempowerment is also possibility: both a bride who proves to have been unchaste, or a groom's failure to deflower her, call into question the general *and* particular associations of men with male dominance and construct subordinate masculinities.

The category 'women' is no more monolithic than that of 'men'. A hegemonic femininity (cf. Giovannini 1981) is also produced by the rituals of defloration, and women, too, are active participants in its construction. 'Honourable' women – those who seem to conform most closely to the ideals of chastity and who are fertile – gain privileges and social precedence. The bride is certainly an interested party. If she successfully loses her virginity on her wedding night, she demonstrates her prior chastity, her husband's virility and the honour of their respective families; she is likely to retain both her husband's and her family's support later in her marriage. Moreover, her wedding-night transformation from virgin to non-virgin confirms her adult status and the possibility of legitimate fertility. The celebrations also associate all other women with those privileges of marriage which depend on the salience of gender difference. Whether we consider what Rogers calls 'myths of male dominance' (1975), or Kandiyoti's notion of the 'patriarchal bargain' (1988a), it is clear that an emphasis on the separateness of men and women sustains the rhetoric and practice of male dominance while simultaneously creating domains in which some successful women exercise control over both material resources and other people.

There can be no doubt that the rhetoric of honour is politically effective because it operates at a level of abstraction which hides classificatory ambiguities and alternative points of view, while empowering some fortunate men and women. A bride's defloration by penetrative sex is a ritual moment when, ideally, a 'real' man is potent and a 'real' woman is chaste, when gendered difference and hierarchy can be experienced as quintessentially real. Undoubtedly, this is one aspect of what honour is 'for' (cf. Davis 1969: 79). However, even the quintessential moment of defloration defines other, subordinate identities. And, of course, everyday interactions produce an even wider range of ambiguous and ever-changing masculinities and femininities.

NOTES

Many friends helped me write this chapter. I am particularly grateful to Leila Zaki Chakravaty and Mary Hegland for their lively observations, while special thanks are due to Andrea Cornwall, Veronica Doubleday, Dale Eickelman, Peter Loizos, Pierre Centlivres and Sue Wright for their incisive comments on earlier drafts. Fieldwork in Afghanistan was funded by the SSRC (Project No. HR 1141/1). The paper was first read at the SOAS anthropology department seminar on 'Com-oddities' in November 1991.

1 Models which emphasize an extreme dichotomization of gender reinforce heterosexual biases, and other sexualities are often ignored or inadequately described.

For instance, Wikan's suggestion that male homosexual prostitutes in Oman constitute a third sex does not do justice to her own more complex ethnography (1977; Shepherd 1978, 1987). However, there are some exceptions: cf. Delaney's (1991: 50) discussion of the relation between body morphology and gendered identities in the case of male homosexuality and sex-change operations in Turkey.

2 Another topic which deserves further research concerns the close parallels often found beween rituals of boys' circumcision and those of marriage. See e.g. Kennedy 1978: 155 ff. or Tapper 1979: 168–9.

3 We know little of how subordinate and variant masculinities are refracted through hegemonic notions of fatherhood. Certainly men who have not fathered children are often deemed less than 'real men' and the stigma may be such that sterile men connive with their wives to gain heirs (cf. Peters 1980: 145; Tapper 1991: 125). But what of the masculine identity of those men who never marry or those whose children do not survive infancy or prove defective in some way?

4 Delaney's rich ethnography of a Turkish village (1991) offers another detailed account of how embodied experiences create and sustain gendered difference. See also Good (1977) on other aspects of embodiment in the Middle East.

5 The recreation of virginal potential may take other, less literal, forms. In Afghanistan, a man may both address and refer to his wife using the word *pegla*, which may be translated as 'virgin'. Or, in Greece, married women refer to each other by a term which may be translated 'daughter/virgin'. Here I wonder if the women are not referring to the same kind of self-contained, sterile sexuality that Greek men are marking when they use the term 'masturbator' among themselves (Loizos and Papataxiarchis 1991: 227, 229; cf. Loizos, Chapter 3 in this volume).

6 Deniz Kandiyoti, personal communication.

7 There are of course some exceptions: see e.g. Wikan 1977: 308–9.

8 My thanks to Pierre Centlivres for bringing this to my attention. The ballad was translated by Darmesteter (1888–90).

9 Peter Loizos, personal communication.

10 The various contexts in which different, competing and sometimes contradictory theories of conception are expressed remain largely unexplored. Some theories of conception reproduce versions of hegemonic masculinity (cf. Delaney (1986, 1991; Musallam 1983: 52ff.), while others, perhaps articulated by the same people to a different audience, disrupt dominant notions (cf. Musallam 1983: 52ff.; Tapper 1991: 57, 70).

Chapter 5

'We're here, we're queer, and we're not going shopping'
Changing gay male identities in contemporary Britain

David Forrest

SETTING THE SCENE

> Oh a great deal of pains he's taken and a pretty price he's paid
> to hide his poll or dye it of a mentionable shade;
> But they've pulled the beggar's hat off for the world to see and stare,
> And they're haling him to justice for the colour of his hair.
>
> (Housman, 'O who is that young sinner', 1988: 217)

It is tempting to draw an analogy here between the poet's young sinner and the contemporary gay[1] Londoner, assuming that a representative of the latter can in fact be found. He could be said to have changed the image he projects to the broader society, as well as his own self-perceptions, to ones which can be seen as more acceptable. Those aspects of his identity which centre upon his homosexuality – his same-sex desires and behaviour – may have become more prominent of late, but he appears to have moved away from seeing himself, and being seen by others, as a 'gender invert', a 'feminine' soul in a 'male' body, and towards seeing himself and being seen as a complete (that is, 'real') man: a union of his biological sex with what he perceives to be, and what he assumes to be socially accepted as, the natural mental, physical, individual and social characteristics of men. In a move variously documented as 'the butch-shift' (Segal 1990; Fernbach 1981) or as the 'masculinization of the gay man' (Gough 1989; Marshall 1981), the last three decades have seen the emergence of such 'macho' figures as the moustached 'clone', the tattooed 'leatherman' or 'biker', and more recently the all-American 'jock'. Gay men, it now seems, are going to the city's gyms in droves. In virtually all gay erotica and in the advertisements for gay chat-lines, escorts, and bars and clubs, macho posturing, bulging biceps, sculpted pectorals and lashings of torn denim, black leather and sports gear appear to be the norm rather than the exception.

However, when we take a closer look at these representations things appear much less straightforward. Personal ads in the gay press appeal for 'similar straight-acting' partners – sexual or otherwise. Gay men still behave in 'un-manly' ways. Many of us frequent 'drag shows', applauding and mimicking the artiste who struts around in his exaggeratedly 'feminine' attire. We still hear many gay men referring to others as 'she', and hear talk of 'drama queens' (emotionally charged men), 'size queens' (men who like big cocks) or 'muscle queens' (body-builders). The last seems to make nonsense of the traditional association between muscles and physical (masculine) toughness, since 'queens', enthroned or otherwise, are hardly synonymous with muscles. In addition many gay men like to be fucked, behaviour, as Pronger points out, seen by much of mainstream heterosexual society (and some 'homosexuals' too) as 'the deepest violation of masculinity in our culture' (1990: 135; cf. Loizos and Cornwall, Chapters 3 and 6 in this volume). Here the recipient is seen as the 'passive' (and therefore 'feminized'?) object of an 'active' and penetrating 'male'.

Inside a typical club our gay macho man might be seen drinking mineral water rather than strong lager. His perfectly sculpted chest may be shaved and oiled; his hair neatly gelled. He might own a 'camp' flat off the King's Road. He may be a stockbroker from middle-class suburbia, but he could just as well be a make-up artist from an inner-city slum. He may still see himself as a 'real man', but in what sense? Surely, as Quentin Crisp remarked with regard to 'homosexual' men desiring 'real men': 'If they succeed, they fail. A man who "goes with" other men is not what they would call a real man' (quoted in Pronger 1990: 141). Which of his personal attributes, then, is our gay man drawing upon in an effort to portray his 'masculinity', his 'manhood' or his 'maleness'?

Before pursuing these questions further it might be useful to return to the analogy with the poet's young sinner. Our gay (male) Londoner is still able to draw upon his social status as a man and so reaps the benefits that such subscription can bring in an unequally gendered society like Britain. In addition, he has recently received a certain amount of respectability, even legitimacy, with the elevation of his kind to what I call 'community' status. The 'gay community' now 'exists', at least within political, academic and liberal discourse, alongside the 'Afro-Caribbean community', 'the mining community', 'the business community' and so on. Similarly, businesses owned by heterosexual men or women in those areas with a large, con-centrated and relatively affluent gay population are not averse to appealing to the 'gay consumer': 'A buck is a buck', writes one contibutor to a Toronto newspaper, 'Who the hell cares if the wrist holding it is limp?' (Altman 1982: 18).

Yet once again our gay man's true colours also continue to provide a basis for his continuing persecution. Either he remains ridiculed by many hetero-sexuals as 'not quite a man', a comical type of figure, habitually accustomed to dressing in 'female' clothes and typically employed in the more 'feminine' professions such as hairdressing or the fashion industry, and the 'less serious' world of the arts in general; or he is portrayed as some sinister pervert lurking in alleyways, a threat to 'public morality', 'our children' and 'traditional family life'. In their unelected and largely unaccountable role as custodians of public decency, national and local newspapers are unrelenting in their pursuit of 'queer' vicars, 'perverted' schoolteachers, 'kinky' judges, and gay politicians and celebrities.

Such are the paradoxical and contradictory 'realities' of 'gay life' in London. Clearly then, any analysis of the changing nature of gay male identities must be able to confront, problematize and deconstruct 'traditional' key concepts such as 'identity', 'the masculine' and 'gay oppression'. Such concepts must never be taken as undifferentiated and unproblematic wholes, partly because it is bad anthropological practice to do so, and partly because their hegemonic meanings are often framed in terms favourable to the dominant powers in society. I therefore have no intention of inventing some sort of monolithic model or series of models into which all gay men are to be squeezed. But neither is it my intention to get 'lost' within the frenzied postmodernist pursuit of difference, deconstruction and ambiguity. This chapter considers the constantly evolving nature of gay male identities, as well as our shifting interpretations of such phenomena, not in isolation, but as part of developments occurring within the economic, social and political structures and practices of the broader society. A look at the complexities of a particular historical trajectory – the dialectical relationship between the gay man and his environment – ought to be central to any understanding of this far from straightforward 'gay present'.

It is within this framework that I take a closer look at what we mean when we talk in terms of 'the masculine' and 'the feminine' and at how the apparent 'masculinization of the gay man' fits in with such gendered categories. I begin by looking briefly at the emergence of the gay man, and at the way in which the identity of this historical figure has moved from that of the 'effeminate' and so-called 'gender invert' towards that of the 'macho man'. I then consider how such a butch-shift has been enhanced by, and in turn helped to develop, what has become known as the 'commercial gay scene' and the gay man's sense of 'community'.

IDENTITY, THE INDIVIDUAL, AND THE EMERGENCE OF THE GAY MAN

All people have a sense of self and their place in a given social order, however confusing or complex the setting or context. In this sense then, identity may be seen to be as integral to our psychic being as our capacity to reason. This, of course, says nothing about its varying content, something to which Jeffrey Weeks is referring when he writes:

> Identity is not inborn, pregiven, or 'natural'. It is striven for, contested, regulated, and achieved, often in struggles of the subordinated against the dominant. Moreover, it is not achieved by an individual act of will, or

discovered hidden in the recesses of the soul. It is put together in circumstances bequeathed by history as much as by personal destiny.

(1989a: 207)

Marx reminds us in his *Eighteenth Brumaire of Louis Bonaparte* that, 'Men make their own history, but they do not make it just as they please; they do not make it under circumstances chosen by themselves, but under circumstances given and transmitted from the past' (1959: 320). In other words, human agency must be placed firmly *within* the ideological *and* material structures and practices of the past and present. Present gay male identities are social because they emerge and are sustained by a process of regulation and interaction with others, *within* a given economic and ideological environment. For most gay men their identity as gay men hinges on their same-sex desires and behaviour. In other words, their 'sexuality' is *the* critical factor in the way they perceive themselves. Any account of the development of a '*gay identity*' must therefore include a look at sexuality in general, and homosexuality in particular.

Moreover, as Foucault (1984) and Weeks (1977, 1989b) have illustrated, such phenomena must be historically and culturally situated. Foucault, for instance, posits the constuction of what became known as 'the homosexual' firmly within the legal, administrative and social changes brought about by the advent of industrial capitalism; crucially he recognizes the bureaucratic capitalist state's increasingly zealous intrusion into the sexual mores of a rapidly expanding, and frequently discontented, population.

Regulation of sexual behaviour, of course, was nothing new. But as Foucault points out, prior to the late eighteenth and early nineteenth centuries *all* non-reproductive sexual relations were regulated under the prevalent canonical, pastoral and civil rules. By the Victorian era, monogamous heterosexual marriage was 'legitimized' as 'natural' by the powerful medical and psychiatric institutions, and tended to function as the norm. 'What (now) came under scrutiny', Foucault notes, 'was the sexuality of children, mad men and women, and criminals; the sexuality of those who did not like the opposite sex' (1984: 318). Legal sanctions against minor perversions multiplied: sexual irregularity was annexed to mental illness; 'from childhood to old age, a norm of sexual development was defined and all possible deviations were carefully described' (1984: 316). Accompanying this encroachment of powers, scattered sexualities rigidified, became stuck to an age, a place, a type of practice. Moreover, 'perversions' such as homosexuality were stigmatized not just as a series of sexual acts, but as *a state of mind*. This, claims Weeks, was crucial, 'indicating a massive shift in attitudes giving rise to what is distinctively new in our culture; the categorization of homosexuality as a separate condition and the correlative emergence of homosexual identity' (1977: 81).[2]

Most importantly, though, the emergence of 'the homosexual man' –

someone able *and* willing to define himself as a distinct type of individual on the basis of his same-sex desires and behaviour – took place within a largely middle-class, metropolitan milieu. It was a milieu in which those men who habitually 'went with' and desired other men became seen as 'gender inverts'; they were seen to have the appropriate social (gendered) qualities of the female sex (qualities which were themselves based upon an evolving hegemonic bourgeois ideology of womanhood). Bourgeois women, for example, were expected to be confined to the 'less serious' task of home-making; the 'feminine' becoming synonymous not only with certain 'weak' physical appearances, but also with a similar state of mind. And so too the homosexual man.

Male same-sex behaviour and desires, as both Weeks (1977; 1989b) and Gough (1989) have noted, were not, however, confined to those who self-identified as homosexual. On the contrary, perhaps until as late as the 1950s, 'the norm' usually necessitated the formation of sexual relations with a different type of man – a man who did not live within, nor identify with, 'feminized' homosexual milieu, but who none the less had sex with other men. Usually he was from the lower classes, was married and did not see himself as homosexual. The latter, by forming sexual relations with 'effeminate' homosexuals, whether for economic gain or otherwise, was able to see his own sexuality as at least quasi-heterosexual, and himself as the 'man' in the encounter. Of course it was also true that the 'visible' or 'self-identified' homosexual would possibly see himself as a real man, in spite of his milieu, if he had sex with younger/socially inferior men and/or was the penetrator in the encounter.

Nevertheless, many men who self-identified as homosexual also self-identified, to some significant degree, with the psychiatric and medical establishment's notions of sexual perversion and gender inversion. In other words, the hegemonic model was, until very recently, that of the gender invert. As we saw at the start of this chapter, this association has continued through to the present, most overtly within right-wing heterosexual dis-course. But since the 1970s there has occurred a marked shift away from the old stereotype towards a 'masculine' one. The contemporary 'masculin-ization' of the gay man, then, involved the weakening of the link between male homosexuality and the female gender. The link between sexuality and gender has of course remained, but what has obviously changed, as Gough points out, is the fact that this new 'masculine' identity – in style, mannerisms, certain forms of social behaviour and so on – has become rooted in male physiology rather than a peculiar 'feminine' psyche: 'the social in the biological' (Gough 1989: 120).

In certain respects, as Humphries has noted, this butch-shift is a 'direct response to the popular view that homosexuality involves at a very deep level a lack of masculinity' (1985: 71). But the question remains: can this move be posited *solely* within some sort of mythically autonomous free market of 'good ideas'? If so, how do we explain the particular timing and rather contradictory outcome of consumer choice? Essentially, as Gough points out, this 'idealist' perspective tends to reverse the real relation of the social form of sexuality – the 'masculine' gay man (fundamentally the effect) – and the material relations of gender – the unequal structuring of capitalist society along certain lines (fundamentally the cause) (1989: 133).

Gough (1989) notes how the butch-shift emerged from major social and economic changes brought about by the economic boom of the 1950s and 1960s; changes which made it easier to drive a wedge between gay male sexuality and 'effeminacy'. First, there has occurred an erosion and blurring of the sexual division of labour, whereby women have moved increasingly into the more 'serious' male world of waged work, with demands for equality of opportunity, pay parity and the like. We now have female judges, astronauts, electricians and so on, despite enormous discrimination.

Secondly, the increasing use and availability of contraception has tended to separate heterosex further from reproduction, thus 'freeing' female and male sexualities. It has become acceptable for women to have overt desires themselves. The 'objectification' of 'the woman', long a legitimate feminist target, has been joined by the objectification of the male, although the implications are not the same.

Thirdly, this 'objectification' of the male body has undoubtedly been given much greater significance by the ever-increasing commoditization of social relations typical of late/consumer capitalism (Jameson 1983; Harvey 1989). Athletic-looking male models are increasingly being used in advertising, and there can be little argument against the notion that sex/(hetero)sexuality 'sells'. As Pronger points out, 'commerce has taken sex not only as a commodity in itself, but also as *the* enticement by which it transforms products into objects of desire' (1990: 42). Male nudes appear in art galleries, on posters, cards, etc. (notwithstanding continuing official censorship), while semi-nude male dance troupes and male strippers such as the Chippendales illustrate that the contours of the male body are now 'hotter' property than ever before: 'man the hunter' has now also become 'man the ("feminized"?) prey'.

As part of a broader societal trend, Altman points out that, 'as Western countries became societies of high consumption, rapid credit, and rapid technological development, it was not surprising that the dominant sexual ideology of restraint and repression . . . came under increasing attack' (1982: 90). The eroticization of a 'consumer ethos' is more pronounced today in the so-called conservative 1990s than in the pre-AIDS, 'permissive' 1960s and 1970s.

Fourthly, this shift towards the commoditization and sexualization of social relations in general has been accompanied by a correlative deepening and widening of heterosexual (as well as homosexual) male identities. One of the consequences of these changes, as Gough points out, has been that fewer nominally 'straight' men are now perhaps willing to be stigmatized for having occasional/casual gay sex. In this sense, over the last twenty or so years homosexuality may be considered to have become *more* 'deviant', and the sexual pool on which nominally gay men depended has narrowed. Conversely, the correlative growth of a distinct 'gay scene' since the 1960s has probably weakened the view of gay male sexuality as an obscure and 'deviant' entity. At least in large urban areas, London in particular, gay men have become much more visible and 'accepted' as part of a tolerated sub-culture. This is not to imply, however, that homosexual behaviour is therefore considered an 'acceptable' practice for *everyone*.

Participants in 'the scene' are now able to seek sexual partners amongst other identified homosexuals. Male homosexuals, in effect, became desired as well as desirers (Gough 1989: 129). Moreover, they become desired as *men*; as 'real/complete' men. Self-conceptualization as either distinctly 'masculine' (and therefore 'active' and *not* homosexual) or 'feminine/gender-inverted' (and therefore 'passive' and *distinctly* homosexual) appears to have given way to a more uniform, if paradoxical, masculine identity.[3] It has enabled, 'many men . . . to come out of the closet by thinking that (their) homosexuality poses no threat to their masculinity' (Pronger 1990: 76). But this begs the question of *why* such 'masculine' characteristics (however ambiguous and contradictory) have been desired, adopted and consciously reinforced by gay men. In other words, why is there this need to be seen as or feel like 'real men', and how possible is it to meet this need?

HIERARCHY AND GENDER: SUSTAINING AN IDEOLOGY OF SEXUAL DIFFERENCE

We are all socialized either as men or women. It is very difficult to think ourselves outside what Pronger calls 'the filter of gender'(1990: 1). 'It is gender' he notes, 'that makes physical sex meaningful in social, cultural, and sexual contexts' (ibid.: 49). This 'gender myth exaggerates the minor physiological differences between male and female, transforming them into opposites' (ibid.: 51). Moreover, it helps to divide power unequally between men and women, notwithstanding the way gender is extricably linked with class, race, region, nationality, age, ability, disability and so on. It is not surprising, therefore, that gay men wish to be seen as 'real men'. As Segal points out, in a hierarchically gendered society such as ours, 'to be masculine is not to be feminine . . . or gay; not to be tainted with any marks of "inferiority" – ethnic or otherwise' (1990: x). Women's associated gender characteristics – such as gestures, concerns, dress, mannerisms, language and the like – are seen as inferior ways of behaving, regardless of whether they are taken on by a man or a woman, and regardless of whether they originate within a working-class or middle-class milieu.

This hostility directed towards the 'feminine' cannot be overestimated – there remains this tight connection between misogyny and hatred of homosexuals. As Segal points out, 'although the persecution of homosexuals is usually the act of men against a minority of other men, it is also the forced repression of the "feminine" in all men' (1990: 16). It continues in spite of the significant inroads women have made into the public (waged) spheres of British society, and in spite of the increasingly outward 'masculization' of gay men in general.

Probably nowhere is this forced repression of the 'feminine' more evident than in our military institutions. Segal points to the paradoxical tolerance (in a very limited sense) for actual homosexual behaviour within the army despite rigidly enforced taboos on tenderness and a rampantly homophobic [4] ideology. Here 'femininity', it would appear, belongs more to the realm of 'unmanly' feelings than to the perversity of certain sexual acts themselves. Segal adds that, 'in institutions committed to "making a man" out of young men, those who suffer the most from homophobia, routine bullying . . . are . . . as likely to be heterosexually as homosexually inclined' (1990: 143).

Male bonding and intense male friendship, Foucault suggests, are inimical to the smooth functioning of many modern institutions such as the army or educational and administrative bureaucracies. 'Heterosexual' men are expected to be aware of how different they are from both women and homosexuals – between being a homosocial man and a homosexual man, or, to put it another way, between being a 'man's man' and 'interested in men'. The ideological construction of 'homophobia' serves to tell us how different the two are. Yet 'homophobia' continues to flourish, remaining implicit in much government legislation covering female and gay male sexuality, and frequently explicit in the right-wing press, in school playgrounds, at the pulpit, in men's clubs and in the military.

The problem of 'bonding' is now confounded by the fact that western men individually and competitively seek proof of their 'manhood', through sporting achievements, sexual exploits and the restructuring of their bodies (through weight-training, body-building, even plastic surgery). Initiations of this sort, together with this simultaneous erosion of the sexual division of labour and the emergence of the male body as a 'desired' and 'objectified' commodity, seem to have produced a certain recentring of the masculine arena. We may be witnessing the proliferation of certain identities based on sexual practices, fashion, life-styles or certain fetishes, but these revolve around the athletic male body. This shift cuts across class and cultural boundaries. The 'functional Rambo' is not only a North American phenomenon.

Yet commercial appeals to man's 'masculine' heritage often seem little more than a parody of a mythic past. *Rambo* star Sylvester Stallone refused to visit Europe because of his fear of 'terrorists'; hunky male models for Levi Strauss jeans may reveal their 'ideal' athletic bodies on our TV screens, but their sex appeal also relies upon make-up artists, male toiletries and the like. Whatever its contradictions or changing characteristics, 'male masculinity' is tied to a masculine body. This body is hard, muscular and athletic; a symbol (if not a guarantee) of power within a hierarchically gendered society.

Gay men may be attracted to different degrees of masculine expression, of which the body is just a part. But by enhancing our physical 'manliness' we have done much to dilute the myth of our 'womanly' and inferior nature. Yet through our 'masculinization' are we not also reinforcing the very gender categories which are frequently the source of that oppression? Surely, as Marshall has pointed out, 'the emergence of [gay] "macho men" illustrates the extent to which definitions of male homosexuality continue to be pervaded by the tyranny of gender divisions' (1981).

However, we also need to be aware of the paradoxical nature of this gay masculinity. Pronger claims that, 'Masculinity *is* the source of homoerotic desire' (1990: 130), yet it is a masculinity, he insists, which is fundamentally at odds with what he calls 'orthodox masculinity'. For example, homoeroticism violates the difference of manhood from womanhood because it is directed towards gender *affinity*:

> Because homoerotic desire focuses on manhood but ignores the sexual acts that bring about manhood, homoeroticism reflects a paradoxical sense of what it means to be a man. Because it both embraces and violates masculinity, homoeroticism is a paradoxical eroticism.
>
> (Pronger 1990: 71)

Pronger also highlights its potentially subversive nature. He notes,

> In our culture male homosexuality is a violation of masculinity, a denigration of the mythic power of men, an ironic subversion that significant numbers of men pursue with great enthusiasm. Because it gnaws at masculinity it weakens the gender order. But because masculinity is at the heart of homoerotic desire, homosexuality is essentially a paradox in the myth of gender.
>
> (1990: 2)

It would be safe to say, then, that gay masculinity must be seen simultaneously as both subversive (in that it challenges orthodox masculinity) and reactionary (in that it reinforces gender stereotypes – a crucial factor in the oppression of gay sexuality). To suggest that this butch-shift is one or the other is to ignore the paradoxical nature of masculinity in general, and gay masculinity in particular. The same sort of dilemma, it is useful to note, forces attempts at understanding the gay 'camp' alternatives of the 1960s and 1970s and the more recent 'queer' movement. 'Camp', as Segal points out, may enable gay men 'to be different and proud of it' (1990: 145), but some of its key 'attributes', such as artistic creativity, 'queerness' and 'femininity', are still seen as somehow less serious or important than the 'masculine' world of work and reason. It was hardly surprising, then, that such movements in the 1970s remained largely in the domain of the urban middle class: students, academics, artists and others with perhaps less to lose in adopting such an identity. Aside from the very real threat from 'queer-bashers' it is important to remember that most gay men can, and often do, pass as 'straight', and in doing so continue to reap the advantages awarded to them *as men*.

Even camp's positive features, such as insistence on one's 'otherness' and a refusal to pass as straight, remain 'irredeemably compromised by complicity in the traditional, oppressive formulations of that "otherness" ' (Blanchford 1981: 202–3). As such, camp can be seen as replacing the signs of 'masculinity' with a parody of the signs of 'femininity', therefore reinforcing existing social definitions of both categories. Conversely, it may act as 'little more than a kind of anaesthetic, allowing one to remain inside oppressive relations while enjoying the illusory confidence that one is flouting them' (ibid.). Even camp's more 'masculinist' successor – the 'queer' movement which has emerged over the last few years – seems to *attempt* little more than to 'dethrone the serious' in a self-conscious and very postmodern 'form-is-content' style (Pronger 1990: 229). What is crucial is that politicized movements of this sort, failed or otherwise, must not be looked at in isolation.

THE POLITICIZATION OF THE GAY MAN

As we saw in the second section, the emergence of the masculine *gay* man could not have take place without the coming together of large numbers of otherwise isolated homosexual men. The emerging 'gay scene' created an arena for a particular masculinization of the gay male. With its bars, night-clubs, magazines and newspapers, bookstores and various groups – political and otherwise – there is little doubt that 'the scene' succeeded in meeting some of the most basic needs of its young, predominantly (but by no means exclusively) white middle-class participants. It has also played an important part in what has become a sort of collective gay identity. It has deepened our sense of gayness and to some extent reinforced essentialist notions of difference, where sexuality has been seen as the main determinant of this difference.

Although written with reference to the development of ethnic identities, Comaroff's excellent analysis of group dynamics and identity formation (1987) may also be applied to the emerging collective gay identity. Once 'ethnicity' is seen by a group as the factor determining its particular (in this case, subordinate) place within the social system, events may then conspire to perpetuate *and* deepen such an identity. Moreover, as Vance suggests, within an ideological and political context it is often to the advantage of all groups struggling for resources to stress not only group unity (in this case based on same-sex behaviour) and historical privilege, but also their status as an essential group to which members have no choice in belonging (1989: 27–8). We may note, for example, the instant (if cautious) welcome given to the recent 'discovery' of what scientists in America termed 'the gay gene'; the main response appears to have been 'told you we couldn't help it' (LeVay 1992).[5] In addition, a 'gay history' is being slowly assembled around 'outed' public figures from King Edward II through to William Shakespeare and Field Marshal Viscount Montgomery. In certain fundamental respects categorization not only seeks to deter people from drifting into 'deviancy', it appears to foreclose on the possibility of drifting back into 'normality' (MacIntosh 1968: 32). However, I would suggest that gay identity depends on context. Moreover, I am not so sure we can be certain that gay men make such conscious distinctions in the first place.

Nevertheless, as Altman argues, this collective identity, for all its benefits, also has the effect of reinforcing prejudices that homosexuals are a distinct group rather than 'a potential open to us all' (1980: 56). Whether homosexuality is a 'potential' open to us all is not the point. What is important is that this construction of an exclusive, mythical past and present must be seen in its wider social context. This relationship has been well documented,[6] though several issues deserve emphasis here.

Collective lesbian and gay 'resistance' has been very much a part of the alternative, non-class-based strategies emerging in the late 1960s. Strongly influenced by the feminist movements, political programmes were, and continue to be, propagated by the unelected and largely white, male, liberal, middle-class 'leaders' who incline towards the view that, 'whatever income bracket lesbians and gay men enjoy, their sexuality expunges privilege and expels them from class' (*Rouge* 1990). True, gay sexuality is rigorously policed and regulated to the point where most gay men experience some degree of oppression and discrimination *as gay men*, but *pace* such arguments, it quite clearly fails to deny gay men most of the privileges associated with manhood, and clearly does not expel us from class. Nevertheless, comparatively wealthy professional middle-class and upper-class gay men – highly vocal and powerful within 'the community' – are expected to coexist with unemployed white or black unskilled workers. Yet the former, on account of their position as *class subjects* in a class-divided society, do not automatically lose all the material and social benefits awarded to them even though the dominant social practices of that very same society are instrumental in sustaining their oppression *as gay men*. For them, capitalist social practice may not seem too bad even if it tends to be policed by bigoted 'homophobes'. In addition, both unemployed gay men, who otherwise have very little at stake in the present system, and wealthy gay men benefit from their position *as men* in a society with a massive history of sexual inequality. Perhaps, as Eagleton observes, 'it is because being oppressed sometimes brings with it slim bonuses that we are occasionally prepared to put up with it' (1991: xiii).

Given the long tradition of suspicion and even contempt our white, liberal, middle-class political elite (gay or otherwise) has towards the collectivist working class, the personalizing tendencies in the gay movement are hardly surprising. The success of this process in imperializing the political consciousness of the gay movement and of ordinary working people in general, though, is as much to do with the fact that gay men, like women and ethnic minorities, constantly have to face a personal and private struggle as it is a reflection of broader global defeats of collectivist class action (especially since 1968). Transcending this 'personal-problem' perspective seems quite difficult. As Denneny points out, there appears to exist a 'widespread tendency to believe that once we have accomplished the psychological ordeal known as "coming out", we are suddenly and magically free of the negative conditioning of our homophobic society' (1983: 420).

One bonus western capitalism seems to have delivered (if reluctantly) is a highly developed 'gay scene'. As part of 'the gay community', we join a whole host of apparently free and equal 'elective communities' or 'communities of choice' (Weeks 1989a). 'Community' status can be based on ethnicity (the Asian community) or occupation (the mining or business community) as well as sexuality.

For most gay men a sense of community has always been centred on a commercial scene – pubs, clubs, bookstores, porn movies and so on. Since the late 1970s, however, there has been a proliferation of such commercial activities. Gay businesses in London have mushroomed, while mainstream businesses are not slow to latch on to the 'high disposable income' of many single gay men in work. From gyms, through certain 'men's magazines' with their homoerotic undertones, to music and TV shows with large gay followings and even the sale (as in some Canadian gay bars) of a beer called 'Pride' (*Rouge* 1992, no. 11), business appears keen not to drive away 'the pink pound'. Our sense of a gay community is increasingly determined by commercial interests. And for some gay men for whom community emphasis predicates political action there has been a 'shifting stress from the language of oppression, liberation, and "the movement", to one of discrimination, rights, and "the community"' (Altman 1982: 21). This, Altman suggests, 'indicates the new integration of gays through the commercial world into mainstream society' (ibid.).

Though some gay groups see assimilation into mainstream commercial society as undesirable, they challenge neither the new consumer ethos nor the idea of a separate or exclusive gay culture. Such is the case with the 'queer movement' that appeared in Britain at the end of the 1980s. Anti-assimilationist groups such as 'Homocult' and 'Outrage' promote the concepts of 'queer' and 'difference', but do so using commercial means – fashion, night-clubs, cinema and so on. Like the politicized camp of the 1970s, the queer movement's activists appear to subscribe to the philosophy that if they are loud and outrageous enough, they will be able to promote a different or better kind of 'gay culture'. Mass kiss-ins, outrageous attire at gay weddings and male 'nuns' on roller-skates make good copy for newspapers, but it is doubtful whether they change the behaviour or psyche of those gay men or heterosexuals outside 'the queer movement'.

Of course, whether we are talking about the mainstream 'gay community' or the antics of 'queer life-stylers', we must recognize the porous nature of such cultural boundaries. 'Community' membership overlaps with membership of other 'communities' and frequently cuts across class and gender divisions. A sense of community membership is situational and fluid. It differs from individal to individual and can only be one facet of identity. Like 'masculinity', 'community' may be seen as very 'real' in that it has a real impact on our lives. But, equally, it is a myth, something forever beyond our grasp.

CONCLUSIONS

Throughout this chapter I have attempted to draw out the key elements in the formation of a distinct and hegemonic masculine gay male identity in Britain, both in the personal/individual sense and in its collective/political manifestations. This notional identity is far from static, monolithic or context-free, and the constructs on which it depends, such as 'the masculine' and 'the community', do not have a reality outside the contexts in which they are ascribed particular meanings. A more detailed analysis would look at the effects of class, ethnicity, religion, age, ability/disability and regional environment upon identity formation and composition. Nevertheless, I argue that even the most elementary understanding of the changing nature of gay male identities can only progress when we start to consider such phenomena in the broader context of a 'total society'; as a 'product' of both the underlying material and ideological (that is, 'social') practices and what constitutes human praxis – the on-going struggle between individuals, groups and classes in their widest setting.

NOTES

1 The words 'gay' and 'homosexual' are frequently used interchangeably in present discourse, though it might be useful to note one or two distinctions. Humphries suggests 'Gayness' ought to be seen as the *'social form* of homosexuality, whilst homosexuality is a part of sexuality' (1985: 74). Similarly, Cass notes how 'the proponents of the homosexual/gay dichotomy suggest that a gay identity is (also) a more "advanced" identity since it reflects the individual's development of strategies for effectively dealing with a stigmatized status' (1983–4: 117). Denneny insists that '"homosexual" and "gay" are not the same thing: gay is when you decide to make an issue out of it' (1983: 409). Similarly, Pronger claims that by 'becoming "gay" one cultivates a positive attitude towards the homosexual paradox by asserting one's legitimacy in thought, word, and deed' (1990: 121). Both words will be used during the following discussion, but I will try to adhere to the above-mentioned distinctions where possible.
2 Three more recent and particularly poignant examples of this regulation exist in the shape of Section 28 of the 1986 Local Government Act, under which it became illegal to 'promote' homosexuality as a 'pretended family relationship'; and

clauses within the more recent Criminal Justice Bill (1991) and Children's Act. Even the apparent liberalizing laws (regulating male homosexual activity) of the 1967 Act (England and Wales), must be seen as 'not so much an acceptance of homosexuality as a change in its official definition' (Weeks 1980). Homosexuality now becomes a 'condition' to be partially accepted, but the rest of society (this is made clear by the distinctions made in the Act between 'public' and 'private) is to be warned against it. Following the passage of the Bill, as Weeks notes, there occurred a tripling of convictions for consenting homosexual acts in what were defined as public places. Whether we wish to read into this a particular sinister intentionality on the part of the authors of this Act is largely irrelevant for the purposes of this discussion. It is important to note, though, that the continued regulation of sexuality and the clear distinctions before the law between homosexual and heterosexual serves to reinforce those tendencies which make for a separate homosexual identity; as a discriminated minority in a society which frequently distinguishes its subjects in terms of their sexual preferences (Weeks 1977, 1989a; Shepherd and Wallis 1989; Gough 1989; Plummer 1981; Altman 1982).

3 Of course role playing, particularly in 'sado-masochistic' practices, may establish differences in the physical sense of passive versus active. But there is little evidence to suggest that such roles are carried beyond the sexual act itself. Indeed, even within such sexual acts the 'active' dominant partner may deal out 'punishment' to his dominated captor, but the latter may be seen by both of them as 'man enough' to take the physical pain and punishment willingly. The important point is not that some acts may be seen as 'passive' or some as 'feminine', but that both gay men would identify themselves as *men* and masculine men at that.

4 'Homophobia' is an awkward construction in that it suggests a hatred of both lesbians and gay men. Yet, as Bristow has noted, 'anti-lesbianism' and 'anti-gay-maleness' manifest themselves very differently. Lesbians, for example, are at the receiving end of misogyny, which can come into operation to enable men to control a situation whether at home, at work, or in the street (1989: 57). In fact gay men can be part of this sexual hatred. Pronger also makes the point that many 'out' gay men are themselves homophobic in their hatred of those who are 'effeminate' or 'camp'. Many of us hold a fear of our 'masculine' violation; a fear of loss of patriarchal power – we cannot ignore this aspect of the term.

5 A review of these developments can be found in Ray (1992).

6 See Weeks (1977), Plummer (1981), Shepherd and Wallis (1989).

Chapter 6

Gendered identities and gender ambiguity among *travestis* in Salvador, Brazil

Andrea Cornwall

The main road leading from the old centre of Salvador, Brazil's fifth largest city, heaves by day with shoppers and hawkers. By night scantily clad feminine figures cluster to sell sex. Ambiguity is part of the game on the *trottoir*: these glamorous 'women' are often *travestis*, with the allure of a phallic femininity.[1] Also at night, in any of the hundreds of temples (*terreiros*) of the Afro-Brazilian religion of *Candomblé*, *filhas de santo* (literally 'daughters of the saint', devotees) clad in white lace dresses take to the floor as they receive their deities (*orixás*) in possession. In most *Candomblés*, it is only 'women' who can be 'mounted' (*gún*, Yoruba) by the *orixás*. In many *terreiros*, *travestis* enjoy this privilege.

On the *trottoir* and in the *terreiro*, *travestis* adorn themselves in feminine trappings. They shape their bodies to exaggerate the curves identified with the female body, with a 'hidden extra': bodies with breasts and a penis. They do not self-identify as *homens* (men) or *mulheres* (women), but as *travestis*. According to Grupo Gay da Bahia (GGB), a prominent gay rights group in Salvador, an estimated 90 per cent of *travestis* are devotees of *Candomblé*.[2] Yoruba language is used in ritual in many *terreiros* and can be heard in street slang. Members of GGB suggested that: 'the gay community have adapted Yoruba to their daily lives and realities, according to their own subculture'.[3]

The literature on prostitution (e.g. Espiñeira 1984; Bacelar 1982; Oliveira 1986; Pereira 1988) and on *Candomblé* (e.g. Bastide 1978; dos Santos 1988; Segato 1986; Teixeira 1987; Fry 1982) contains scant but suggestive references to those who move between the domains of the *trottoir* and the *terreiro*. My interest here is in the gendered identities *travestis* assume and are accorded by others as they traverse these spaces. I examine gendered identities and gender ambiguity in street prostitution and in the performative and ritual domain of *Candomblé* in order to raise wider questions about processes of gendering. This brief analysis aims to open areas for further exploration.[4]

So pervasive is the gender dichotomy within western discourse that anthropological accounts of cross-gender behaviour have either re-created it using different, but equally fixed, criteria (Whitehead 1981; Devereux 1937),[5] or defined an intermediate 'third gender' (see Wikan 1977; Mageo

1992): that which Carpenter (1919) called 'the hybrid kind of life'. Recon-figuring the gender dichotomy or placing the *travesti* in the category of a 'third gender' implies that the terms 'men' and 'women' have some kind of presence outside their situational usages in different activities and arenas. Creating a 'third gender' merely reinforces an essentialized notion of gender. Also, such a move side-steps the issues of power in the attribution and enactment of gendered identities.

The apparent gender ambiguity of *travestis* poses several theoretical challenges for analyses of gender. I begin by considering some of these issues. Setting *travesti* prostitution within the wider frame of prostitution in Salvador, I explore representations of adult 'masculine' and 'feminine' prostitutes who possess penises. I go on to examine what Foucault (1978) terms the 'historical apparatus of sexuality', looking first at hegemonic discourses about sex and gender and then at subordinate variants that establish alternative frames of reference within *Candomblé*. Taking up the issues that arise from the intersections of these schema in different settings, I explore implications for analyses of gender.

MALE WOMEN OR FEMALE MEN?

In western European discourse, the term 'transvestism' carries with it a sense of dissonance. To call someone a 'transvestite' involves making a series of prior assumptions about them. These cluster around the notion that there is some original 'sex' or 'gender' to which they 'really' belong: transvestites *cross*-dress, they do not just dress. Transvestites transgress, moving across the boundaries marking gendered difference. In doing so, they pose a challenge to the taken-for-granted association of 'men' with 'male' and 'masculinity', and 'women' with 'female' and 'femininity'. Dislocating the markers of femininity and masculinity from the bodies of females and males, transvestites represent 'gender' as not only achieved, but actively fashioned.

In Britain and North America, forms of male transvestism vary in both degree and kind (Prince 1957; Woodhouse 1989; Stoller 1976; Butler 1990; Baudrillard 1990). Transvestite men may be defined or may self-define as heterosexual, bisexual or homosexual. Male transvestism can range from (hetero)sexual fantasies staged in the bedroom, to dressing up, to performing on stage in 'drag', to attempts to 'pass' as 'women' in a range of social settings. Most transvestites do not wish to *become* but to *perform* as 'women'. Transsexualism, on the other hand, has been treated as the clinical category of 'gender dysphoria' since the 1960s (Stoller 1976; Raymond 1979). Trans-sexuals do not wish just to perform but to *transform* themselves, to assume what they regard as their 'natural destiny' (Raymond 1979). Representations of the feminine are constructed and lived out by those who feel 'trapped in a male body'. Male to female transsexuals may self-define as heterosexual or lesbian, identifications based on a conception of themselves as 'really female'. While the availability of silicone implants and the use of hormones can simulate or stimulate signs of a female body, notions of the 'sex change' dwell less on addition than on subtraction: of the penis. Both male transvestites and pre-operative male to female transsexuals still tend to be ascribed membership of the category 'male' by virtue of possessing male genitalia.

In Salvador, several kinds of cross-gender behaviour can be observed. *Transformistas* can be compared with the UK/US category of 'gay drag artiste'. Most *transformistas* confine cross-dressing to an evening's work; presenting male femininities within a particular temporal and spatial context. *Travestis* adopt clothing, gestures and styles gendered female in Brazil, make permanent or semi-permanent body changes and attract feminine terms of address. For the most part *travestis* do not think that they are, nor are they taken to be, 'really' women or men (Oliveira 1986). The term *transsexual* has now entered the language to denote those who wish to submit or have submitted to the surgeon's knife. Yet it is unclear whether *transsexuals* regard themselves as 'women' (*mulheres*). As one *travesti* pointed out, 'real' women can give birth: *transsexuals* can never attain 'true' femaleness. Further, Acosta paints a different picture of the social worlds of Brazilian *transsexuals* to that found in British or American accounts (e.g. Raymond 1979):

> I know various post-operative cases, none of whom have ceased to seem to be *homossexual*, despite having had it all cut off; they move in the *homo* scene, they are the friends of *homos*, and continue to cultivate the same old myths of the *homo* through their lives and beyond. They might change their appearance, but underneath this what continues to exist is a pretty *bicha* ['homosexual'], castrated or not.
>
> (Acosta n.d.: 5)

Despite the apparent similarity to western European categories, differences emerge. One of these differences is particularly salient: neither the *transformistas*, the pre-operative *transsexuais* nor the *travestis* describe themselves, nor are they referred to by others, as *homens* ('men'). Rather, they are classed in a residual category marked by the pejorative term *bicha* (literally 'pest', 'bug'). This term denotes a wider class of persons and subsumes those who live their lives in clothing gendered male, who may behave 'effeminately' and who have sex with men. Homoerotic encounters between men do not necessarily mark both parties as *bichas* or as *homossexuais*. 'Being a *homem* [man]' is defined less in terms of 'sexual orientation' than in terms of an imputed preference for the insertor role in sex. Such men are not considered to be *homossexuais*.

One variety of cross-gender behaviour escapes pejorative labelling in Salvador: that associated with the explosion of colour and chaos of *carnaval*. Parodying selected and exaggerated feminine attributes, cross-dressed men take to the streets. Most of these men are not regarded as *bichas*, but as *homens*. They appear to perform neither as if women nor as women, but as 'not not men', to borrow Schechner's (1985) phrase: hairy chests are displayed, beards retained, genitals bulge from under lycra. Trevisan argues that *carnaval* 'proclaims the rule of ambiguity' (1986: 156), permitting the ambivalence that runs as a strong undercurrent in Bahian sociality a legitimate space to emerge. *Travestis* carry the fantasies of *carnaval* and of their clients outside the space marked by *carnaval* for the containment – and toleration – of ambivalence, into the domain of everyday activities. They embody a paradox of desire and denial.

The Brazilian *travesti* is neither a 'transvestite' nor a 'transsexual', as defined in western terms. There is a degree of overlap between the cluster of notions used in attributing sex and gender in contemporary mainstream discourse in Britain and North America, and in Salvador. Closer inspection reveals some significant differences. Applying western European notions of 'sex', 'gender' and 'sexuality' would impose a number of problematic presuppositions. Considering how *travestis* can be located in terms of theoretical approaches to 'gender' raises further problems, to which I now turn.

RETHINKING SEX AND GENDER

The polarized debates between 'essentialism' and 'constructionism' (see Vance 1989; Wieringa 1989; Gatens 1983) reveal the extent to which presuppositions based on binaries of sex and gender pervade the theorization of difference. In drawing 'a distinction between sex, in the physiological sense, and gender, which is a cultural construct' (Caplan 1987a: 1), constructionists present 'gender' as constituted in various ways in different social, cultural or historical settings. Rather than dispensing with essentialized ideas about the 'natures' of women and men altogether, such accounts tend to reinstate essences elsewhere. As Butler notes, 'the presumption of a binary gender system implicitly retains the belief in a mimetic relation of gender to sex whereby gender mirrors sex or is otherwise restricted by it' (1990: 6). And 'sex' narrowly refers to the biological material onto which 'gender' is inscribed in variant ways: 'anatomical sex differences' become given, fixed, biological 'facts'.

Accounts of the construction of 'gender identity' tend toward the assumption that once formed, such identities are fixed and coherent. In descriptions of people in similar social, cultural or historical settings, 'gender' often emerges as a stubbornly static entity. The notion of 'gender constructs' obscures, rather than illuminates, processes of gendering over people's life-courses, in different spaces and through different activities. People gender others and actively create, perform and modify their own gendered identities in different settings. Bodies are not mere biological material providing a canvas for the bold strokes of gender to be painted on. They can be reshaped and modified to em*body* discourses about sexuality or gender literally. In different settings, to different actors, parts of the body may be alternately marked or disregarded in attributions of gender (Kessler and McKenna 1978).

Gatens (1983), Grosz (1987) and other feminist theorists of difference have argued there is no such thing as an unmarked body; 'anatomy' is necessarily as cultural as 'gender'. As Gatens (1983) points out, the alleged neutrality of the body carries with it the implicit rationalist assumption that posits a split between body and mind, physical presence and consciousness. This denies the active subjectivity of the person inhabiting a body, which is always already a culturally and historically *sexed* body. Foucault (1977) identifies the body as the site on which discourse is inscribed, yet does not account for the agency of subjects in choosing the body they inhabit. Using Lacan's notion of the 'imaginary body', Gatens takes this a step further. She suggests that subjects actively develop socially and historically specific images of the body, marking certain bodily experiences and attributes as 'privileged sites of significance' (1983: 149). Thus, she suggests, the experience of being feminine or masculine in a *female* or *male* body is qualitatively different.

This raises the further question of how 'female' and 'male' bodies are defined and differentiated in different domains of discourse. Gatens suggests that images of the body are 'constructed by a shared language; the shared psychical significance and privileging of various zones of the body; and common institutional practices and discourses on and through the body' (1983: 152). I would go further than Gatens' rather problematic notion of 'shared' understandings. The body may be talked about, constructed, imagined and given psychical significance differently by different actors in different domains of discourse. Accordingly, the 'site[s] of significance' that are 'privileged' by particular actors also vary.

Kessler and McKenna (1978) illustrate the extent to which western distinctions privilege the presence of male genitalia in categorizing two 'sexes'.[6] Definition of what is 'male' by the possession or absence of the penis is, they argue, no cultural universal. The possession of a penis, it seems, is only contingently linked with attributions of 'male gender'. This provokes a number of questions about the 'sex' as well as the 'gender' of *travestis*. Defining the *travesti* as 'really male' in terms of some original state or by virtue of possessing a penis raises difficulties. *Travestis* are made, not born. Initiated by older *travestis*, the transformation is called 'making the *travesti*' (*feito travesti*). This process is conceived as a rebirth and, significantly, bears striking similarities to initiation into *Candomblé*. 'Being made' brings a new name, a new body, a new identity. Defining *travestis*, then, in terms of a prior state is problematic.

Further, *travestis* possess penises, but the 'privileged site[s] of significance' of that which is designated 'female' equally form part of their simulations of femininity. 'Partible' (Strathern 1988) 'female' attributes are literally in*corpo*rated by the *travestis*, who shape their bodies not only by mechanical means, but also with hormones.[7] *Travestis* have the bodies of 'males' *and* of 'females'. Their 'sex' or 'gender' is not something that can be defined in abstraction. *Travestis* may adopt and be ascribed a range of gendered statuses in different settings. Only in certain contexts or activities does the penis take on the indexical load associated with the male gender (cf Garfinkel 1967).

'Masculinity' is often conflated with being 'male' or 'being a man'. These notions lack any single definitional ground and may be more usefully regarded as loosely bounded clusters of 'family resemblances' (Wittgenstein 1963). The meanings ascribed to these terms by different actors may overlap to a certain degree, but also vary significantly in different domains of discourse. Dislocating 'masculinity' and 'femininity' and taking a closer look at the ways these terms are defined and attributed reveals the power effects of gender attributions. Gatens (1983) contends that it is not masculinity *per se*, but *male* masculinity that is valued in mainstream western discourse. And, while male masculinit*ies* are always also plural, particular representations of the masculine – what we term 'hegemonic masculinity', following Carrigan *et al.* (1985) – may be deployed in ways that marginalize and do violence (literally, in this setting) to others.

Attributions of 'sex' or 'gender' vary according to the frame of reference within which they are made. So too, then, do associations of particular, gendered attributes with agency or power. By examining the masculinities and femininities represented by *travestis* on the *trottoir* and in the *terreiro*, I seek to disrupt any essential ground for defining a singular 'masculinity', as well as a unitary and unmarked notion of 'maleness'. In doing so, I explore alternative models of agency that displace the hegemonic association of 'masculinity' with power.

FAZER VIDA: CONTEXTS OF PROSTITUTION IN SALVADOR

The old centre of Salvador, whose decaying elegance serves as a chilling reminder of the transatlantic slave trade that brought the city to prominence, has long sustained a population regarded by outsiders and some locals alike as *marginal*. The Brazilian term *marginal* (plural *marginais*) carries with it connotations beyond that of its English equivalent. It is often used in expressions of disgust to describe those considered as the lowest form of life: comments about the *marginais* of the centre often refer not only to the prostitutes, dealers, hustlers, thieves and *travestis* in the area, but, by extension, to most of its inhabitants.

The district was marked out in the 1920s as an area for containing prostitution, and by the 1960s, 'prostitution and the activities that revolve around it . . . formed [its] ambience' (Bacelar 1982: 54). Initiatives to restore the *centro histórico* ('historic centre') began in earnest in the 1970s and

1980s. This set in motion a mushrooming of enterprise, supplying attractions for the streams of visitors seeking 'Africa in Brazil'.

Once repressed by the state, Afro-Brazilian religious cults, *Candomblés*, have now acquired semi-official status and cachet for the fashionable. Tours are laid on to visit the most 'traditional' cult houses (*terreiros*). Waitresses and street-sellers (popularly known as *Baianas*) dress in the white lace and beads of *Candomblé* to serve secularized 'African ritual cuisine' to tourists. Images of *Baianas* feature on postcards and holiday snaps, marketed as 'cultural symbols' of the nation. Official tourism offers shows or courses of Afro-Brazilian dance, music and *capoeira*, an acrobatic blend of dance and self-defence developed by slaves in the interior of Bahia. Formerly the target for police repression (Landes 1967), *capoeira* has become part of the presentation of 'African Bahia' and features in adverts and political propaganda. Street youth perform *capoeira* in the squares for tourist audiences and in shows for the wealthy, where their uniforms of calico may be swapped for 'African' leopard print.

The 'discovery' of 'African Bahia' has brought wealth to some. Yet the shift from stigmatization to celebration of black Bahia has done little to ameliorate racist discrimination or the hypocrisies of the masculinism that permeates all sectors of Bahian society.[8] *Travestis* and gay men continue to be beaten up, murdered and harassed (Mott 1988; GGB, personal communication, 1991).[9] The growth in the number of *Baianas* reflects not only increased interest in their product, but also the lack of alternative employment for women of colour, whose lot has barely improved. And despite having been 'discovered', the *capoeristas* of the centre continue to be regarded as *marginais*.

The sale of sex continues to play an important part in the economic lives of the inhabitants of the district. Although the market in sexual services has diversified to capture opportunities from tourism, changes appear to have been inspired more by the desires and *fantasias* of local clients. Female prostitutes (referred to by the derogatory term *putas*) work the bars in the port area attending to a stream of foreign sailors and local regulars. In the backstreets of the centre, the clientele is local, while in the bars of the main squares a more lucrative trade for the younger *puta* lies with tourists. The tourist market has created in addition a new, more subtle, form of prostitution framed around the 'holiday romance' (see Loizos, Chapter 3 in this volume).

Male hustlers, dealers and 'guides' often derive their income from 'holiday romances' with tourist women. Gathering outside bars or performing *capoeira* in the central squares, they often do not have to move any further to make their catch. Accommodation and sustenance (and the occasional jackpot of their lovers' possessions or a trip to Europe) are exchanged for protection and a well-rehearsed patter about the Afro-Bahian secrets of the quarter. Symbols of Africa enhance their allure, from beads, to *berimbaus* (instruments used in *capoeira*), to the now fading fashion of a rastafarian image: all of which quickly begin to be associated with *marginais* and are cannily abandoned in trade-offs between success with clients and problems in gaining entry to the cheap hotels housing the stream of backpackers.

In the alleys away from the central squares, boy prostitutes loiter at night in darkened doorways. Older male prostitutes, *bofes* (also called *mîches*), ply the side-streets. Most are in their late teenage years. *Travestis*, once so repressed by the police that they could not emerge from their houses by day, now form part of the colourful confusion of the area. The tourist trade, with its glamorization of the exotic, may have permitted more of a space for *travestis* to move. Their clients, however, are more often locals than foreigners. Characterized as *marginais par excellence* and barred from gay clubs and bars, *travestis* work the streets and are subjected to police harassment and violent attacks (Mott and Assunção 1987). Most of the *travestis* on the streets of Salvador are in their twenties, many are black. It seems that over the last decade growing demand for *travestis* has ousted *putas* from the marketplace. The title of one newspaper article makes this explicit: 'Prostitution: *travestis* are the new owners of the night: with love and silicone' (*Correio da Bahia* 1980).

The market in sexual services in Salvador is complex and diverse. For the purposes of this analysis, my focus is on two categories of adult prostitutes – *travestis* and *bofes* – those who possess penises and service a predominantly local clientele.

DISLOCATED DICHOTOMIES

In Brazil the cult of the body beautiful has long had an enthusiastic following. Representations of the feminine dwell on curvaceous bodies in figure-hugging clothes; images of the masculine portray sculptured torsos, taut, tanned and muscular. Gender attributions based on clothing, style and looks would appear extremely straightforward, so limited is the scope for apparent ambiguity. Two sharply differentiated genders are presented, which, while inviting play, also bound its possibilities. *Travestis* and *bofes* appear to embody these two alternatives.

Travestis, clad in miniskirts and high heels with curls and vivid make-up, pose to striking effect. Their depilated bodies are clenched at the waist to produce curves, their breasts accentuated. The glamour of an exaggerated femininity carries with it a sense of both fantasy and artifice. For while they present the codes of femininity, it is the presentation to excess that renders them identifiable as *travestis*. As one remarked to Oliveira, she could see no merit in being a *mulher* ('woman') as, 'when a *mulher* passes no-one bothers to look, but when a *travesti* passes everyone wants to look, to have . . . to be a *travesti*' (1986: 84). *Bofes* present the figure of the *macho* with muscular bravado. Lounging on street corners, often wearing body-sculpting trousers revealing every detail, *bofes* represent an archetype of virile male masculinity.

Representations of gender difference in mainstream discourse do not only draw on appearance and anatomy. They present *homens* ('men') and *mulheres* ('women') in terms of agency and its apparent absence. The hegemonic version of masculinity portrays strong, capable and virile protectors. The term *homem*, as noted earlier, carries with it explicit reference to how 'real men' are expected to behave in bed: as *ativo* ('active') and as *comedor* (literally 'eater'; insertor), irrespective of whether their sexual partners are women or men. *Mulheres* ('women') are represented as those who inspire or are the subjects of the actions of others, and are portrayed in sex as in life as acted on, as *passivo* ('passive'), as *doador* (literally 'giver'; insertee). Despite Brazil's libidinous image, purity and innocence still appear to be valued in women of all social classes; and may be fiercely protected by patriarchs. Yet in cultivating and displaying sexual allure, many women play to notions of the irrepressible desire of the *macho* and the inherent desirability of the sensuous woman. These notions offer a glimpse of a potentially alternative model of power, raising questions about the imputed lack of agency of those who 'give'.

Stereotyped notions of *travestis* and *bofes* draw on these representations of the 'natures' of the feminine and the masculine, transposed onto male bodies. Appearing to signal embodied femininity, *travestis* are widely believed and expected to participate as insertees in the sexual act. Correspondingly, *bofes*, with their swaggering virility, are envisaged as insertors. These polarized extremes appear to preclude spaces in between. Matters are, however, rarely as straightforward as these rigid dichotomies might suggest.

A closer look at issues surrounding attitudes to the so-called 'sex-change' operation is revealing. Many, although not all, *travestis* are against the idea. It appears that the primary concern in 'having it all chopped off' (as one put it) is material, rather than psychical or even physical. A 'sex change' is an option that requires not only a large amount of money, but also the ability to sustain a livelihood outside prostitution. One Bahian *travesti*, Vera, reveals one reason for rejecting the operation: 'I would never want to cut off my penis . . . I think that it is [my penis] that makes me most interesting, it is that men see the whole of me, with this penis in the middle' (Oliveira 1984: 3). The juxtaposition of male and female attributes forms part of the allure of the *travestis* and defines the value of the commodity they sell. Further and more compelling reasons exist, however. *Travestis* talked of the operation as rendering them 'useless' in sexual transactions with clients and drew attention to the loss of potential for orgasm through ejaculation (cf Oliveira 1984, 1986). This hardly seems to support the notion that *travestis* act as if 'female', acting as insertee or fellator to clients or lovers. By all accounts, it appears that the converse is usually the case. According to members of GGB, services involving the *travestis* performing in the 'active' role provide about 90 per cent of their custom.[10] The following description, given by a São Paulo *travesti*, Luana, makes this explicit: 'At the moment my penis is like a workman's drill; unless he opens holes, he doesn't get paid' (Acosta n.d.: 5). Penis size plays a part in determining the market value of *travestis* as well as *bofes*: clients judge both by their 'virile member'. Almeida (1984) details strategies adopted by *bofes/miches* for enhancing apparent penis size through padding or by standing hands in pockets to maintain an erection as clients pass. In the case of *travestis*, Pereira (1988) reports that clients stop their cars to feel what they are paying for before negotiating a price.

Sexual services are offered according to a menu, termed the *programa*. Not only sexual activities but notions of gendered sexual behaviour determine the pricing system. *Chupetinha* and *punhetinha* (blow and hand jobs, respectively), perhaps the most frequent services performed, are the cheapest. Where clients request penetrative sex, two distinct pricing systems exist, corresponding with hegemonic notions of the feminine *passivo* and the masculine *ativo*. In the case of *travestis*, Mott (1982) and Oliveira (1986) describe a sliding scale of prices. This runs from *chupetinha* and *punhetinha* to *bundinha* (being penetrated), *programa completo* (*bundinha* and other services as '*passivos*', including an overnight stay), *sacanagem completo* (which can include penetrating the client, being fellated by the client) and *troca-troca* (involving both/neither *ativo* and *passivo* sexual roles). For *bofes* too, deviation from the normative '*ativo*' sexual role commands a higher price (Almeida 1984; McRae 1985; Pereira 1988).

Who, then, are the clients of *travestis*? I spent a lot of time in bars talking with *putas* and their clients. The clients of *travestis* are less easy to find sitting around for a casual drink. Many have cars and custom is solicited at the roadside. Most clients seem to be middle-aged, middle-class, married men (Mott 1982; Oliveira 1986). Some are older men who have problems in achieving erections; some caution the *travestis* never to mention that they are *travestis* and not women; and some just want to gape at the bodies of the *travestis* (Oliveira 1986).

Clients are, however, cast in the popular imagination as the ones to act as insertors in sex and 'remain *homens*'. *Travestis* talk of such clients with disdain and call them *mariconas* (glossed as 'closets'), feeble creatures who take advantage of the veneer of respectability attained by marriage and procreation. Rather than despising such men for not 'coming out' as *bichas*, however, the disgust *travestis* display toward *mariconas* draws on the very masculinist attitudes that render the *travestis* themselves objects of abuse. Oliveira cites one *travesti* who remarked: 'At heart they are much more *veados* [literally 'deer'; derogatory term for homosexual] than us' (1986: 194). *Putas* had similar views on bisexual men, terming them *giletes* (after the double-sided razor). Some *giletes*, I was told, make love with *putas* and then produce a dildo and request the women to penetrate them with it. One friend was particularly dismissive: 'These kinds of men are all *bichas*! They want to be fucked and pay women to let them seem as if they are not *bichas*.'

A further, albeit very rarely found, type of client is female. For them, the *programa* is called *suruba* and is one of the most expensive (Oliveira 1986). Oliveira reports that clients are often female prostitutes and that, 'this is considered among the *travestis* as the maximum in eroticism and the height of inversion' (1986: 189). This, she argues, reflects the notion that love between two *travestis* or a *travesti* and a *mulher* is considered scandalous. Unfortunately, I was unable to find out more to shed further light on Oliveira's comments. I was, however, told on several occasions that *travestis* may set up home with *sapatões*, so-called 'butch' lesbians. This was considered acceptable, a marriage between male femininity and female masculinity.

The feminine appearance of *travestis* and their association with idealized femininity masks homoerotic desire. Clients, with a beautiful 'woman' in their passenger seats, appear to be enacting the 'myth of the macho'. Some *travestis* counted this as one of their major attractions, although, as one informant put it, 'everyone knows: no-one is fooled except them!'. Others declare that although dissimulation is one aspect of the encounter, the allure of the *travesti* lies in the perceived eroticism of the female form endowed with a penis. 'It is the ultimate fantasy', one remarked. The femininity of the *travestis* re-creates the 'male' in their clients; what Mott refers to as 'restor[ing] their camouflaged masculinity' (1987: 52).

With the repositioning of assumed sexual roles in relations with clients comes an adjustment not only of the pricing structure but also of the behaviour of the *travestis*. Prices rocket. Sometimes *travestis* increase the price after sex, as well as when additional services are requested in the privacy of a hotel room or car. There are occasional reports of *travestis* extorting all the valuables the client is carrying, through threats of violence or exposure. Oliveira cites a *travesti* who tellingly described her/his reaction to clients who do not pay up: 'When they don't pay, one forgets what is feminine and *vira* (turns) into a *homem machão* (he-man) and it becomes necessary to smash his car and his face in' (1986: 181). In 'forgetting what is feminine', *travestis* '*virar machão*': they (re)turn to dominant, powerful and violent behaviour. The perceptions of outsiders and locals echo this image, dwelling on the aggressiveness and violence of the *travestis*, as thieves, muggers and the most *marginal* of *marginais*. Through displays of violence towards *maricona* clients, *travestis* replicate hegemonic masculinism. This creates a number of interesting paradoxes. *Travestis*, in taking on a 'male' sexual identity adopt its corollary attributes – such as violence – in such situations.[11] They reinstate the dichotomy, in reverse.

The male masculinities displayed by *bofes* are similarly compromised by the demands of their clients. Again the weight of masculinism is brought to bear on clients. *Bofes* refer to such clients as *bichas*, rather than 'real men'. The pleasures of many customers do indeed lie in what one informant described as 'the fantasy of *submeter ao macho* (submitting to the macho)'. A significant number of clients, however, prefer to take the '*ativo*' role. This, as McRae (1985) stresses, is no secret. *Bofes*, however, do not regard themselves as *homossexuais*, but as *homens*. They vigorously defend their *macho* image, often adopting strategies such as bragging about the women they have toyed with to reaffirm their 'maleness' (see Pereira 1988). The sale of their bodies is strictly defined as 'work', a means of earning cash (McRae 1985; Almeida 1984). Detaching commoditized desire defers responsibility: 'they think that if they receive money in return, it isn't them, but the person who pays, who is the "*homossexual*"' (Pereira 1988). Denial and the contradictions of desire can have explosive results. *Bofes* may turn to vicious assaults on those who appear to embody the possibilities of homoerotic desire: again, re-turning to violence to assert a particular male masculinity.[12]

The expected sexual roles of 'man' or 'woman' set the classificatory frame in these transactions, despite the array of sexual practices. Rather than stepping outside this frame, variations become inversions which replicate notions of how a 'man' or 'woman' should behave in bed. In 'off-duty' relationships, this framework persists. *Travestis* who gain their income from acting as insertors in commoditized sex talk of their 'husbands' who are 'man enough' never to wish to be penetrated. *Bofes* sometimes cohabit with *travestis*, or with *bichas*, whom they may dominate and disrespect; playing out the stereotypical *macho*.

The association of *homem* with 'active', dominating, male masculinity and the residual category not-*homem* with its lack has arisen through particular historical circumstances. Turning to the 'historical apparatuses' of sexuality in Salvador, further issues arise.

'SINS OF THE FLESH': DOMAINS OF 'DEVIANCE'

Foucault argues that 'sexuality must not be thought of as a kind of natural given which power tries to hold in check, or as an obscure domain which knowledge tries to uncover' (1978). Foucault's emphasis is on the often discontinuous production of categories which are deployed in processes of 'normalization' within particular 'regimes of truth'. Inspection of the production of homosexualities in Salvador from the sixteenth century to the present reveals shifting frames of reference.

The arrival of the Inquisition in 1591 produced the first documentary evidence of attempts to categorize and control sexual behaviour in Brazil. Prior legislation had marked out forms of 'deviance' which said more about non-reproductive sexual acts than actors: sodomy, the 'abominable sin', and mutual masturbation attracted penalties for both parties (Mott 1988). Cross-dressing was criminalized as a separate offence: the 'sin' of 'pretending to be in a different state and condition' (Mott 1988: 32). The 1603 Ordinance narrowed the terms of reference, directing attention to what would now be termed homosexual relations, interestingly making reference to what is now called lesbianism. This set the frame for later refinements, yet continued to refer to acts rather than 'types'.

The terms *comer* (literally 'to eat'; to penetrate) and *dar* (literally 'to give'; to be penetrated) appear in confessions. The Inquisitors classified those who engaged in sodomy accordingly: as *agente* (active) or *paciente* (passive). Inquisition records referred to *pacientes* 'performing the duty of a female' and 'acting as a woman' (Trevisan 1986: 55). Interestingly, a third category emerges from the records, Mott (1988) reports, accounting for a significant 25 per cent of confessions: *troca-troca*, both/neither *agente* and *paciente*.

Independence from Portugal in 1820 brought new legislative measures, which took their point of reference from nineteenth-century European discourses on the 'family' (cf. Foucault 1978). The 'abominable sin' became one of the 'crimes offending morality and good custom' in 1830, tellingly replaced in the 1890 Republican Penal Code by 'crimes against the security and well-being of the family' (Trevisan 1986: 68). Punishment for cross-dressing remained, meriting a less severe penalty; as 'wearing clothes inappropriate to their sex in public, in order to deceive' (Trevisan 1986: 69).

Above all, the emphasis was on procreation within marriage, with a corresponding emphasis on a hierarchical and mutually exclusive 'masculinity' and 'femininity'. 'Homosexuality', defined by Kertbeny in 1869, began to be used as a psychiatric category in Brazil in the late nineteenth century, along with notions of the 'pervert' and the 'invert' (Trevisan 1986; Foucault 1978; Marshall 1981).

The focus had shifted away from the act to the actors: the categories *agente* ('active') and *paciente* ('passive') now came to refer to persons rather than sexual positions. *Troca-troca*, with its implication of a less hierarchical model for sexual – and, by extension, social – relations, disappeared from the frame. The (imputed) act of penile penetration became synonymous with male gender and became prominent in defining 'masculinity'. Two categories emerged: *homens* and *bichas* (Fry 1982). *Homens*, glossed simply as 'men', were assumed to be '*ativo*' and therefore not '*homossexuais*'. *Bichas* were typed as the '*passivo*' partners of *homens*, the 'other half' of a heterosexual model of submissive femininity and assertive masculinity. Only *bichas* were considered to be *homossexuais*.

'Deviance' was recast in terms of relations between 'people of the same *gender* identities' (Fry 1982: 91). *Bichas* became objects of persecution and ridicule, while *homens* retained the privileges of 'male' status. *Travestis* were now doubly offensive, cast as *bichas* and as committing the 'crime' of cross-dressing. As the example *par excellence* of 'deviation' from 'normal' familial relations, the *travesti* – more even than the prostitute identifying as female – came to carry the symbolic load of and stigmatization for alternative forms of desire.

In the south of Brazil (Fry 1982) and increasingly outside radical activist circles in Salvador, 'homosexual' men have come to embrace a new *geui* (gay) identity. However, in Salvador, in 1990, the classification of men into 'real men' and *bichas* was still pervasive. Use of the category *homem* continues to turn on the act of penile penetration allied with the possession of a penis. In one emotionally charged discussion I had with a mixed group of neighbours, for example, all agreed that a man who lets himself be penetrated, a dildo-wielding woman who penetrates her male partner or women who have penetrative sex with other women were all classed as not-*homem*. As one man exclaimed, when I asked if his comments on *bichas* applied to lesbians: 'No, women who have sex with women are still women, but a *bicha* is *no longer a man – he has become a woman* as he lets himself be fucked' (my emphasis).

From this brief account, it becomes apparent that shifting discourses have produced variant sexualities and genders over time. Sexual and gender identities may be regarded as the effects of discourses, but there is never only one option available. Hegemonic discourses on sexuality and gender clearly impinged on relations of sociality among non-white Bahians, yet are part of a more complex picture. The emphases on reproductive sex and on marriage through different periods were as much concerned with maintaining a white/ non-white boundary as with the production of appropriately servile reproducers. The disciplining concerns of the wealthier classes are not so easily extended to those outside these groups.

Accounts dating back to the early days of slavery and colonial occupation suggest that among several African, as well as indigenous Amerindian, groups 'homosexual' relations were by no means uncommon. Nor were such relations described as a source of stigma or social condemnation within these communities (Oliveira Marques 1971; Mott 1988; Trevisan 1986). Inquisition records refer not only to confessions of 'the abominable sin' between whites and other races, but also among and between *negros* (blacks), *mestiços* (bi-racials) and *indíos* (indigenous Amerindians). Cases of transvestism appear in these records from the sixteenth century onwards (Mott 1988). Of particular interest is the connection which emerges between African *feiticeiros* (medical and ritual specialists) and the wearing of 'female' clothes.

The association of African religious practice with alternatives to heterosexual marriage appears to have become significant as black communities reconstructed 'tradition' during the following centuries. Devastating rates of infant mortality and the separation by slavers of couples from their offspring and each other (Woortman 1987), as well as demographic gender imbalances between towns and rural areas, affected the stability of heterosexual partnerships in black communities. Discourses about homoerotic desire, which recognized and affirmed the possibilities for alternative partnerships, appear to have become prominent.[13]

Religious expression played an important part in the process of re-creating 'African culture'. The systematization of religious practice during the nineteenth century drew on the symbolic media of 'African religion' and the

Catholic church to form *Candomblé*.[14] One of the major influences on the development of *Candomblé* appears to have been the religious practices of the ethnic group spanning present-day Nigeria, Benin and Togo, now referred to as Yoruba.[15] Women, numerically and economically dominant within Salvador's black communities during the eighteenth and nineteenth centuries, played major roles in these cults. As vessels of the deities and as traders or vendors, women held considerable power relative to men, who had limited economic opportunities in the cities (Herskovits 1966; Woortman 1987). These were not the submissive wives of the bourgeoisie, but assertive and purposeful agents in their own right. *Candomblé* became a sphere in which women consolidated their power. Women could gain status and influence as devotees or priestesses and benefit from the web of informal social and economic networks which ramified from the cults (Herskovits 1966).

Landes, researching in the 1930s, dubbed Salvador 'The City of Women' and wrote of the 'cult matriarchate of *Candomblé*' (1940). She noted that while cult membership consisted mainly of women, there were also 'notorious passive homosexuals' (1940: 393) in the cults. Ribeiro (1970) and the Leacocks (1972) confirm, for Afro-Brazilian cults further north in Recife and Belem, both the presence of *bichas* and public perceptions to this effect. These men were often possessed by 'female' deities, in an arena which was dominated by powerful women. Landes, Ribeiro and the Leacocks offer the explanation that *Candomblé* provides a space for 'homosexual' men to express their 'femininity'. As such it is portrayed as a palliative, to provide them with temporary solace from societal persecution. This line of argument resembles that of Lewis (1971) and has similar problems. For, in viewing the participation of the marginalized from the position of the powerful, alternative perspectives are not brought into the frame. Segato offers quite a different view. Cult members she worked with in Recife referred to 'homosexual' relationships, particularly those between women, as a 'custom'.[16] Further, Segato contends, 'Homosexuality [is] not accidental or superfluous to, but a structural aspect of understanding the *Weltanschauung* of the cult' (1986: 75).

Karin Barber (1991) makes the interesting observation that among Nigerian Yoruba:

> Gender classifications are not organised in fixed schema: they are ambiguous and fluctuating. This . . . must be understood in terms of the importance placed . . . on the maintenance of a multiplicity of differences and alternatives.
>
> (1991: 277)

Through an exploration of the multiple differences offered within *Candomblé*, alternative frames of reference emerge. Within these the *travesti* as devotee may be attributed 'sex' and 'gender' according to quite different criteria.

'THE LIFE OF THE SAINTS'

The 'saints' of *Candomblé* appear in images and writings as a fusion of Catholic saints with counterparts from the anthropomorphic pantheon of Yoruba deities (*orisa*), referred to in Brazil as *santos* or *orixá* (Bastide 1978). Devotees (*filhas de santo*) venerate the deities who 'call' them to become their vessels and 'mount' them in possession trance. Initiation is described as 'making the saint'. The devotee's *orixá* is not an essentialized given. Rather, each individual creatively styles her/his *orixá* from a diverse collection of attributes. Although devotees are 'mounted' and 'possessed' by their *orixás*, they may also reject particular *orixás* for others: they are not merely passive vessels. Each *orixá* has a sex, gender and personality, which his/her devotees enact in trance and often carry into their interactions outside the space marked by possession.

Among Yoruba, individual *orisa* form the focus of separate cult groups and the constellation of deities varies widely from place to place. In *Candomblé*, however, the *orixás* are represented as part of a family and each *terreiro* propitiates and celebrates a restricted pantheon of deities. Fictive kinship bonds between devotees replicate the *família de santo* (family of saints) (Costa Lima 1977), forming part of an extensive informal network with close affective ties. Myths and oral art within *Candomblé* portray a different image of the family to the bourgeois model. Heterosexual partnerships are presented as fragile and fraught and descriptions of the actors in these scenarios present alternatives to the hegemonic version of masculinity and femininity (Segato 1986).

Representations of the *orixás* in myths, paintings and ritual objects subvert hegemonic notions of gender. They establish masculinity and femininity as fluid, rather than fixed: offering gender as a continuum of qualities found in both males and females. Masculinities are associated as much with emotion and softness as with forceful dominance; and femininities include images of the fierce and the powerful, as well as the sensuous and gentle. Notions of masculinity and femininity are represented as interchangeable, contingent options, displacing the assymmetry in mainstream discourse of a hierarchical 'masculinity' and 'femininity'.

Personalities, rather than sexed bodies, sexualities and social gender, form the key principle for attributing *orixás* (cf Lepine 1978). While the personalities of the *orixás* cover the entire range of human experience, each is usually ascribed a mythical 'sex'.[17] Definitions draw on Yoruba language and mark three categories: *aboró* (male), *íaba* (female) and *méta-méta* (literally 'half-half'; intersexual) (Teixeira 1987). Initiates acquire *santos-homens* ('male saints'), *santos-mulheres* ('female saints') or the intersexual *santos* according to the correspondence between elements of their personality and that of the respective deity.

In the selective recombination of gendered traits, the sexuality and sex of the *orixá* replaces that of the devotee for certain purposes and in particular settings. These permutations and substitutions are open to play, presenting a range of choices and alternatives within which people can locate themselves. Dressing for the *orixás* lends legitimacy to the identity of *travesti*. Intersexual saints, such as Logunedé and Oxumaré, enable devotees to conduct their lives as 'women' *and* as 'men'. As one *geui* male informant suggested: 'Logunedé sets an important precedent. People can't then discriminate or they would be sending Logunedé out into the street. It is a question of identification.'

A further classificatory level gives both a name and a legitimate space to homoerotic relationships and cross-gender behaviour. This framework distinguishes not two, but four 'genders': *homens* and *mulheres*, *adés/adéfontós* and *monokós/monas do aló* (Teixeira 1987). From Teixeira's (1987) description, it appears that these categories collapse the axes of difference used in western classifications – those of sex, gender and sexual orientation – into a scheme for describing both the 'gender' and the 'sexuality' of devotees. These distinctions overlap with those based on the attribution of *orixás*, whereby *adés* and *monokós* are often (although not always) possessed by *santos-mulheres* and *santos-homens* respectively.[18] *Adés* are generally identified as *bichas*, or *travestis*, *monokós* as *sapatæs* ('butch' lesbians) and, in that, as symbolic possessors-of-penises.

Possession and performance in rituals are usually limited to the two categories of women and *adés* in many *Candomblés* (although, these days, only those professing to be 'the most traditional'). As vessels of the gods, women and *adés* hold spiritual power and attain respect and recognition. As 'women', *travestis* can enjoy the privileges this brings. A further system of classification appears to emerge from consideration of the non-ritual tasks performed by initiates. The division of labour within *terreiros* appears to intersect with classification of initiates in terms of the 'mythical' sex of their *orixás* (Teixeira 1987). Hegemonic distinctions between 'men's work' and 'women's work' are, however, replicated within the practical arenas of the cults. The tasks of cleaning, sewing, cooking and washing fall to women and *adés*, while only 'men' perform the more prestigious duties of sacrifice, protection and patronage. The least valued tasks fall to women with *santos-mulheres*; those with no claims to 'mythical', biological or classificatory maleness.

Whereas *adés* are permitted the scope to become as if 'women' where it is desirable, options for *monokós* to become as if 'men' are limited. For certain purposes it seems that classification according to 'biology' takes precedence, where two 'sites of significance' are privileged: the possession of a penis and the capacity to extrude menstrual blood. Teixeira reports that in terms of practical activities, those without penises are barred from taking on certain tasks irrespective of their 'mythical sex', sexuality or possessing deity. Even where women are allowed to perform certain duties as *monokós*, this is strictly limited to the periods during which they are not menstruating or to those among them who are past reproductive age. Costa Lima (1990) notes the description of the latter class of women as 'a woman who has already become a man'. Such women, like the *adés*, are ambiguously gendered and can cross the boundaries which mark appropriate tasks for men or women. Yet certain activities are still categorically denied to them. This would seem to suggest that their transition to 'maleness' is incomplete. They may be possessors of 'mythical' penises and no longer fulfil the principal criteria of 'femaleness' as they are no longer able to procreate, but they do not have the physical organ itself.

In the different activities and contexts within the *terreiro*, it seems that *adés* have the best of both worlds:

> *Adés* possess flexibility, or better, an ambiguity which permits them to be seen sometimes as women, sometimes as men, according to what is being valorised at that moment, whether it is the state of biological maleness [which they retain] in non-religious activities . . . or of femaleness which is adopted in religious activities.
>
> (Teixeira 1987: 43)

Within this space, possession of a penis again does not in itself signal 'maleness'. For a feminine devotee of a *santo-mulher* the penis ceases to have any significance. Yet in contests over the allocation of prestige or power, possessors of penises have the advantage of being able to make claims to a 'maleness' which is defined in different ways to those that would be outside the *terreiro*. A 'sex change' would do nothing to enhance their status. They can draw on and inhabit representations of the feminine to consolidate their positions in some situations, with no concomitant impact on their status in activities where being 'male' offers advantages.

While a range of alternatives and possibilities is offered within the domain of the *terreiro*, its members are agents in more than just this sphere. The attitudes and values of the mainstream impinge on and intersect with the alternatives offered within *Candomblé*, as they do on the ways in which its members interact with others both within and outside the cult. Alternative models of power and agency may supersede those of mainstream society in certain respects. However, hegemonic notions of masculinity continue to impinge, providing possessors of penises with strategies for repositioning themselves within these different frames.

COMPROMISING POSITIONS?

Travestis move from ritual to secular space and back again: within and between different, although not entirely discrete, frames of reference. Bürger puts forward the notion of 'the dialectic of the boundary' (1990: 49), whereby boundaries persistently defy abolition and are instead constantly reinstated. This may be usefully applied not only to the boundary between subordinate and hegemonic discourses about sexuality and gender, but also to that between 'masculinity' and 'femininity', 'male' and 'female', *ativo* and *passivo*: the contested sources of these representations. The dissonance generated through boundary flux gives *travestis* the scope to enact a range of gendered identities in different situations.

In the context of street prostitution, it is not possession of a penis that confers 'maleness'. Rather, it is in the *use* of the penis to penetrate that the *travesti* crosses the boundary. *Travestis* called upon to service their client in this way may *virar machão* (re-turn to a violent, male masculinity) only to take on the part of the glamorous belle in negotiations with the next client. In the *terreiros* of *Candomblé*, 'mythical' penises may be attributed to those who lack their biological counterpart, while possession of a physical penis may play no part in attributions of 'sex' or 'gender' for others. Conversely, possession of a penis may provide sufficient grounds to claim 'male' status in the absence of most of the elements associated with hegemonic versions of 'masculinity'. It is again the possession of a penis that allows the *travestis*, generally inhabiting the ambiguous category of *adé* within *Candomblé*, often with *santos-mulheres* (female deities), to cross the boundaries between 'women' and 'men'. By retaining the penis *travestis* defy the rigid boundary that mainstream gender ascriptions create and benefit from strategic boundary crossings within *Candomblé*. In doing so, they juxtapose femininity and maleness: to strategic ends that do not always cohere with the egalitarian promise that this might suggest. For, as Bürger (1990) suggests, the boundary is never removed, merely repositioned.

Strathern contends: 'Idealised masculinity is not necessarily just about men, it is not necessarily just about relations between the sexes either' (1988: 65). The slippage of *travestis* between these different frames of reference suggests the power effects of acts of classification. The mutually exclusive categories of *ativo* and *passivo* that form part of mainstream gender attributions have less to do with sexual expression than defining and normalizing gendered relations of power. The use of the notions of *comedor* and *doador* extends beyond the frame of sexual interaction to describe appropriate displays of hegemonic masculinity – or its lack. Thus, winning football teams 'eat' their opponents (see also Archetti 1992). However, to regard the giver as passive, powerless and merely a patient would deny, and obscure, more subtle relations of power between the actors (Hobart 1989). A giver, after all, gives something *to* someone else. Domination, like sub-mission, is situational: differently understood and continually re-evaluated and disputed.

Attributing passivity as an essential attribute of a particular category is, then, an act of power that serves to legitimize inequalities rather than define them. The conflation of sexual acts with gendered identities locates the submissive (as well as the 'deviant') as residual to the category *homem*. This preserves the space for 'straight-acting' men to take full advantage of the privileges offered to them as *homens* (cf Forrest, Chapter 5 in this volume). The ritualized inversions of *carnaval* may open a space for wider expression of gender dissonance. However, both these and the everyday transgressions of *travestis* do little more than reinforce and restore, rather than redress, gendered inequalities. In representing femininity as passive, subordinate and a mere object of masculine desire, the *travesti* supports – and exemplifies – a particular version of patriarchy. In re-enacting male masculinity, both in their attitudes toward women and their relations with *mariconas* (closets/clients), *travestis* reaffirm the 'myth of the macho'.

Within mainstream discourse and on the streets a particular variant of masculinity – that of the idealized *homem* – is associated with agency and with power. Alternative conceptualizations of power within *Candomblé* dislocate these associations. Individuals may be attributed different 'sexes' and 'genders' according to the context. And opportunities also exist for those of apparently ambiguous status to benefit from a range of gendered identifications. *Candomblé* offers a continuum of gendered attributes. The alternatives offered within the *terreiro* resist the closure implied by hegemonic masculinity and femininity and expose the contingency of the relation between men and masculinity, women and femininity. Within this space, the association of the *travestis* with the feminine and their positions as devotees of powerful female deities locate them within a different model of agency. Submission to the *orixás* does not connote the powerlessness associated with *doadores*, who are 'mounted' by their lovers. Yet neither this domain, nor the actors within it, exist in isolation from wider society. Gendered hierarchies which draw on, rather than subvert, masculinist values also form part of the repertoire: both those inscribed within the recreated 'Africas' of the *terreiros* and those which carry the hegemonic principle of male prerogative into these spaces.

Travestis move between these spaces and are gendered by others according to overlapping, yet conceptually discrete, sets of criteria. In the domains of the *trottoir* and the *terreiro*, it is not what *travestis* 'are' but what they *do* which confers their 'sex' or 'gender'. *Travestis* resist an essential definition as 'male' or as 'female', but are certainly not neuter (*ne-uter*; neither one or the other). The mutability of 'gender' in this case raises the wider question of how useful an analytical construct this term really is, when abstracted from the setting in which it is used. As Butler suggests:

> Gender ought not to be construed as a stable identity or locus of agency from which various acts follow; rather, gender is an identity tenuously constituted in time, instituted in an exterior space through a stylised repetition of acts.
>
> (1990: 140)

NOTES

Many people have contributed to the writing of this paper. I am especially grateful to Grupo Gay da Bahia, Vivaldo da Costa Lima, Robson 'the Baiana', Maria, Antonio and Snr Geraldo and his *filhas de santo* for all their help while I was in Bahia. I would like to thank Kit Davis for her help with an earlier version of this chapter and Hermann Bennett, LaRay Denzer, Richard Fardon, Angie Hart, Mark Hobart and Nancy Lindisfarne for their insights and comments. I am grateful to Luiz Mott and Peter Fry for their encouragement.

1 My reservations about using the terms 'men', 'male' or 'masculinity' and 'women', 'female' or 'femininity' have been expressed in the introduction to this volume.

2 One of the first gay activist groups in Brazil, GGB works principally in gay rights and HIV/AIDS education and outreach work. GGB works with a wide range of people in Salvador, including *travestis*.

3 Yoruba terms are used as slang to exclude outsiders, shout warnings and provide a language to flirt, joke and mock. To give some examples: *okó odara* (tasty man), *okossi* (money), *ajé-ô* (food); shouts of 'cuidado *mona ali bá*!' warn of the approach of police. *Travestis* and gay male devotees also use gestures from *Candomblé* to ridicule each other; performances are used in play in everyday life.

4 Fieldwork was carried out in Salvador from July to October 1990. This was preceded by a period of five months' residence in the central prostitution area in 1987 and a visit for *carnaval* in 1988, during which I first became interested in these questions.

5 See Kessler and McKenna's (1978) critique.

6 They report an interesting experiment. A mixed sample of Americans were shown two pictures: one portrayed a long-haired, depilated, curvy body with a penis and the other a short-haired, hirsute body without a penis. They were asked to gender the figures. Responses to the first picture were almost unanimous; 96 per cent thought it represented a male. The second picture produced a more mixed response, with 72 per cent of men and 57 per cent of women suggesting that this figure represented a female (Kessler and McKenna 1978: 145).

7 Informants told me that *travestis* either take oral contraceptives or buy injectable hormones, which are sometimes locally administered to the bust. See also Oliveira (1986).

8 I use Brittan's (1989) term 'masculinism' here as the term 'homophobia' implies a fear of 'homosexuality', already a problematic notion in this setting, rather than what appears to have more to do with the pervasive enforcement of hegemonic masculinity.

9 GGB keep a record of all murders and assaults which are reported. It is of alarming dimensions.

10 It is unclear how much this has changed with increasing HIV infection and HIV/AIDS education.

11 Oliveira (1986) cites an interesting comment made by a *travesti* that assuming the sexual role of insertor would result in losing her breasts, as it would reverse the effects of the hormones she was taking.

12 Mott (1982) reports that most of the murders of gay men in Salvador at that time had been committed by *bofes*.

13 This raises many questions, which I cannot consider here. Several writers (Landes 1940; Woortman 1987; Segato 1986) have given causal explanations for an alleged 'collapse' in male masculinities, which Segato goes on to relate to an increase in homoerotic expression. These accounts, on closer examination of west

and central African literature, appear both ethnographically and historically dubious. All assume that 'the African family' and 'African marriage' (already problematic unitary notions) resembled that of the Portuguese model of patriarchy. The idea that changes which undermined male prerogative and control could produce expressions of 'homosexuality' is particularly questionable (see Brittan 1989 on the inadequacies of 'male crisis theory').

14 The term *Candomblé* is an umbrella term which denotes certain family resemblances between a number of forms of religious expression. Three major 'types' are usually identified: Angolan, Caboclo and Nâgo/Jeje. It is with the third type that this analysis is concerned. I use the generic term to denote this form, but do not wish to suggest that this analysis can be extended to cover *Candomblé* in general: clearly, this is an area for further research.

15 Many reasons have been suggested for this and a complex debate surrounds this issue, which I cannot enter into here (see Dantas 1988). For whatever reasons, Yoruba religious practices are most readily identifiable within 'traditional' *Candomblé*.

16 This raises a number of fascinating historical questions, which require further research.

17 In addition, Kinni-Olusanyin (n.d.) suggests that at some times it may be a particular aspect of an *orixá* which is referred to as a 'man', where the 'sex' of the *orixá* is established as 'female', and vice versa.

18 Several people remarked that *bichas* come to the cults to be initiated as *filhas* of Oxum, whose representations include the most conventionally 'feminine' of attributes. A person cannot simply choose an *orixá*, however, but must be chosen. Nevertheless, due to the confluence of their characteristics with those of the deity, it is common to find *bichas* as *filhas* of Oxum.

Chapter 7

Pandora unbound

A feminist critique of Foucault's *History of Sexuality*

Lin Foxhall

It is rare that we who study past societies can claim any analytical advantage over colleagues who work in the present. But however much we do not and cannot know about a culture long dead, we have a panoramic view of social landscapes which those caught in the on-going flow of the same present as the people they study can never catch.

The influence of Foucault's writings on sexuality, especially *The History of Sexuality* (1978–86), on subsequent studies of sexuality, gender and the discourses of power and oppression has been profound. In particular, Foucault has revolutionized the study of the social history of classical antiquity, where, with fifth–fourth century BC Athens, he ultimately decided to begin his investigations. Foucault's intellectual framework is a maze in which a large amount of recent work on gender in classical antiquity is trapped. But every maze has a way out. Here I will argue that there are considerable difficulties with Foucault's historical construction and con-textualization of the discourses of sexuality and the implications of these discourses for both past societies and our own. This is not to say his contribution has been negligible; far from it. Foucault provides an analytical framework which can be expanded to explore the implications of sex and gender in the whole of social life.

Foucault fashioned his analytical 'techniques' over a lifetime of archae-ology, geneology and ethics. This is grossly oversimplified, but archaeology (to maintain the metaphor) consists less of the systematic excavation of discourses than of remote sensing: of inferring the meanings of hidden landscapes of the mind by the lumps and bumps on the textual surface. Geneology is the progenesis of power in discourse: the uncomfortable kindred relation between claims to authority and the use of power. Ethics first emerges in Volume 2 of *The History of Sexuality*; its development as an analytical technique seems to be entangled with the major change in scope and design of his project. Ethics is best summed up by Foucault's own phrase, '*rapport à soi*'; that is, the relationship of the self to itself and the concomitant creation of moral systems. All these techniques have opened new directions in historical and cultural analysis. But the weakness of archaeology and geneology is that in both Foucault's usage and other senses of the terms they are modes of enquiry founded in a past which has only a tenuous sense of the breadth and complexity of *their* present. Ethics, in contrast, collapses in on itself. The revelation that there is a reflexive dimension to morality is an immensely valuable insight. But the exercise falters in the absence of the protean 'others' which are part of the self's reflexive definition. Foucault produces a sophisticated history of ideas but ignores the complex ethnographic settings of these ideas. In the case of classical Greece (as laid out in *The History of Sexuality*, Volume 2) it is especially crucial that the reflexive self has been limited to an idealized male self – a limitation totally unjustified by the historical evidence. This kind of masculinist reflexivity underwrites and absorbs the masculine ideologies of the past as part of the process of living out those of the present.

The dimension of enquiry I add to redress the balance could be called ethnography; that is, a consideration of the synchronic, simultaneous, changing contexts in which conflicting (often incompatible) discourses operate. Here I re-evaluate sexuality as a part of personal and political identity through the social acts of constructing gender, whose meanings change with context. Being a man or being a woman, male or female, boy or girl does not always mean the same thing.

Not that the Greek sources give us much positive assistance in such an exercise. For specific reasons, all sorts of text from classical Greece are largely the products of a dominant masculine ideology. One can hardly blame Foucault for taking them literally. So do virtually all other scholars. I have tried to circumvent this problem by searching for the meanings of actions as well as ideologies, without delegating preferential constitutive status to either.

I have also tried to avoid a mistake made by Foucault and others in working with Greek material – that of construing the part for the whole. Even for ethnographers (in both a metaphorical and a practical sense) working in contemporary societies, not all contexts are accessible or are equally accessible. For ancient Greece only a limited number of contexts can be explored. Precisely because of the nature and context of the production of virtually all our sources, the touchstone of understanding is always the free, adult, male citizen. Hence discourses on power, love and life itself frequently take on the form of hierarchical definitions of 'otherness' in polar opposition to the pivotal pillar of society: the adult, free, male citizen. This illusion, partly a consequence of the production of the sources themselves, blurs our vision of the intricate detail of lived reality, if we allow ourselves to be swallowed up in it (Foxhall: forthcoming b).

The 'other' of man is not only woman, but also slave, child, old man, god, beast and barbarian. But what is the 'other' of woman? For Foucault, she has no 'other'; only male selves are admissible in his analysis, and he never questions whether women complied with this negation of female selves. It is indeed harder to perceive woman as a first element from the texts alone. So, for example, women are never the starting point or focal person for defining an *ankhisteia* – which is the formally structured bilateral kindred that children of first cousins used to determine inheritance and funerary obligations. In anthropological terms a woman can never formally be 'ego', because 'significant' kinship networks were seen to link men. None the less, women were essential for connecting the *ankhisteia* together. Indeed, it could not work without them and frequently female links were chosen as a means of emphasizing relationships between men who had no male link. Moreover, there were alternative social and kinship structures, which operated in particular contexts. These were just as real in people's lives as those governed by the ideology of the adult male citizen. What is interesting is that they are not openly expressed in the texts. But if we start instead from the viewpoint that a number of significant aspects of social life were governed by feminine ideologies, an entirely new set of contemporary and simultaneous contexts is opened up in an ethnographic way.[1]

There are three aspects of life in which male and female discourses are at cross-purposes, to the point that they are sometimes mutually unintelligible. One is the relationship to time and hence to monumentality. Another is the constitution and political construction of households, and the relation of individuals to them. The third is the area problematized (but not so con-textualized) by Foucault: the development and construction of sexuality *vis-à-vis* social and political relationships.

TIME AND MONUMENTALITY

Women and men experience time in different ways. I think this is probably true in many societies, but it is certainly demonstrable for classical Greece. There are two areas where gender-specific relationships to time are most obvious. One is the different ways men and women pass through life stages; the second is the way individuals access the past and the future (which are different pasts and futures for men and women) beyond their own life spans.

One can still read that Greek women were considered to be permanent children (Sealey 1990: 40–2; Foucault comes close to arguing this). This is surely incorrect. Xenophon in the *Oikonomikos* portrays a newly married woman as an adult (albeit a young adult), who is taking on adult responsibilities with her marriage: women are realized, children are potential. Of course adulthood did not mean the same thing for women as for men. But it would seem that in general girls were felt to reach adulthood sooner than boys (cf. Aristotle, *de gen. an.* 775a.5ff – females take longer to generate in the womb, but grow up faster; female diseases work on different time spans from male diseases). Girls might be 'finished off' after marriage under the tutelage of a mother-in-law (e.g. Lysias 1), but they were fully adult when the babies started to arrive, within a few years of their marriage shortly after puberty

(12–14 or so, so they were 'adult' by the time they were 15 or 16). Boys slid more gradually into adulthood over a longer period of time, through a process which began at around age 17 or 18 (cf. Vidal-Naquet 1981). They might not reach full adulthood until around 30, and few Athenian men married much younger than this. Similarly at the other end of life, women frequently remained powerful and active in their world of the household longer than men remained powerful and active in the world of the city. Men faded out of politics when they were no longer militarily active, but women's influence over their younger kin increased as they grew older. The corollary of these differences in life cycle must be that the meaning of being a man or being a woman itself changed in relation to the other over time.

Individuals' contact with the past and the future is similarly gender specific, and related to gender-specific life cycles. Women projected themselves into the future directly via their children and grandchildren, especially their sons (Hunter 1989). In most of the contexts of everyday life, classical Greeks rarely had much concern for a past or future reaching out more than three generations (Foxhall, forthcoming b). So, for example, the *ankhisteia* comprised the group of people who shared an ancestor three generations back; concomitantly one planted olives for one's grandchildren and great-grandchildren. Indeed much of a household's social and economic activity was for the sake of its children; that is, its own immediate future. Because of the special role of women's relationships in directing and managing households, much of the practical direction of life on this three-generation time scale was in women's hands. I shall return to this point, though it is worth noting that in a Greek context household management means much more than simply doing the housework, since a family's economic enterprises (including factories and farms) were conceptually contained within the household – no notion of independent, corporate, economic institutions existed (see Foxhall 1989).

Men were dependent on women for access to the three-generation time scale which framed most of everyday life (some of the later discussion about sexuality returns to this theme). But the formal network of kinship was appropriated by men. This was the *ankhisteia* (mentioned earlier), which was most often invoked when kinship affairs became public matters (as in funerals, or in the marriage of brotherless, fatherless girls, which could become a state problem). Men also appropriated a larger-scale past and future, which existed in a rather undifferentiated way beyond the three-generation limit, and excluded women from it. The way in which this kind of time was used I have called monumentality (see Foxhall, forthcoming b). This notion of monumentality is explicit throughout Greek literature, art and inscriptions. It becomes entwined with a complex rhetoric about fame, glory, reputation and memory. For example, the (male) historical/journalistic writer Thucydides describes *his* account of the Peloponnesian Wars as *ktema eis aei*, 'a possession for eternity'. Many other examples of male monumentality could be cited, in forms varying from the Parthenon to individuals' grave stelae or vases inscribed with graffiti. Virtually all of the literary and epigraphical sources for ancient Greece emanate from this context of male monumentality, generated by men in their relatively short period of full, powerful adulthood. More specifically, they are the artefacts produced by the purveyors of a (perhaps 'the') 'hegemonic masculinity' which attempts to dominate, subordinate and feminize the rest, and their production is an intrinsic part of this process of domination (see Cornwall and Lindisfarne, Chapter 1 in this volume).

Similarly with access to the past, because men married older than women and older men married much younger women, children were likely to have contact for longer with a grandmother than with a grandfather. Thus part of classical Greek socialization processes would have been learning about the short-term past from women in the household.[2] The past and the future (on this roughly three-generation scale) were thus more accessible to women than to men, and it may be partly because of this that women had special roles in marking the passage of time in human lives – in *rites de passage*, notably weddings and funerals and most obviously in childbirth.

These contested discourses, the problematizations of gender and time, also reverberate in the relationship between the ritual and the agricultural calenders of ancient Athens. There were three major festivals of Demeter and Kore, which related directly to crucial periods in the growth of cereals, the main food staple, and to a lesser extent grapes. The Thesmophoria was celebrated in late October over five days just before the start of the sowing period, which was also the busiest period of the year for agricultural work. The festival excluded men (virtually no Athenian festivals excluded women), and during this period women took over the city, held sacrifices, fasted, and performed magic to infuse the seed corn with fertility. The Haloa, a rowdy women's festival (again excluding men) celebrated at the end of December in honour of Demeter and Kore and Dionysos, marked the end of the autumn agricultural work (sowing and vine pruning). The third festival of this type was the Skira in June, which was tied to the ritual plastering of threshing floors towards the end of the harvest.

Significantly, in all of these festivals women displayed their sexuality to, among and with each other in the absence of men – Aristophanes depicts 'homosexual' as well as heterosexual desires and behaviour between women in these gatherings, and this is supported by the anxiety with which other sources document these festivals. It is also significant that immediately after the Thesmophoria and shortly before the Skira there were festivals to Apollo which were centred on the phratries (patrilateral clans) and thus celebrated the principles of male descent. The Apatouria (immediately after the Thesmophoria in early November) also celebrated the moment at which youths were becoming men (beautifully analysed by Vidal-Naquet 1981). The Thargelion came in mid-May, just before the cereal harvest. Though it included a sacrifice to Demeter Chloe (Green Demeter), the victim was a ram – one of the very few occasions when a goddess received a male animal. Perhaps most important in relation to the Thesmophoria were Haloa and Skira (the women's festivals to Demeter and Kore): all of the agricultural tasks at the heart of the rituals were men's jobs.

Over and over, women's ritual activity was essential for men's work to be effective. That ritual activity consisted in large part of women constituting their sexuality. The core of Greek social continuity was symbolized by Demeter and Kore – the relationship of mother and daughter. This became symbolically tied up with the continuity of the physical body through the social activities of food consumption and production: Demeter was the *kourotrophos*, the nursemaid, of humanity (this was one of her cult titles). In contrast, the celebration of the generations of men in festivals to Apollo complemented, or perhaps resisted, the centrality of continuity and kindred through female links which excluded men. Demeter and Kore – lines of mothers and daughters spanning generations of men – thus provided alternative kinship structures to the male-dominated *ankhisteia* (three-generation kindred) and phratry (patrilateral clan). Women might almost be said to control time in some contexts, but hegemonic masculinity wrested the control of one kind of eternity from them. Monumentality in the public sphere, the struggle to achieve glory, fame and remembrance, largely excluded women.

THE CONSTITUTION AND POLITICAL CONSTRUCTION OF HOUSEHOLDS

Even for Aristotle (*Politics* 1), the fundamental sociopolitical unit of Greek city-states was the household (*oikos*), not the individual. The household was not simply 'the private sphere' to which women's activities were relegated, leaving it as 'other' to the public, political world of male citizens (usually defined as more important by modern academics). 'Public' and 'private' were interleaved in a complex way, and were not always hierarchized with the 'public' holding sway over the 'private'. Depending on the context, the household was itself a public entity, with political significance. The adult male in his prime[3] held a privileged position *vis-à-vis* the household in that as *kyrios* (literally 'master', head of household), he could move freely between the contexts in which the household behaved as the private sphere and those in which it became a public entity (Foxhall 1989).[4] Much of the power of the *kyrios* derived from his ability to transcend contexts and to mediate in this way.

In spatial terms, it has been observed that in Greek town planning, household space (houses and fields) dominated over public space (Jameson 1990a, 1990b). And houses themselves contained space which was, at different times, sometimes defined as 'private' and sometimes as 'public', though on the whole exclusively male activities were marginalized within

Greek houses. It was the aggregate of household decisions which formed the economy of Greek city-states, since economic enterprises largely existed and were managed within the structure of households. Similarly, it was households that were represented by individuals in the assembly, the law courts and the agora, as well as at the Thesmophoria. And households could not be constituted without their women; indeed women might be said to have constituted the household more fundamentally than the men who spoke for it. 'Plato is wrong to argue that women and men can do the same work on the analogy of animals', says Aristotle. 'Animals don't have households to run' (*Politics* 2). Interestingly, Aristotle's objection to Plato here is not that women are physically or even mentally *inferior* to men (though he certainly implies this elsewhere) or that they do not have the capacity to do men's work, but that culture is 'biologically' intrinsic to humans as it is not to other animals, and people 'naturally' live in households in societies (so 'humans are political animals', *Politics* 1). Hence the nature of man is culture, and without woman that culture is impossible.

It was households which reproduced the political institutions of a city, for descent was one of the most crucial tenets of citizenship in all Greek city-states (though its precise significance varied). Citizens emerged from households and claimed their right of citizenship by virtue of the place they held in a household. Obviously women were essential to physical reproduction. And clearly men attempted to appropriate social reproduction, especially its public and political aspects, by monopolizing civic life. But I would argue women were central to other, equally important aspects of social reproduction, because of their special relationship to time. *Oikoi* (households) did not stretch themselves into the past and the future in simple linear continuity. Rather, when property and social roles passed from one generation to the next, *oikoi re-created* themselves, rather than continuing indefinitely. This is reflected in the naming system: people died in the household in which people named after them (their grandchildren) were the next step in the re-creation process (Foxhall 1989). *Oikoi* were then really re-created every *other* generation. But because women's life cycles were 'out of synch' with men's, they married earlier, they were 'adult' for longer and they had a different relationship with the past and future of lived life; so it was that women were most likely to be the ones bridging the two generations it took to re-create the household. In other words, men lived within one generation while women's lives spanned over two formal generations of men. This also reinforced the special relationship already noted between women and *rites de passage*, and their relation to time. In a sense this relation of women to time might be said to be at the heart of the social reproduction of the household. And, as I shall discuss in more detail below when I come to sexuality, men's institutions of male social reproduction could be seen as an alternative discourse to those of the household in its communal setting, which centred on women.

Women (as constituents of households) penetrated even apparently exclusively male, 'public' arenas. In Athens and Corinth and other Greek cities the earliest public buildings in the agora (datable to the seventh and sixth century BC) were not law courts or council chambers or stoas, they were fountain houses. And women used fountain houses. These were areas of female public space in zones of male activity. Here women met, talked (away from men), and filled their jugs with the water necessary to keep their households operating. Tyrants like Peisistratos in sixth-century BC Athens rated the building and upkeep of fountain houses high among their most important public works, essential to the identification of themselves with the community of the *polis* and hence to their maintenence of power. To what end? That women could keep the households of the city running and reproducing.

Foucault has construed the household as a male-dominated institution whose bars between itself and the outside world confined women's lives, including (perhaps especially) their sexuality and its expression. But the bars separating off households were different ones for women and for men. Men traversed them, but the only unproblematic way in which they could do so was as *kyrioi* – heads of household. But while men usually lived out their lives in one household, women lived in two: their natal and their marital house-holds.[5] This left open an avenue with the potential for some autonomy which many women seem to have traversed with alacrity (for example, Demos-thenes' mother; see Hunter 1989). Women became related (in terms of kinship) to their husbands, their mother-in-law, and their marital households through their children, while they also maintained their relations of kinship and affect with their parents and siblings from their natal household, especially with female kin. Women's networks of alliances, then, ranged quite widely beyond the confines of their own households. Men could suppress these bonds so long as they were formed so that women remained nested in their 'proper' place within the *ankhisteia*. From here, women's bonds strengthened the household unit against threatening competition from other households outside. Women kept to their place, and that place upheld men's individuality.

But women were not always passive and families and households were not always ideally configured. Women could and apparently often did form relationships with other kin, especially female kin, with slaves (especially female slaves) and with children, which contravened the interests of men and their positions of authority *vis-à-vis* their household. Men's control over women's relationships and bonds was in fact often tenuous. This is perhaps what spawned the male fantasies of women conspiring against men which are prominent in comedy (Menander, *Samia*; Aristophanes, *Clouds*, *Ekklesi-azusai*, *Thesmophoriazusai*, *Lysistrata*), tragedy (*Medea*, *Agamemnon*, *Anti-gone*, *Bacchai*) and law-court speeches (Lysias 1; Antiphon 1; Demosthenes 41; cf. Foxhall, forthcoming a). In most of these examples, women are perceived and portrayed as acting against the autonomy and the interests of an individual man (or men) via relationships and bonds over which the man is not fully in control. Male individuality appears as a discourse incompatible with the bonds and relationships, generated by women, which ran so much of men's everyday lives through household structures.

For men, kinship within and beyond the household was an important tool for maintaining their political and economic status and autonomy. The interesting thing is that though women's manipulation of kinship ought to have been subject to male authority according to the dominant masculinist ideology, patently it often was not.

SEXUALITY, SOCIALIZATION AND POWER

Greek male ideologies of sexuality have a lot to do with notions of control, autonomy and individuality, as Foucault has quite rightly argued. A very important source of men's power and authority as heads of households was that (ideally, at least) they could control the sexual activities of other household members (including animals and slaves), but that they themselves were autonomous and no one else could dictate their sexual activities. But reality, however hard to get at, is usually more complicated than ideology. And this ideology works only as long as women are assumed to be passive and boys obedient. I shall consider women's sexuality first, then boys'.

That women's sexuality was not passive is clear from the sources. Sexual offences by men involving women (rape, adultery, seduction, even sexual insults) were offences against men's *authority* over their households and against their *power* to control the sexual activities of household members, as Foucault argues. So, for example, in a law-court speech, a man arguing that he had caught the man he killed in bed with his wife says: 'he committed adultery with my wife, and he violated me inside my very own house' (Lysias 1.29). *Moikheia* (usually translated 'adultery', but probably really sex with a woman in someone else's charge) was committed with the wife, and this was *hybris* against the husband (see Cohen 1991; Cantarella 1991; Foxhall 1991).

But *moikheia* was not legally worse than rape nor were legal penalties in Athens more severe, as Foucault (and others) have maintained. The situation is more complicated and more interesting. Rape was not isolated as an offence, nor was it specifically construed as a crime against women. Generally it came under the category of *hybris*, 'assault', in legal terms. Hence boys and men, as well as women, could be victims of what we call 'rape'. Moreover, *moikheia* and rape were legally not very clearly distinguished, and the punishments were the same most of the time (Harris 1990). The reason for this was almost certainly that from the point of view of the laws the victim of both crimes was not the person attacked but the man in whose house she dwelt. But when we turn to the moral assessment of rape and *moikheia* (at least in terms of male ideologies), a different picture emerges. Women (like boys) who were objects of rape were pitied (Cole 1984: 111–13) and gratuitous violence against free women was despised. Women could be moral, if not legal, victims.

But in *moikheia* both parties were considered despicable (for different reasons). This difference in moral attitude between *moikheia* and rape has as much to do with the reality of women's behaviour as with ideologies of male superiority. In *moikheia* it was less easy to maintain the ideology that women had no well-defined sexuality of their own but were merely the passive vehicles of men. *Moikheia*, at least in the few cases where we have some details, implied a longer-term, larger-scale relationship, with a more active rôle played by women (and female networks). For example, in the case I have just cited, the wife was said to have been close to (and attended a major religious festival with) the mother of the murdered adulterer, while a slave girl acted as go-between for the lovers. The husband claimed he was finally informed about what was going on by a disgruntled ex-lover (female) of the adulterer. And perhaps most significantly, all the trouble with the wife started (so the husband says) when his mother (who lived with the couple) died. A woman with a lover (*moikhos*) has taken control of her own sexuality, and has taken that control away from the man who purports to dictate her sexual activity (cf. the women in *Lysistrata* who swear to have sex with neither *moikhos* nor husband). A woman with female lovers takes her sexuality away from men altogether. The paucity of references (though there are a few) to female homosexuality may represent the threat it posed to male individuality and autonomy, and its removal from male spheres of activity and knowledge.

Foucault argued that adultery depended on the behaviour of only one marital partner: the woman. In fact, it seems to have depended more on whether the existence of a wife's lovers were acknowledged by her husband. There was an uncomfortable subtext for the man whose authority and power was penetrated by a *moikhos*. A public accusation of *moikheia* must have elicited the communal question of whether the control exerted by the accuser was ineffectual. A man whose wife took a *moikhos* was a cuckold. Was the accuser, then, considered to be as much at fault in a social sense as the accused might have been at fault legally? It is hard to know the answer to this. But this aspect of *moikheia* allows for a slightly different interpretation of the interesting penalty problematically referred to by Demosthenes (59. 66–7) and Aristotle (*Ath. Pol.* 51.2), permitting the wronged husband to attack the guilty *moikhos* and 'to use him however he wished without a knife'. Was this a chance for a cuckolded husband publicly to re-exert his sexual authority and his autonomy via his own physical strength and personal courage, as well as having the more obvious aim of taking revenge for the *hybris* committed against him? The unflattering implication that a man might not be looking after his authority very well, the potential messiness of divorce, and, in perhaps a number of cases, status differences between the offended party and the *moikhos* all provide reasons why real cases involving *moikheia* are thinly represented in our sources. This is certainly implied in Aiskhines 1.107, where he suggests that the cuckolded husbands of Andros would not be willing to expose themselves to testify to Timarkhos' iniquities with their wives. Whether or not this is a spurious excuse on Aeschines' part to account for lack of witnesses, it was meant to sound plausible to jurors. It is probably significant that the one victim of *moikheia* of whom we can be certain, Euphiletos (Lysias 1), had to choose between representing himself as a cuckold and the possibility of execution for murder. Again this disjuncture of incompatible discourses made room for women to wrest some autonomy from men.

But male sexuality, especially the emergence of male sexuality from boyhood, was also problematic in relation to notions of adult male control and autonomy. By Foucault and some of his commentators (e.g. Poster 1986: 213; Seidler 1987; Winkler 1990) this was considered the central problematic of Greek sexuality. What he did not consider was the connections between the emergence of male sexuality, the tension it created between the development of a male, autonomous individual from childhood, and the relationship to household bonds and structures of this new person (with a new notion of self) who came out of the chrysalis of a very long male 'adolescence'. We can still, with Foucault, avoid the long line of psychoanalytic explanations of the development of male sexuality from Freud to Chodorow, for the issue is not the separation of the male child from his mother but the life cycle of socialization which excluded fathers (by the self-separation of a boy from the household) as it came to include mothers.

The creation of female sexual identity took place within the household (indeed within two households: marital and natal). But the creation of male sexual identity happened out of reach of the household, in the gymnasium and in other public places, at a time when a boy or a young man was still part of a household which he did not 'control' (that is, he was not the head who spoke for it and represented it). This is at the heart of the problematic nature of male erotic and 'romantic' love which Foucault persuasively identified. The whole process of the emergence of male sexuality happened over a long time, starting before puberty and culminating in marriage around age 30. The emergence of female sexuality was much faster, and seems to have taken only the couple of years around puberty (though it probably continued to develop within marriage).

Although boys were ideally not supposed to take pleasure from their passive role in sex, they are sometimes shown with erections during the sex act. Further, among the numerous depictions of sex between males in Athenian vase painting, a large minority do not show the canonical *erastes/eromenos* (lover/beloved – older/younger male) relationship, but men or boys who are closer in age. Moreover, boys and adolescents are frequently shown having sex with girls and women. This shows up the cracks in the dominant masculine ideology of the *erastes/eromenos*, so prominent in the literary sources. Though boys were subordinate in certain circumstances to older men (who might also often have been of higher status),[6] they were neither entirely passive nor fully feminized. Boys and women shared some traits in masculine perceptions, but they were inherently different. Overly feminine boys were disdained, and a boy was beautiful specifically because he manifested the acme of masculinity, just as a girl or woman was beautiful through her femininity.

The development of adult male sexuality pulled a boy away from his household (as it took place outside it), most especially away from the authority of its head (usually his father). The conflicts between sons entering adulthood and fathers losing control are highlighted in Attic comedy, a literary genre which by its nature frequently homes in on the critical structural tensions of Greek social and political life (Aristophanes, *Clouds*, *Wasps*). A father's authority became weaker as his son's sexual identity (and with it autonomy and individuality) grew stronger over time. Foucault's paradox of the *eromenos* (the beloved) who evades his father to submit to a lover (*erastes*), and who must submit without being seen to do so too easily or dishonourably, is not, as Poster argues, simply the problematization of the sexual passivity of free boys and thus the implication of unfree status. Status was relative and so boys submitted to men. It is in fact also another paradox: submission to unrelated male lovers from other households weakened the ties of authority to a boy's own father (who resisted the infringement of his authority). Yet this was essential to the development of a young man's own sexual identity, autonomy, and his ability to become the head of a household of his own and a political person in his own right.

Adolescence presented similar tensions, though in a different sociopolitical context, to the association of 'ritualized' homosexuality with entry into adulthood which Herdt (1987) has identified among the Sambia in New Guinea. This process of developing autonomy was complete or near completion when the son married and became an autonomous head of his own household. And the ramification, the really crucial paradox which Foucault did not take on board, is that this culmination, which put the newly matured son almost out of reach of *paternal* authority, brought him back into the *maternal* fold. When he married, the network of female bonds of his household and that of his mother (and other female relatives) took responsibility for socializing his wife into her new household, and ultimately his children as well (as in Lysias 1, the adultery case mentioned above). His mother's authority might be enhanced at this time relative to his father's.

In summary, the gymnasium, like other institutions of male social reproduction, pulled young men away from the dominion of their households, thus encouraging their development as sexual and political individuals. The irony is that the end of that process brought a new kind of tie to the household, which was rooted primarily in female links. It is significant that it is these masculine institutions of social reproduction which are monumentalized and celebrated in art and in literature, to the near- exclusion of female roles in social reproduction.

CONCLUSIONS

Seidler (1987) has argued on rather different grounds from me that Foucault's attempt to analyse discourses of sexuality fails because it is divorced from structures of gender. Gender was probably the most important organizing principle for Greek society, both on the level of everyday life and on the level of metaphor. It is clear that the complexities of gender were the template for expressions of power. I have tried to show that most aspects of life in classical Greece consisted of complex discourses and 'conversations'. Though the dominant masculinist ideology of the elite, citizen, adult male shouts loudest, this voice never quite overwhelms the others, though it certainly configures their speech. No voice can shout continually, and when the dominant one pauses for breath, the others are ready to fill the gap in their own way, even if they can never permanently win. It is my task as a feminist scholar to listen for the other voices and report what I hear.

Foucault's arguments and methodologies in *The History of Sexuality* are significantly flawed. One aim of this revised account of Greek 'sexuality' has been to make manifest these problems, by examining the intricacies of gendered roles in areas of Greek life that went beyond 'sexuality' in a narrow sense and yet were intimately entwined with it. The wider context of the household in its temporal, spatial and political settings provided the context in which sexuality was expressed and developed. Foucault illegitimately removed masculine sexuality from that context.

The most fundamental problem remains: that the nature of the historical sources and the contexts of their production and survival emanate from, and indeed celebrate, only a very small slice of male life and power. The contexts of the production of these texts happen to be the ones that our culture privileges: I am not sure this was so in ancient Greece, and there is enough evidence of other discourses to problematize Foucault's privileging of these. Is it possible that Foucault's intellectual methodology itself, in isolating the discourse as the object of analysis and interpretation, succeeds in de-contextualizing discourses from their social setting precisely because alternative discourses are not always mutually audible or intelligible? In refusing to hear alternative discourses he has deprived Greek women of their selves, he has left them passive and compliant in the face of male ideologies of oppression, and he has robbed them of their recourses to autonomy. I would not argue that women in classical Greece were not oppressed, but I would maintain that they resisted suppression. The dominant masculinist ideologies which ruled political life and serve as the context for the creation of most of the surviving source material never completely drowned out the other voices in the Greek conversations we can still hear.

NOTES

1 I do not use the unmodified terms 'man' and 'woman' in an essentialist way. I refer specifically to persons of the citizen category. Of these, the best-documented group are the wealthy elite of Athens; their behaviour was not necessarily typical of less well-off citizens of their own or other cities.

2 Contact with the past via older men may have been largely outside the household, in a context that pulled young men away from it, as is described below with respect to sexuality.

3 Sometimes more than one adult male resided in a household, but this could cause trouble, as I discuss later. Long adolescence usually prevented more than one household head.

4 Like many words in ancient Greek, *kyrios* is protean and context-specific. It also refers to a man who acted for a woman in a public capacity in contexts from which women were excluded. Although it is often translated as 'guardian', no fixed relation to the woman is implied and the relationship was negotiable – see Foxhall (forthcoming a) and Hunter (1989).

5 This, at least, is the ideal. In practice, the man who married an *epikleros* (a fatherless, brotherless girl) and/or was adopted by another household did not live out this ideal, and may have had a different relationship to the women of his household.

6 Frequently the man or men who were a boy's lovers became his political and economic patrons when he grew up.

Chapter 8

Men don't go to the moon

Language, space and masculinities in Zimbabwe

Chenjerai Shire

In this chapter my concerns are with the widest range of linguistic and spatial representations of masculinities in Zimbabwe. My account is auto-biographical and what I describe has my own experiences and memories as its referent. General terms like 'Zimbabwean', 'Shona' and 'masculinity' mask fragmentary contexts. There is no universalized 'Zimbabweanness' or 'Shonaness', just as there is no single, universalized masculinity. I use the term 'masculinities' here to examine male preoccupations as celebrations of ideals of maleness, pluralized to render a definition as fragmented as the many domains in which men are constructed as 'men' through language and space.

The noun *murume* (man), apart from being a designation of anatomy, has connotations of not only gendered difference but specific functions. To women in spaces designated as female, *murume* is a site of bother. The term used to describe what men do in courtship, *kuruma* – to seduce or literally to sting, bite, stimulate – defines masculinities in terms of activities and actions addressed to women. *Mukadzi anoruma* (the woman is seduced) shows, by use of the passive, the woman as being acted on. *Kuruma* can also be that which has potency. These idealized representations portray men as active and in control, yet they also carry with them a sense of the dependency of men on women and of the ways in which masculinities are defined and shaped through interactions with women. As I will go on to suggest, women are far from passive in these processes.

Masculinities are negotiated and constructed in different areas through specific language usage. Spaces designated as male, such as the *dare* (traditional meeting place of men) and the beerhall, are places in which men can show their prowess through the skilful use of language and embellish particular masculinities. In these domains, definitions and descriptions of *murume* create ideals of autonomy. In proverbial self-definition, the 'Shona' say '*murume murume, anoti chamuka inyama*'. A free translation would read 'a man is a man, he asserts that anything that arouses is fair game', meaning that it is a prerogative of men in their own spaces to take whatever is placed before them. The use of metaphor to define maleness in this sense alludes to various ideals. The use of the word *nyama* (game, meat) not only defines men as masculine subjects in terms of their hunting prowess, but alludes also to anything discursive as fair game. The use of language in these domains marks out a space in which men contest and confirm particular masculinities through shows of verbal versatility, competence in the 'language of men' and the use of particular forms of discourse.

As they grow older, boys learn what it is to be a *murume chaiye* ('real man') not only through their interactions with those who profess to embody these ideals, but also through the myths of masculinity which are spun by female relatives. In spaces designated as female, in which men are not welcome, the discourse of women shapes the masculinities of boys as they move in and out of these and other gendered domains. Female relatives – particularly the *vatete* (father's sister) and *ambuya* (paternal grandmother) – impress certain masculine ideals on young boys, instructing them in what it takes to 'be a man' and in the arts of courtship and love. Women, as custodians of the praise poetry which marks the particular masculinities of each totemic group, celebrate and affirm men in the language of *mutupo* (totems) in public places, and between lovers in private, through praise poetry known as *madanha omugudza*, 'lovers' discourse under the blanket'.

THE SHAPING OF 'SHONA' MASCULINITIES

My analysis draws on my own experience and that of my generation, rather than on published sources. My narrative describes a past in which I, as a young boy living in a rural area in the south of Zimbabwe, moved within gendered spaces learning the language of men. This experience is characterized by colonial occupation, under which 'Shona' men's lives were in perpetual motion between a number of places. As men moved from rural communities to be relocated in farming compounds, mines, town locations and schools, their identities shifted. Ideas about *zvechirume*, freely translated as 'male preoccupations', were dislocated as a result of this movement. They remain in constant motion, as different identities are being defined.

With the changing circumstances brought about by the colonial presence, *zvechirume* underwent dramatic modifications. The descendants of chiefs became subjects in circumstances which altered the physical nature of the spaces in which men expressed and learnt what it was to 'be a man'. Men who once constructed their identities through the rich vocabulary of totemic connectedness were renamed using a term signifying an area for colonial government: the 'Shona'. My use of the term 'Shona' here refers only to the cluster of totemic and language communities in a geographical area now known as Zimbabwe. The definition and meaning of this term are embedded in colonial power relations. Opinions differ as to its original meaning. I suggest that it derives from the name 'Shona', the feminine version of the Gaelic man's name 'Sean' (cf. Doke 1931a, 1931b; Chimhundu 1992).

'Shona' men, within this setting, internalized a masculinity designed to place them in emasculated, subordinate relations with the colonial power. This does not mean that *zvechirume* were equally emasculated. They were, instead, transformed.

In traditional 'Shona' society, power relations did not necessarily follow a single-sex hierarchical structure. Masculinities, in this setting, could be organized as much around female as male dominance. Patriarchal masculinity was embedded in British colonial discourse, and the internalization of a masculinity based on war and phallocentrism became a part of social reality during the period of occupation as a result of the Zulu and Boer wars of the late nineteenth century. The presence of the British settlers in southern Africa led to concepts of masculinities based on weapon-centred ideals. Settler fantasies about Zulu warriors systematically undermined and effaced 'Shona' masculine ideals. Language in places where men spent their time reflected the masculinities of the men of the *assegai* and the rifle. Unlike the Nguni, whose masculinities were constructed around the period when the Shaka's defiance of the colonial invasions shaped views on the Nguni male, the absence in male spaces of weapons as objects of fantasy had an impact on 'Shona' men's preoccupations.

Elsewhere, and especially in towns, 'Shona' men became the 'boys' of the colonizers. Colonial discourses impinged on their masculinities, expressed and contested in beerhalls and other places where 'Shona' men gathered. In the rural areas, where the bases of 'Shona' masculinities were more systematically eroded by interventionist legislation, identities were reconstructed around borrowed notions of defiant aggression. The great patriarchs of the 'Shona' resorted to telling tales about the Nguni *assegai* or *muscet*: objects of desire, which symbolized the machismo of the warrior and resistance to colonial domination. Others expressed this identification through the use of the Ndebele language. SiNdebele signified the epitome of a very physical masculinity: an ability to use the knobkerry and the myths of the Zulu fighters like Shaka. SiNdebele related to organized male space and about organizing to fight. As I grew up, most men in the Zvishavane and Mberengwa area spoke SiNdebele while among other men, whether or not they themselves were Ndebele. I remember SiNdebele because of these men; men who felt that they were male enough to speak SiNdebele. Anyone who could not speak it fluently was not treated as a *murume chaiye*, a 'real man'.

The changes brought about by colonial rule make the exploration of what was once a traditional, gendered cultural identity, represented most vividly in various instances of language use, little more than a romantic recovery of the past. This account is neither a project of recovery nor an attempt to capture or distil 'Shona' ideals of masculinity through use of the ethnographic present. In choosing instead to draw from my own experiences, I speak as a 'Shona' man who grew up in and moved between rural areas and towns, between male and female spaces. During this period, resistance to colonial rule produced

multiple, changing masculinities: manifestations of the experience of domination and of struggles appeared in many domains and helped to define what it
took to 'be a man'.

MEN IN THEIR SPACES

As I grew up the most important male space was the *dare*. As boys, we started
to spend more and more time in the *dare*, moving between this 'outside' space
and the 'inside' space of the hut, the domain of women. The *dare* was used to
structure various ideas about maleness. It was a place used to debate and
assess masculine ideals, for judicial matters and for relaxation. The *dare* was
always located far away from the women's spaces, such as the kitchen or the
women's sleeping quarters. Women were not denied access to this space, but
their approach was limited to those occasions when they entered the *dare* as
victims, victimizers or jurors in judicial matters or when they brought in food
for the men.

The prerogative exemplified by *murume murume, anoti chamuka inyama*,
which could mean something very different when used in another space, was
validated within the *dare*. Masculinity was often shaped here through the use
of metaphor and proverbs, whose meanings we began to understand as part of
the process of achieving linguistic competence as 'men'. Men who were
unable to demonstrate verbal prowess, whether in terms of command of
SiNdebele or in skills of argumentation and use of proverbs, were challenged
in this space. Those who were unable to compete would be labelled 'boys'
(*mukomana*) and sent away to run errands and to enter women's spaces. By
contrast, no matter what age boys were, if they could speak well and had a
strong opinion to voice – whether on the subject of herding cattle or
elopement – older, less fluent people might be sent for errands. Having strong
views and the verbal agility to argue a point meant that boys as young as 8 or
10 were listened to and taken seriously. The *dare* was very much a space for
talking rather than doing. Here we were taught manners and formalities, as
well as skills for fighting, hunting or grazing. We would go out and
experiment with what we had learnt there, sometimes re-creating the stories
from the *dare* in fights with boys of other areas.

As boys passed into the *dare*, they were taught about the gender of certain
material objects which were of importance in constructing male identities.
Apart from the *assegai*, which signified Nguni military machismo, objects such
as *munondo* (sword), *shahu* (axe) and *pfumo* (spear) were to be found in male
spaces, for use by men. These items had metaphorical associations with the
changing forms of *zvechirume* which emerged during the colonial era, defined
in terms of a weapon-based masculinity. For example, when men talked about
pfumo (spear), they did not only talk about the weapon, but also referred to a
military regiment. Proper names such as *Pfumojena* (the-radiant-spear) or
Chinemukutu (one-with-an-arsenal) could also refer to related notions. These

are gender-specific and constructed from military historical folklore; they are sometimes evoked in praise of the male descendants of such men.

The *dare* was also the space in which men exchanged experiences and learnt about making love and pleasing women. Men did not exclude boys from these conversations, or from hearing about their physical or sexual problems, unless those boys were seen as spending too much time in women's spaces. Gossip was something that took place only in the female domain, so the talk of men was regarded as something which needed to be contained to prevent its transformation into gossip. The notion that 'real men don't tell' was impressed on boys, and those who did talk about the news they heard in the *dare* were termed 'weak hearted' or *matera* (cowards) – a term which can only be used of men. At times they would be chided and mocked by other boys and men, who might ask: 'Are you a *musikana* [girl] then?'. Such characters were not given a place in the male space, but were sent away to run errands, leaving the men free for discussion. As boys, until we were able to prove that we were not spreading information left, right and centre, we were not allowed to spend long periods of time in the *dare*.

Within this space, differences between men extended beyond those of 'boys' and 'men'. Specific discourses also marked out and addressed particular groups of men. At times, certain forms of language were used by married men or those whose advanced age threatened sexual potency to exclude younger, single men. These discourses concerned ways of improving love-making and giving sexual pleasure to women, and involved the passing on of knowledge about aphrodisiacs to 'strengthen the spine'. Men were treated differently not only with regard to their age or status, but also according to their kin positions relative to other men. These defined the particular parts men played in dealing with one another, irrespective of their age. Relationships with different types of kin produced different kinds of masculinity, both within and outside the space of the *dare*. Masculine identities that related to being raised by maternal relatives differed from those produced through relationships with paternal kin.

Closely linked with the embellishment of aspects of manliness in the *dare* was the killing and eating of a beast there. Different parts of the beast's body signified different masculinities. Young boys were encouraged to roast and eat the *gakava* (sinews) of the beast to acquire vigorous argumentative skills. A *mazondo* (cow's foot) was regarded as an aphrodisiac which bolstered sexual performance for married men. Certain cuts of meat were given to men who occupied different positions within the family, marking relations of junior and senior men and defining their masculinities within this relation. The *rwatata* (pancreas) was given to nephews and grandsons. The *chisusu* (first stomach) was for herdboys, the *tsvo* (kidneys) for the father. The male in-laws took the *bandauko* (shoulder) to their wives. The distribution of meat within this space, and of the food cooked by women in their spaces, reinforced both gendered divisions and relations of authority among men.

These relations were disrupted by the changes brought about by colonial occupation. The *dare*, once the site of contests over power for 'Shona' men, no longer formed the only arena in which men gathered to display and discuss *zvechirume*. Younger men were sent off to towns in search of wage labour to pay the colonial taxes, away from the sphere of influence of their elders. If an older boy went to town he would come back with trousers and the young women would be attracted to him because he had something new. This in turn influenced younger men who also wanted to go to town. Men returning from town with only a bicycle and a watch to show after fifteen years of work would stay for a while, then go to another town to keep up the role people admired. Women and children were left behind in the rural areas to work the land. Since the women soon found out that they could do things for themselves, men were no longer able to command the same kind of respect from women.

The city was a space inhabited mostly by migrant labourers. As migrants, they were travellers who expressed their masculinities by identifying with the ideals which privileged roving. In 'Shona' nomenclature, a man who disappears to the city is referred to by the same term as one who is broke: *muchoni*. Rural men addressed men born in cities or towns as '*mabhonir-okisheni*' ('born in locations'). The plural prefix '*ma*' communicates a negation of cultural authenticity, defining them as 'objects' and devaluing the manner and place in which they were born. The masculinities of urban 'Shona' men were constructed from their wage-earning power and through the assimilation of colonial definitions of masculinity. Men were no longer 'men' because they belonged to a totemic group or were the heads of lineages. They became instead chattels, slaves. Their sexuality and gendered expectations were structured by colonial discourses on 'African' men. Thus in terms of gender, men in towns could take on a variety of roles. When working for wages, they did not mind cleaning and cooking for their masters, yet at home they would not contemplate doing the same for their wives.

In male urban spaces, then, the discourse of men underwent significant changes. Their masculinities reflected what was on offer in towns within a settler-colonial discourse. Dress codes took the form of *mabhogadhi* (tight jeans), important because of the maleness of film heroes such as Humphrey Bogart. In style, they were regarded as *matsotsi* (rebel males) who wore *masatani* (blue jeans), signifying a 'satanic' masculinity (this, itself, an effect of colonial Christian discourse) or something foreign. My generation got its macho-ness from the swagger of cowboy movies, and from rock-and-roll bands with their guitars as a kind of phallic symbol. We wore headbands and Afro hair: with one pair of bell-bottomed trousers and flip-flops we were kings. We also had to fight for our own independence.

Stripped of their totemic masculinities, urban males inhabited a masculinity that regarded women as *mahure* (whores) whose presence in male spaces, such as beerhalls, evoked extreme forms of misogyny. Any form of violence was legitimized within the male space of the beerhall. Male attitudes towards women in towns were reflected in the language of the beerhall: '*ihure rega rirohwe*' ('it's a whore, let it be beaten') and '*mukadzi ibhiza kupingudza rinoda kukwigwa*' ('a woman is a horse, to be broken it needs to be ridden'). Such attitudes remain entrenched in male spaces. Any gender-specific role structured by rural 'traditional' culture was discarded in favour of a masculinity which was both phallocentric and macho. This is not to suggest that these attitudes remained unchallenged by women, particularly those with an independent income. In both urban and rural areas, women continued to shape masculinities through their interactions with both men and the boys who spent so much time in their charge.

BECOMING A MAN IN WOMEN'S SPACES

Women constructed masculinities right through the lives of men, from birth to adulthood. Women, in their spaces, had a material culture that was exclusively used by women. Objects such as *musika* (whisk), *mugoti* (wooden spoon), *guyo* (grinding stone), *duri nomutsi* (mortar and pestle) and *mutsvairo* (broom) were taboo in male spaces. And men were excluded from using objects belonging to and for the use of women. By reinforcing the femininity of these objects women also defined masculinities. This was done in two ways: on the one hand their use was associated by men with the idea of men becoming female, and on the other women used such objects as weapons to drive young boys and men out of women's spaces. Our fear as young boys was twofold; we feared being beaten by a woman's object and we feared being rendered effeminate and growing breasts. In spite of this, there were boys who through the patronage of the grandmother or aunt had access and were able to remain close to women's spaces. The name given to such boys was *nzvengamutsvairo*, literally 'broom-dodger': a man who evades male spaces.

A man did not brag about his masculinity in women's spaces since male discourse was severely restricted by women in such domains. In speech and deed men were not taken seriously once they entered the women's domain. Men were a bother to women in domains like the kitchen. It was not only that male discourses were ignored or restricted; none of the material objects celebrated as markers of masculinities was of any interest within the women's sphere. The construction of masculinities through processes of exclusion was enforced in these spheres, and the gender identities which were produced by these processes were taught to young boys and girls within the domain of women and reinforced by senior women, particularly the paternal aunt (*vatete*).

The power of the *vatete* to enforce traditional cultural practices derived, in some part, from her status as *muridzi womukadzi* (literally 'the owner of the wife'). All women married to her brothers were regarded as her 'wives'; in divorce cases, in particular, the *vatete* held great influence and power. The spiritual power of ancestors was mostly evoked through the *vatete*. Before 'Shona' power structures were broken by the colonial onslaught, there were aunts who never married and who became heads of households as *mbonga* (female spiritual leaders). *Mbonga* held responsibility for the continuity of the family, as well as success in social and political organization. A chief or king could not exercise his patriarchal power without evoking the *mbonga's* spiritual powers. In war the *mbonga* were supreme; if they were sexually violated by the enemy, the king's *pfumo* (regiment) were emasculated. In peaceful times, the *vatete* united families through her power over her brothers and their wives. Not only was her approval and assistance required for marriages to take place, but often it was also difficult for any of her brothers to divorce their wives without her agreement.

Within women's spaces, *vatete* held great influence over their brothers' wives and over the boys who spent time in these spaces. Through teaching wives the praises and the histories of their husbands' lineages, *vatete* also vested in these women the potential to contest the masculinities created through lineage associations as well as to celebrate them, in discourses about love and sexuality. We were made aware of the power women had to undermine men's sense of themselves, particularly when men transgressed in women's spaces. It was the *vatete* who taught us about *mupfuwira*, the love medicines women were said to use to render men amenable to them. *Mupfuwira*, regarded as the weapon of women, seduced men away from a power-based masculinity. Its effects were to make men behave in ways which displayed docility, rather than dominance, in the presence of their lovers or wives.

And it was from the *vatete* that we learnt, as boys, about the ways to treat women. They taught us about all kinds of things, about practical matters such as contraception and also about sex: about what kinds of character to marry, the kinds of pleasure which would stop women from leaving, and ways in which women could be handled or controlled. In this way, the *vatete* instilled particular expectations about women in boys. For example, one aunt of mine always told me that if you argue, a woman will always leave. You might want to beat her up, but at the end of the day she might just disappear or she can use medicines to poison you or make you insane. It was the *vatete*, more than anyone else, who reinforced myths of maleness.

BOYS 'OUTSIDE': EXPERIMENTATION AND DISCOVERY

Maternal uncles (*sekuru nomuzukuru*) also played an important part in teaching boys about sex and sexuality even while they were still spending a lot of time in women's spaces. From the *sekuru*, we learnt about a masculinity whose discourse centred on giving pleasure to women. The learning process took us into spaces where we learnt about medicinal plants and acquired ideas about sexual prowess. Outside the *dare*, in places where boys herded cattle and played, masculinities were structured in activities which centred on the admiration of the body and its sexual parts.

From an early age, boys engaged in games which were concerned with ensuring procreation in adulthood. Certain fruits and pods signified potency and formed the basis for activities which centred on notions of sexual competence. For example, the *mumveva* (*Kigelia pinnata*) fruit was regarded as signifying this kind of masculinity. When the fruit was in season, boys would bore a hole in the young fruit, into which they would insert their penises. They would then wait to see whether the fruit matured or died. If the fruit died or became deformed, this signified a threat to their sexual potency. If it grew to maturity, this was seen to result in sexual competence and an enlarged penis.

We played games which grew out of our awareness of our bodies as different and of the changes which they underwent. One of these games was to piss as high in the sky as we could, without it falling back down on us. The kinds of game we played as little boys were ones we knew girls could never play – this was a time when we began to look at our private parts and start to think about how they actually worked. In order to be able to compete, the penis could not be flaccid. One would have to wait until it was hard enough to be able to aim straight. Also, we soon found out that it was hard to do a jet without pulling back the foreskin, so we learnt how to do this. And – something grown-ups did not teach us, but which was passed down by older boys – we learnt how to perform a painful operation with a thorn and a bull's hair to free the foreskin. It hurt a lot, but after that it became easier to compete and win the competition. This operation had significance beyond the contexts of these games, in its association with the passage of semen in adulthood. Boys who did not want to have this operation were teased and laughed at; they were called 'chickens', told that they were not really boys and that all they wanted to do was to stay home and look after chickens.

There were many more games which we played as young boys in our own spaces, games in which we learnt about our bodies and our sexualities. For boys of 8 or 9 it was acceptable, even expected, to spend time together playing in this way. For boys to continue with such games into puberty was, however, regarded as deviant. Such boys were called names alluding to bullocks with only one testicle, which are unable to fend off other bulls that mount cows, and which were only able to mount oxen. The term, *ngochani*, has now become the word for 'homosexual'. While I was growing up, homosexuality was never talked about. The first I learnt of it was when I was sent to a mission school, where the boys who did not have school fees would stay with the priests. We thought of it then as something which was connected with Christianity.

As we grew older, girls were more often involved in our games. In one, we would catch a certain kind of beetle which was found in the river, living on the surface of the water. We would put them on our tongues so that they would bite. After this, we would be able to whistle like men. We did this at an age when boys and girls were still allowed to swim together in the river and girls were just starting to develop breasts. The same beetles would be caught and given to girls to bite their breasts and make them swell up. The boys would then tease them and touch them, finding out about their bodies. Other games boys played with girls involved acting out 'pretend' marriages and setting up a home together somewhere in the bush. These games, *mahumbwe*, could at times end up provoking jealousies as it became obvious that people were not just playing, but that something else was going on.

At the same time as we played these games 'outside', while herding cattle or goats, we were learning to be men in gendered spaces. We were gradually expelled from women's spaces to spend more and more time with boys and other men. Our sense of ourselves as men, as we moved away from the domains in which women held sway, was embellished and reinforced not only in male spaces but in places where men and women came together as lovers. As adult men we draw on a complex and overlapping repertoire of masculinities to fashion our present gendered identities as men.

CELEBRATING MASCULINITIES: LOVERS' DISCOURSE UNDER THE BLANKET

Using the language of *mitupo* (totems), learnt under the tutelage of the *vatete*, women as wives and lovers celebrate the variant masculinities of men of different totemic groups. In private spaces, women's praises both create and affirm particular masculinities. Women use this information to bolster their husbands' sense of themselves, but also need it to survive within their husbands' families. The term for these praises, *madanha omugudza* ('lovers' discourse under the blanket'), carries a specific reference to the spaces in which men and women meet to make love. Within these praise poems, metaphors allude to the maleness of the different totemic animals. Within each totemic group, there are a number of *chidao* (sub-clans), all of which have their own particular praises, which invoke potent images of various masculinities.

Those of the *Ngara* (porcupine) totem receive praises which boast of their sexual prowess and fertility. Terms are used which display the sharpness of the porcupine quill, likening it to an arrow: '*Vakapfura dombo nomuseve rikabuda ropa*' ('those who struck the rock with an arrow and drew blood'). The penis of these men is likened to an arrow, so sharp and so rampant that it penetrates through impossible obstacles. In this case *dombo* (rock, stone) alludes to a sterile woman to whom fertility is restored by the sexual prowess of the *Ngara* man. In war, the spines which protect the porcupine itself denote *Ngara* men as *vakuru vehondo* (magnificent men of war).

The masculinity of *Hungwe* or *Shiri* (bird) men is celebrated in a language which is regarded as shameful in everyday speech. However, there is nothing shameful about that language when it is used to praise *Shiri* men for their sexuality. The sexual organs, masked by metaphors in other areas, are openly praised. It is not regarded as obscene or pornographic when these men praise themselves or are praised as '*machende eshumba . . . muranda wemheche*' ('lion's testicles . . . slave to the vagina'), although both *machende* (testicles) and *mheche* (vagina) are regarded as coarse words in everyday language. Those of the *Mhofu* (eland) totem are addressed, if male, as '*mhofu yomukono*' (bull eland). Theirs is a masculinity which is celebrated as secretive and powerful through their knowledge of metallurgy. Discourses regarding their masculinity are held to be sacred.

To cite one example in full, women married to a *Shumba-Mhazi* (lion-amour) man might celebrate her husband in the following manner:

Hekanhi Shumba!	Thank you very much Lion!
Mhazi	Rampant
Maita Mhukahuru	You immense beast
Makashareni shanga mumakoto	You-selected-me seed among the husks
Segukuru remudurunhuru	Like a cockerel in a rubbish dump
Zvamunoti mondigwangura	When you do desire me
Mosvosva nomongo	You delight the marrow
Muchindimatisa senzombe	Provoking me to bolt like a trek ox
Munoti ndivuchire sei she wangu?	How do I show you respect, my lord?
Munondirezva sorusvava	When you fondle me like an infant
Nezvanza zvine nhetemwa dzegwiti	With palms possessing pouched-mouse paralysis
Munoti mandikoda pane shungu dzangu	You titillate me where I am most responsive
Menge mandikanda mudhidho rouchi	And it seems as though you have thrown me in a pool of honey
Hi-i . . . !	Hi-i . . . !
Hekanhi Shumba	Thank you Lion
Ndorobwa nebuka rinoomesa mitezo yangu soruware	I am struck by convulsions that stiffen my limbs like a rock
Radzirai Shumba	Pound it hard, Lion
Musanyenya muchiurura napamusoro	Do not tease and skim on the top
Dzisai murove bwendedszo	Penetrate and strike the target
Ehe-e Shumba	That's it, Lion
Mazobaya mbariro dzechityu	You have now perforated the lath of the breast

Ndokuitirai zvipi	What can I do for you
Zvingaturutsa mate enyu machena anobva mugona?	Which can lure down your clear saliva from its rocky fastness?
E!	That's it!
Ririri rovunga bwusina chirashwa	Burning violently, it bubbles without splash
Maita Tembo	Thank you Tembo
Maita Shumba	Thank you Lion
Maita Chibwa.	Thank you Chibwa.

(Hodza 1982: 9; my translation)

LANGUAGE, SPACE AND MASCULINITIES

In this chapter, I have provided glimpses from fragmentary contexts which reveal the masculine identities of 'Shona' men not as homogeneous, but as associated with particular language uses and particular gendered terrains. In different spaces and at different points in the lives of men they move between these spaces and acquire or are addressed by gender-specific languages. The multiple ways of being a man and the signalling of gender identities through the use of language in different spaces is so central to 'Shona' society that there is little need for macho events to authenticate a notion of 'masculinity'. Women, as well as men, construct and define masculinities, by policing men to keep them out of women's spaces and by creating and affirming a range of male identities through their interactions with men as *vatete*, mothers, wives and lovers.

I would like to end this chapter with an anecdote. I came home from school one day – I must have been about 14 – so excited about the news that the Americans had landed on the moon that I blurted it out to my grandmother in 'Shona'. Her response was swift. She grabbed me by the ear and started to beat me until I retracted my words. I had used a language permitted only in women's spaces; the phrase *kuenda kumwedzi* ('to go to the moon') is used to talk about menstruation. Later, as I sat, still sobbing, she turned on the radio and heard the news. She turned to me and said:

I heard that Americans have gone to the moon. If they are men, how could they? And, if they *have* gone to the moon – so what? Women have gone to the moon every month – so it is nothing new.

Chapter 9

An economy of affect
Objectivity, masculinity and the gendering of police work

Bonnie McElhinny

GENDER AND THE WORKPLACE

Sex segregation in the workplace persists in the United States. Workplaces are gendered not only by the numerical predominance of one sex within them, but also by the cultural interpretations of given types of work. Men's work is stereotypically associated with the outdoors, with strength and with highly technical skills (whether they be mechanical or scientific knowledge). It is perceived as heavy, dirty, dangerous and requiring creativity, intelligence, responsibility, authority and power. Women's work is stereotypically understood as being indoors, lighter, cleaner, safer, repetitive, requiring dexterity rather than skill, having domestic associations, being tied to a certain work station, and often requiring physical attractiveness and charm (Bradley 1989). Important modulations of this generalization are necessary for understanding class and ethnic divisions within the workplace. Middle-class jobs are more likely to allow workers to exercise mental skills (analytic reasoning for men, social and interpersonal skills for women) while working-class jobs require the exercise of physical skills (strength for men, dexterity for women). Because many ethnic minorities tend to have working-class or lower-middle-class jobs, the jobs designates as 'men's' and 'women's' within these communities will often be specified according to community norms about which sorts of work are best done by men or by women. In most cases, men's work, however defined, is rewarded more heavily in terms of money and prestige, because the skills 'men's' jobs require are more highly valued and more likely to be recognized as labour.

Explicit specifications of the sex of workers (sometimes couched as 'protective' legislation) have often maintained this sex segregation of the workplace in the past, though such dictates are increasingly rare in the United States.[1] Today more subtle cultural pressures work to reproduce sex segregation in the workplace, from the tracking of girls and boys into different career paths to unions' and professional organizations' attempts to maintain power and jobs for existing members. Social stigma arising from sexism and homophobia prevents women and men from taking jobs normatively linked to the opposite sex. The fear of being labelled as a lesbian or masculine works to prevent all women from protesting sex discrimination or taking on sex-atypical roles (Pharr 1988).[2]

In this chapter I describe the manipulation of emotion within a working-class workplace that has traditionally been defined as all-male and all-masculine – the police force. My focus is on how women learn to integrate themselves successfully into previously all-male and masculine workplaces, and how the workplaces adapt to them. In 1975 a court injunction was issued to the City of Pittsburgh requiring each incoming police recruit class to be 25 per cent black females, 25 per cent white females, 25 per cent black males and 25 per cent white males. Large movements of women into male-dominated workplaces like those produced by this injunction are rare (the few historical examples include clerical workers, telegraph operators, bank tellers and waitresses), and such movements are usually rapidly followed by the complete reversal of the gender-typing of the workplace (Reskin and Roos 1990: 12–15).[3] In Pittsburgh the quota-hiring system has led to a slow, steady increase of women and African-Americans, so that members of each category now compose approximately 25 per cent of the force.[4] Pittsburgh thus has a larger percentage of female police officers than any other major American city but Detroit (US Department of Justice 1987a, 1987b).[5] This workplace thus provides a unique opportunity to consider how gender norms change as workplaces become sexually integrated. What happens to individuals and institutions when their individual gender identities and the gender of the institution to which they belong are presumptively different? Do women who enter traditionally masculine, working-class workplaces adopt masculine behavioural strategies in order to be perceived as competent by co-workers and customers/citizens? In order to address this question, I begin by describing why police work has traditionally been considered 'men's' work. I then develop an ethnographic fragment which concentrates on one attribute of the gendering of police work – the non-projection of emotion. I close with a brief review of the implications the study of police officers has for the study of the gender of work, as well as for studies of masculinity and femininity more generally.[6]

THE GENDERING OF POLICE WORK

Policing has traditionally been regarded as 'men's work' and, despite increasing numbers of women, it is still so considered by many citizens and by male and female police officers (even female police officers who consider themselves and other females very good police officers). In general, blue-collar jobs like policing are generally thought to be more masculine than white-collar ones, and blue-collar jobs which require strength and/or violence are perceived as more masculine than those which do not. Martin has suggested that:

for blue collar men whose jobs often do not provide high incomes or great social prestige, other aspects of the work, including certain 'manly' features take on enormous importance as a means through which they confirm their sex-role identity. Work that entails responsibility, control, use of a skill, initiative and which permits the use of strength and/or physical agility characteristic of males is highly valued not only for its own sake but for its symbolic significance. Similarly working in an 'all-male' environment reinforces the notion that they are doing 'men's work' and is a highly prized fringe benefit of a job.

(1980: 89)

Police work is defined, in public representations and in many male police officers' minds, by the situations in which police officers are required to exert physical force to keep the peace. Male officers who do not believe women should be on the job often argue that women cannot handle these situations. Most female officers, while recognizing differences in physical ability between themselves and male officers, argue that on serious calls one rarely needs to act without back-up and can cooperate with other officers to bring the situation under control. Female police officers also tend to distinguish between physical strength (which they agree they do not have) and institutional force (which they argue they do). As one woman put it, 'It's never just a fight between a man and a woman – it's a fight between a man and a *police officer*.' This comment points out that police officers have certain tools (nightstick, blackjack, gun) as well as certain extraordinary abilities (the power to arrest and the ability to use a radio to summon, as one officer put it, other members of 'the largest gang in the city'). Female police officers also note that there are some frightened, weak, do-nothing men on the job – a retort to male officers that attempts to suggest that women should not be regarded as a group, but rather as individuals, and which thus contests hegemonic interpretations of gender roles and behaviours.

Many female police officers believe they are more likely to stay calm and cool in conflictual situations than are male police officers precisely because they cannot as easily resort to force, and so must use talk as a tool instead. This claim is difficult for me to evaluate, since despite the images perpetuated by TV shows, situations involving physical confrontation between officers and citizens are relatively rare. The few officers who were identified by other officers as likely to 'go off' (too quickly escalate into use of force) were all men. The few female police officers who are labelled masculine (by male or female officers) are those who are perceived as getting 'too' angry too fast, as 'not treating people right' and as using 'too much' profanity.

There are other differences in how some men and some women interpret the job of policing. More women than men emphasize the importance of report-writing in getting convictions. Men who object to women's presence on the job are likely to say, 'I will give them that – they're good report-writers' – a backhanded compliment, since these men often accord little importance to report-writing. Women are also believed to be better at other tasks like taking reports from rape victims, comforting frightened or abused children and dealing with women involved in domestic disputes. Female officers' emphasis on the bureaucratic (or clerical) and social-work aspects of the job is often shared by younger men and, to a lesser extent, by men with post-secondary education.

That policing can be interpreted as such a wide range of jobs – as law enforcement, as crime prevention, as social work, as clerical work, as therapy – marks a change in progress in the role of policing in American society. Police officers in the late 1960s were associated with considerably more physical violence than they are today.[7] Growing restrictions on and super-vision of police action, as well as increases in the number of civil suits filed against police officers, have led to requirements for written documentation of each action. 'God forbid you fire your gun', said one officer. 'You might as well hire a novelist.'

The beginning of the growth of the modern bureaucratic state, of which police departments are a part, in the nineteenth century required a change in the pattern of gender relations and, crucially, a change in the normative pattern of masculinity from physical aggressiveness to technical rationality and calculation (Connell 1987: 130–1).[8] This in turn led to arguments by, for example, Mary Wollstonecraft and Susan B. Anthony that women should be able to participate more fully in the state. Changes in the normative pattern of masculinity have taken place, however, at different rates in different parts of the state. Only in the late 1960s did changes in the interpretation and organization of policing allow women to become police officers. The inclusion of women has in turn hastened the transition from a physical workplace to a more bureaucratic one.[9]

This transformation of policing is a movement from one masculinity (with an emphasis on physical displays of force) to another (with an emphasis on objectivity and rationality). The workplace may well be perceived as less masculine than before because an emphasis on physical force or strength contributes to a stronger perception of a job as masculine than does an emphasis on emotionless rationality. Rationality and emotional control, however, are gendered masculine in American culture by virtue of their contrast with the emotionality associated with women (see Lutz 1990). This movement from one masculinity to another is evident in macrostructural reorganizations of police departments to accommodate increasing paperwork and court appearances and in individuals' interactional styles and psycho-logical adjustments to the work of policing.

GENDER AND AFFECT AT WORK

The projection of emotion is a type of often uncompensated work shaped by the requirements of work structures within which individuals find themselves. For instance, the display of positive affect is one of the chief privileges of secretaries, one of their chief sources of power, one of their most important tasks and one of their few avenues to professional advancement, since loyalty to and care for a particular boss can lead to promotion when that boss is promoted (see Kanter 1977). Hochschild (1983), writing of how airlines train flight attendants (who are still largely female) in the projection of warmth and cheerfulness, notes that jobs involving emotional labour (especially service jobs) comprise over a third of all jobs, but they form only one quarter of the jobs men do, and over one half of those women do. When men are required to perform emotional labour, it is often the projection of negative emotion (threatening those who have not paid corporate bills, as bill collectors do, or 'acting crazier than they do', as police officers do), or of affectlessness (as in the rationality and impersonality required of businessmen and bureaucrats).

An economy of affect: emotional requirements of policing

The emotional work that policing exacts is quite different from that of the typically feminine jobs described above. One young female rookie (formerly a teacher) describes how she adapted to workplace interactional norms:

(Do you think women who come on this job start to act in masculine ways?) Umhm. (Like what are some of the things you see?) Your language. I know mine, mine changes a lot from . . . When I'm at work I always feel like I have to be so, so like gruff you know. And normally I'm not like that. I'm usually kinda bitchy but I'm not like real. Sometimes I try to be like such a hard ass. I, I don't smile as much. I'm not saying that men, you know that's a masculine trait. I think you . . . you have to pick up maybe not necessarily fighting but techniques to subdue people or just hold them or whatever and I don't think that's naturally feminine either you know. I think it's mostly language. You know . . . My, mine's atrocious sometimes. I've toned it down a lot. When I first started you know cause I worked with a lot of guys it seemed like, they didn't may not even have swore but I felt like I had to almost like be tough or something around them you know. And that was my way of being tough. (Is it like mostly profanity, or do you do it like with tone of voice or something?) Little bit of both. Like I said I've toned down my profanity a lot. I just kinda use it to describe things now, like I don't call people names and stuff. But I don't know. Sometimes I try to like talk to people. Like I said about how black women were able to kinda command respect from people in the projects, I try to like pick up some of their slang, either their slang or their tone something. Then I like I listen to myself sometimes. I'm like God I sound like you know I sound like a HILL person [a person who lives in a largely black, largely poor area of Pittsburgh]. And then I think I should just be able to be me. I shouldn't have to be everybody else.[10]

This police officer feels as though her occupational persona is a mask. She describes learning a combination of emotional skills – emotionlessness ('I don't smile as much'), toughness and gruffness which she does not believe to be natural to her. This sort of alienation from the emotional labour required by a job was also widespread among the flight attendants interviewed by Hochschild (1983) – the ways that they were required to act had little to do with how they themselves felt.

Many officers believe that some sense of reserve is the only way to survive on the job – otherwise it is too stressful. One female police officer who had been on the job for twelve years was describing the amount of drinking many officers do, and the frequency of divorce and suicide. She described her reaction to seeing her first bad accident, and her way of coping with this and other traumatic scenes:

So my first dead body, which was one that was a girl that was very young, 19. . . . And I see ALL this, this pool of blood came all the way down and made a huge pool at the end of the street. So much blood. And I said I don't know if I can handle it or not boss, I never seen one before. [He] said okay, said if you think you're gonna throw up, turn around and don't throw up on my shoes. I remember him saying that. . . . So he pulls back the sheet and I look at this and I was SOOO FASCINATED . . . . I was TOTALLY fascinated and he said THAT'S ENOUGH. He said ARE YOU GETTING SICK? I said NOOO! He said SOMETHING'S WRONG WITH YOU KID – he said YOU SEEN ENOUGH. He put the sheet back on her. . . . That is when I looked and decided that was not a person . . . I don't get emotionally involved. . . . They're like clients. You always have to be impartial. . . . So that's just the way I do it. And it works for me. I don't have to drink myself to sleep at night.

In this case, the older male officer expects the young female officer to react in a stereotypically female way – by shrinking away, by being horrified, by being sickened. When she does not react 'appropriately' he dismisses her from the accident scene. For the female officer, the expenditure of emotion on others, especially sympathy or empathy, is understood as support lost for her. If she allowed herself to feel too much for others she would be torn apart herself, so she has to take care to isolate herself, not to get involved, not to allow herself to see her clients as people. Emotion is here understood as a limited commodity, and using it means losing it. Being impartial and suppressing one's own reaction is in her eyes also being professional, as doctors, lawyers and coroners are with their clients.

In addition to dealing with traumatic incidents, officers often find themselves in situations where seemingly innocuous calls suddenly turn into life-threatening ones. Depending on the situation, caution may manifest itself as emotional guardedness ('flattened affect') or as anger.

Police officers learn to act like 'tough cops' who limit their conversation to the formalities of the investigation because increased interaction offers further opportunities for excuses, arguments, complaints, reprimands, fights or worse (Rubinstein 1973: 264). It is not, then, any marked lack of compassion that produces these interactions. Police officers, male and female, will say, 'When I'm in uniform, I'm not a woman/man – I'm a police officer.' They mean to emphasize that they have set aside personal lives, personal opinions and personalities while they are on the job.

The result of experiences like this is the development of an *occupationally conditioned habitus*, which I will call an *economy of affect*. Habitus is the notion developed by Pierre Bourdieu to describe how experience structures interactional behaviour. Habitus is 'a system of lasting transposable dispositions which, integrating past experiences, functions at every moment as a matrix of perceptions, appreciations and actions' (Bourdieu 1977: 82–3). It is 'history turned nature', interactional experiences incorporated into memory, to form the common sense with which people's expectations about, and reactions to, subsequent incidents are shaped.[11]

Bourdieu's notion of habitus provides an explanation of why a person's interactional style might be slightly inappropriate for a given situation even if she believes she is accommodating to that situation: she has not had experience in producing the appropriate style, or her experiences have conditioned her to produce a different style in the same situation. Bourdieu tends to emphasize the role of family and school in establishing the individual's stylistic repertoires and to define style as use or non-use of standard language. I focus more centrally on the role of the labour market in shaping adults' speech styles, in particular on the ways occupations shape the norms for appropriate expression of affect.

The traumatic, dangerous and hostile interactions which police officers regularly experience produce an *economy of affect*. By economy I mean to suggest the extent to which this style is shaped by the particular nature of their involvement in the labour market, and that officers are economical (in the sense of thrifty) in their expenditure of (especially positive) affect with citizens; and also that police officers understand the expenditure of positive affect in terms of a closed economy (a significant expenditure of sympathy or grief on others means that less is available for themselves).[12] Police officers do express positive affect on the job, but they choose the situations in which they do so carefully – as if they were on a limited budget. They often invest emotion where a pay-off seems most likely – with children, or with an individual clearly needing help. Because the situations in which most complainants meet police officers are characterized for them by high emotional intensity, the businesslike way that officers usually set about taking their reports is likely to strike complainants as cold, or heartless. The possibility for miscommunication is immanent in western interpretations of 'unemotional' as *either* calm and rational *or* withdrawn and alienated (see Lutz 1986: 289–90; Lutz 1990). That which police officers interpret as the first, citizens may interpret as the second.

The linguistic devices used to remove traces of opinion and personality in written language – passive voice, substitution of 'one' for 'I', etc. – have been widely studied (Biber and Finegan 1989; Chafe and Tannen 1987). Because both male and female officers have the same experiences and the same tasks, and interpret these tasks and experiences similarly, they resort to the same linguistic style while making these reports – a sort of bureaucratese, or facelessness, in face-to-face interaction.

OBJECTIVITY, MASCULINITY AND CHANGING WORKPLACES

That women who move into powerful and masculine institutions sometimes adopt the interactional behaviour characteristic of these institutions might disappoint some feminists. But it seems clear that our idea of who can do certain jobs changes more rapidly than expectations about how those jobs should be done. The process of women entering a masculine workplace necessarily includes some adoption, as well as adaption, of institutional norms. I focus here on an interactional style that male and female police officers share, in part because I want to represent their work environment as they understand it, and one of the important ideologies which structure this workplace is that 'it's us versus them', and 'we all wear the blue'. I also, however, focus on these as a response to the extant literature on gender, which often begins by asking what are the differences between men and women, rather than whether or not there are differences between men and women. The focus on women versus men threatens to reify social differences in ways not so very different from sex-based essentialist theories.

I argue here for a more flexible definition of gender, one that recognizes the degree of agency accorded to people in developing a style of living, behaving, speaking and being based upon their own occupational choices, personal histories, sexuality, life-styles and more. Rarely is any given social act interpreted as solely masculine or feminine (Eckert and McConnell-Ginet 1992). Usually it is perceived as conveying a wide range of information about the actor, from her personality to her level of fatigue, from her age and regional background to her ethnicity and class. Close attention to all the local meanings attached to certain actions will produce a more dynamic view of gender and power relations because it can recognize the resources for challenges to hegemonic and binary gender norms that are already available within each community. Although resistances to and reinterpretations of hegemonic interpretations of gender may be particularly evident in some settings – women doing 'men's' work, or lesbian and gay men's choices about how to project their own gender identities – they exist in every community.[13]

In planning this project I set out to discover the extent to which female police officers would manipulate the socio-symbolic resources at their disposal – clothing, strength displays, ritualized ways of handling tools, and use of language – to present themselves as competent workers, which I believed, on the evidence of earlier ethnographic studies of other women in traditionally all-male, working-class jobs (Martin 1980; Williams 1989), and because of the centrality of occupation in defining identity in the west, would mean studying how these women learned to present themselves in masculine ways. This expectation was not entirely fulfilled – not because the behaviours of women do not change to accommodate their jobs, but because they do not interpret their behaviour as masculine. Because masculinity is not referentially (or directly) marked by behaviours and attitudes but rather is indexically (see below) linked to them, female police officers can interpret behaviours which are normatively or frequently understood as masculine (like non-involvement or emotional distance) as simply 'the way we need to act to do our job' in a professional way. The implicit recognition of the nature of this link evident in police officers' own interpretations of their behaviour shows that indexicality can be exploited in ways that foster the integration of women into workplaces from which they were previously barred.

The distinction between referential and indexical markers of gender (Ochs 1992) is crucial for understanding the differences between the ways that academic feminists and female police officers tend to interpret masculinity. Referential markers of gender are unequivocal, unambiguous, categorical symbols of gender (for instance, the terms 'she' and 'Ms' reference female identity).[14]

Indexical markers of gender are non-exclusive (they may mark other kinds of social information like age, sexuality, personality traits, etc.), constitutive (so that one trait ['emotionlessness'] may be linked to another ['objectivity'] which in turn indicates 'masculinity') and probabilistic (as emotionlessness is often linked with masculinity but not exclusively so). When the rookie in my first example says 'I don't smile as much [now that I've come on the job]' but then immediately adds that she does not necessarily believe that not smiling is a masculine trait, she demonstrates an understanding of the indexicality of gender. The fact that not smiling occurs to her in connection with acting masculine is an indication of a probabilistic association; the fact that she is reluctant to say that all men fail to smile is an indication that the link between not smiling and masculinity is not exclusive (since not smiling can also mean one is not happy). Not smiling is also constitutively linked to masculinity in that it is understood as a trait of one who passes judgement or is in a position of great authority, and that such people are often men. Female police officers exploit the indexicality of gender by choosing not to recognize the probabilistic connection between their objective, emotionally distant behaviour and masculinity. In so doing, they are also redefining masculinity and femininity.

Female officers attach less importance to appearance in defining femininity than traditional versions of femininity do (as, for instance, described in Brownmiller 1984) and more importance to behaviour. Attention to appearance may even be understood as excessive attention to appearance, as when police officers (male and female) dismiss some women ('those women with the long polished fingernails') as being unable to work the job. These women are dismissed as *overly* feminine, as in the caricature of the indecisive woman in the example below. This twelve-year veteran female police officer demonstrates that, for her, being tough and being able to handle a man with a gun are not incompatible with being a woman:

> You wear men's clothes. It is predominantly a physical, men's type job you know and you do sorta have to look tough. But it comes with the turf you know. It's not necessarily the job, but the way people treat you, relate to you. You know, you don't want somebody coming on a call where there's a man with a gun going 'oh gee, what do we do now?'. You know, you want somebody that knows how to take control of a situation and handle it. Yeah I think a lot of us do sorta act a little tough. I have no identity crisis, I know who I am, I know I'm a woman and that's just what I want to be. I'm happy to be one.

The redefinitions of masculinity and femininity that female police officers undertake (including their understanding of objectivity) make it possible for them to think of police work as not incompatible with their own felt gender identities.[15]

I conclude by comparing the interpretive work done by female police officers to create a place for themselves in that previously all-male and masculine workplace with that done by feminist scholars to establish themselves in their previously all-male and masculine workplace. For academic feminists, establishing the link between objectivity and masculinity has made possible a critique of prevailing academic practices which have often excluded women and the study of women. Keller (1990), for instance, approvingly cites Simmel's statement that in 'the history of our race the equation objective = masculine is a valid one' (1990: 41), and proceeds to demonstrate how masculinity's connotation of objectivity, autonomy, separation and distance has excluded women (who were presumed to possess other characteristics) from the practice of science, and has contributed to the mastery of a feminized Nature. Critical examinations of 'objective' judgements about which events are important historically, or which literary works are 'great', show how such judgements reflect and support prevailing patriarchal ideologies which devalue, obscure or distort the contributions of women and other marginalized groups as historical and cultural actors (Westcott 1990: 59–60).

Such examinations have also engendered innovative modes of intellectual enquiry that self-consciously scrutinize academic practices, including the relationship between studier and studied (see Nielsen 1990). Instead of asking what is or is not objectively valuable, feminist scholars ask 'valuable for whom?'. In this way they can determine whether 'objective' judgements of value work to promote hegemonic cultural norms about what is historically important, artistically valuable and scientifically unquestionable, and they make explicit the assumption that there is a variety of audiences (not just a single, unified, homogeneous one) whose opinions and value-systems deserve to be taken into account in determining value. These critiques of objectivity have created a space for women and scholars studying women and gender in academic workplaces.

Feminist scholars, then, focus on the ways that objectivity is linked with masculinity and argue against 'masculine' norms by arguing against objectivity. To do this, however, is to leave the association of objectivity with masculinity largely unchallenged, and thus to leave some of the pre-existing dualistic complexes of femininity and masculinity unchanged. It is to treat the indexical link between objectivity and masculinity as a referential one. To insist on a necessary link between 'objectivity' and 'masculinity' (as the terms 'equation' and 'connotation' do) is to refuse to recognize both the historicity and the indexicality of the link between masculinity and objectivity and thus to refuse the possibility of altering these associations, in ways that begin to disrupt the everlasting binary associations we find in our culture between masculine/objective/rational/strong/cultural and feminine/subjective/emotional/weak/natural.

Female police officers adopt a different approach. They challenge the association of objectivity with masculinity by seeing themselves as objective, but not as masculine. In doing so, female police officers, unlike feminist academics, may not question some of the negative effects that acting objective may have, on either themselves or clients/citizens. They may also not recognize the paradox of contributing to the construction of a new 'rational' and 'neutral' masculine workplace as they emphasize their own bureaucratic, social work and mental skills as a way of contesting the older interpretation of the workplace as one which required a physical one.

Neither of the interpretive strategies adopted here by either of these groups of women working to foster their own inclusion in traditionally male environments provides us with a conclusive solution as to how to continue working against sex typing and sex discrimination in workplaces or elsewhere. But the two models do illustrate that different tactics for understanding masculinity can be deployed, and deployed effectively, in attacking different sorts of discrimination. And it shows that neither of the practitioners of the two models – police officers or academic feminists – has or should have a monopoly on knowledge creation, on cultural interpretation, or on the deconstruction of traditional notions of gender.[16]

NOTES

1 Such protective legislation persists in workplaces which prohibit women of childbearing age from working in areas where they might be exposed to chemicals harmful to foetuses. Such dicta usually discriminate against women rather than protect them (Boston Women's Health Book Collective 1984: 89–90).

2 Although fears of being labelled as gay or effeminate also work to keep men confined within traditionally masculine roles and behaviours, Williams' (1989, 1992) comparisons of women in non-traditional jobs (e.g. women who are marines) and men in non-traditional jobs (e.g. men who are nurses, elementary schoolteachers or social workers) demonstrate that men in such jobs may encounter prejudice from people outside their profession, but encounter structural advantages within the jobs which tend to enhance their salaries and accelerate their promotions (cf. Forrest, Chapter 5 in this volume). This is in stark contrast to women in non-traditional jobs who experience prejudice outside and inside the profession.

3 The movement of large numbers of men into all-female workplaces is even rarer. When it does take place foreign-born men tend to replace native-born women, as when Irish men replaced native-born white women in US textile mills as women were drawn to teaching and other jobs that native-born white men were vacating (Reskin and Roos 1990: 15).

4 No separate figures are available to indicate what percentage of women are white and what percentage are black, nor are the categories of black and white police officers broken into male and female.

5 I alternate between usage of 'black' and 'African-American' here. Pittsburgh police officers with African-American heritage almost universally refer to themselves as black, and citizens are also generally described by officers as black or white. I use the term 'African-American' in sections where the voice and opinions are my own.

6 I draw upon a year of fieldwork conducted in Pittsburgh, Pennsylvania, September 1991–August 1992 (cf. McElhinny 1992). My forthcoming dissertation (McElhinny 1993) describes my field methods, police culture and police interaction in more detail.

7 See Westley (1970) for a description of physical force used in one department during the late 1960s.

8 Though the institution of policing was part of the growth of the state and urban economies (see Martin 1980 for a historical review), the aims and attitudes of police officers and the structure of the workplace had and has more in common with the structure and attitudes of military organizations than with industrial bureaucracies, and thus the prevailing masculine norms were associated much more with physical aggression and much less with emotionless rationality than is true in other parts of the state.

9 As women have moved into the police department, some parts of it have become perceived by male and female officers as preserves of (hyper-)masculinity. One such preserve is the City's newly formed Drug Task Force, which is almost entirely staffed by men, and is said to be perceived by drug dealers as the only effective and fear-inspiring part of the police force.

10 In all transcriptions, comments in parentheses are my questions or reactions. Capital letters indicate increased volume.

11 'Common sense' is the police officer's version of the technocrat's 'rationality'.

12 Curiously, anger does not participate in the economy of affect in the same way that sympathy/empathy does. It is not a limited resource, but a dramatic mask. Although all police officers must perform anger or impatience on occasion, they

usually perceive this as a carefully controlled act ('acting crazier than they do').

13 The recent interest in feminist circles in the study of gender ambiguity and cross-cross-gendering (see Butler 1990; Devor 1989; Epstein and Straub 1991; Garber 1991) marks a new era in feminist thought, characterized by attempts to explore the malleability of gender. The rapidly growing field of lesbian and gay studies, in addition to raising its own questions about constructions of heterosexism, homophobia and sexual identity, also raises important questions about the flexibility of gender identity.

14 Though the reference of even these markers is being transformed from female as some members of the gay community adopt female pronouns to refer to one another.

15 At times female police officers try to avoid the label of masculinity at all costs – sometimes it is deferred spatially, sometimes it is deferred temporally and sometimes it is deferred spatially *and* temporally. I have been told that women when they first came on the job had to act masculine, but that women do not need to do that any more; or that 'women at that other rougher station need to act masculine, but that women do not need to do that at this station'; or that, 'I used to act masculine [when I was at that other tougher station] but I don't any more.' This all simultaneously marks the importance that the distinction between femininity and masculinity holds for definitions of self in the US (however masculine and feminine are redefined, the distinction is still retained) at the same time as it marks the difficulty in maintaining the distinction.

16 In 1991, four white men challenged the Pittsburgh police quota-based hiring plan as reverse discrimination. After the courts reviewed the decision, the City was ordered to drop the fifteen-year-old injunction calling for quota-based hiring. The City began to develop an alternative affirmative-action hiring plan. In the same year, the police union negotiated a contract which allowed large numbers of police officers to retire immediately on very favourable terms. Officers with twenty-five years of service who were at least 50 years old could retire with a pension set at three-quarters of their salary, rather than one-half of it. The City was faced with a sudden need to hire officers. It decided to hire the top fifty scorers on the police exam on existing civil service lists. This resulted in an all-male and nearly all-white recruit class. When local civil rights groups protested, the City decided to abandon that plan, and regular civil service procedures, and hire police officers from nearby boroughs and municipalities. Official details on these hirings were not released, but conversations with some applicants suggested that all the applicants were male and about one-third of them were black. The police union is currently protesting this plan. Ironically, the wave of retirements by officers over 50 means that for the first time some of the senior officers in the department will be female, and that the percentage of women will increase to over 25 per cent (all the retirees are male), just as the workplace is in danger of being redefined as one where only men need apply.

Chapter 10

The 'White Negro' revisited
Race and masculinities in south London

Les Back

We are witnessing a considerable growth in academic interest in the politics of masculinity. However, much of the emerging literature on masculinity fails to explore the relationship between racism, ethnocentrism and sexual politics (Carby 1982; *Feminist Review* 1984; Barrett and McIntosh 1985; Ware 1990).

One of the features of the new literature is that it is positioned in a culture which gives priority to individual solutions. In particular, the articulation between racism and masculinity is obscured by the ethnocentric nature of self-centred sexual politics.[1] Mercer and Julien comment:

> the questions raised by race, ethnicity and cultural difference cut across the complacencies of a personalized politics that remains in the prison-house of sexuality and the culture of narcissism. How white feminists and anti-sexist men take on these issues is up to them; the point is that race can no longer be ignored or erased from their political agendas.
>
> (1988: 124)

This chapter explores the interconnectedness of racism and gender in the context of masculine identities among white, working-class young men living in south London.[2]

LEARNING TO LABOUR, LEARNING TO BE MEN

'Masculinity' in conventional usage conveys a unitary idea of maleness. However, in particular social contexts, registrations of masculinity are complex, multiple and contradictory. They are defined in interactive and rhetorical situations and vary over time and across social groupings.

My starting point is the complex ways in which gender and power are articulated in working-class cultures and the varying masculinities this produces. Where men are economically dependent on the sale of their labour, the expression of maleness provides a means to exert power; power is assocated with maleness, its absence with feminization. Such dualism appears in the feminization of young male apprentices (Cohen 1988).

Apprentices in factory cultures are given a variety of trivial duties to perform. The older men define themselves as doing 'real work' and the apprentices are seen as their juniors. However, this is an area of contest and negotiation: seniors compel apprentices to inhabit a feminized position while apprentices strive to transcend it. Apprenticeship is about becoming not merely a qualified worker but also a *qualified man*.

The worker/apprentice division is most apparent in the verbal play endemic on the shop floor.[3] The commonest games in south London are known as 'wind-ups'. These rituals involve publicly losing or gaining face and consist of making the subject angry, then showing this anger to be meaningless: 'It doesn't mean nothin' – only winding you up!'. The dynamics of the wind-up are described by Darren:

Darren: Well me and Rodders we're on the building now ain't we.

Les: Do you like it?

Darren: Yeah, it's alright innit Rodders. Bricklaying, innit alright. Yeah we 'ave a great . . . it's alright you know what I mean. The blokes we work with – they are – na mean – everyone gets the piss taken out of them but they are alright. It's like when you are new they suss you out – make you look stupid. There was this one geezer today and they told him to go down to the stores and get a bag of 'glass nails' and he fell for it. They're always laughing and joking with you but that's the way it is.

Les: Do they do the same to you?

Darren: Me, not really. I remember once they sent me to the stores for a 'rubber hammer' (laugh). Another time they tried to get me to get some holes for a bag of nuts – stupid things like that. But if you don't know what kind of things come out of the stores how are you going to know any better?

Les: Do they get you sweeping up and things like that?

Darren: Na, they have someone else do that because I'm a bricklayer – that's what they've got me there for and that's what I'm going to learn.

As Darren said, 'Everyone gets the piss taken out of them.' The apprentices are made to look stupid, giving them a non-adult/junior/subordinate status and an under-developed masculinity, while the perpetrators reinforce dominant masculine identities. Darren recognizes this but resists it by claiming the skills and knowledge of a worker.

Young working-class men are initiated into this gendered culture long before they enter the labour market. The 'wind-up' is a significant way in which working-class young men explore masculinity and negotiate positions of status. In the following passage, occurring in the youth club of a predominantly white council estate, Bob, aged 16 and of white English parentage, is the main actor and Robert, aged 15 and of Irish parentage, is the wind-up subject. Tony, aged 16, and of Afro-Caribbean and white English parentage, is the observer/foil.

Bob: 'Ere Tony 'ave you seen the size of his hands (pointing at Robert's hands).
Tony: Yeah come here Robert let's 'ave a look at those hands.
Bob: Put your hand down there next to mine (looks at Robert).
         (Robert looks at Bob and puts his hand down.)
         (Bob takes the spoon out of his hot tea and puts it on the back of Robert's hand.)
Robert: Agh – you wanker![4] (Bob and Robert laugh.)
Bob: What a wally. (All three boys laugh.)

Two things are important: first, Tony agrees to enter a group where wind-ups are not insults but a kind of play (Davis 1982: 63–6; Kochman 1972); secondly, within this interaction, Bob and Tony establish themselves as the agents, and Robert – the subject – is shamed. Robert is included in the peer group, but at the same time is temporarily relegated to being a 'wanker'. This process is constantly repeated among young men in public settings: the actors may be agents of wind-ups in one situation but relegated to being subjects in others. In this way peer status is contested and continuously modified. Wind-up rituals are practised by black and white young men alike, providing them with a common sense of identity; and, as we shall see, these rituals also provide the context in which racist name calling most often takes place (Back 1990).

Since I grew up in a white, south London, working-class family, these wind-up rituals are familiar to me. During the fieldwork period I was employed as a youth worker, and I decided to avoid these rituals and play fights. This became evident to some of the young men, especially those I had a poor relationship with, who frequently called me a 'poof' or 'fairy' for not accepting their challenges. This situation changed after a wind-up in which I was sold a free ticket to a football match. In a chip shop where young people hung out, Paul, who had sold me the ticket, shouted at me, 'What a wanker!'. I told Paul that we were not in the youth club now and added, 'You wouldn't get away with that with anybody else and you're not getting away with it with me.' One of the older youths said, 'Watch it, he means it! He'll lump [hit] you!' Paul tried to make light of the situation: 'Alright, don't get heavy, I was just winding you up!'. The next day Paul said, 'Yeah, sorry about last night. I was a bit ready. I was out of order.'

This was a turning point in my relationship with the young men; I had defined myself within their terms of reference. The insult Paul had levelled at me asserted that I did not have comparable public masculinity to that of the young men. I was being vilified as a 'wanker', a feeble outsider. However, when I challenged Paul to a physical confrontation, I positioned myself within the group and as a resident of the estate. My assertion of an alternative masculine identity was quickly accepted.

I have reflected on the gendered nature of these fieldwork relationships elsewhere (Back 1992). The point I want to make here is that these interactions provide a space where the nature of working-class masculine identities is defined. In particular, heterosexual codes are implicit within these rituals and as a result they become statements of what is deemed 'normal' sexuality within the culture. Homophobic assertions and name calling in this context arc used to challenge the status of a young man *vis-à-vis* his peer group. Additionally, participation in these rituals constitutes a kind of communion with these heterosexual versions of masculinity.

Young, white, working-class men do not uniformly embrace 'the street' as a place to act out versions of masculinity. On the predominantly white estate, a folk division exists between young men defined as 'estate kids' and those referred to as 'homebirds'. 'Estate kids' are associated with public spaces (the street and youth club) while 'homebirds' are young men who stay within the confines of the flat or house and are alienated from publicly enacted masculinity.

Deano, a 'homebird', rarely ventured into the youth club although he knew most people who attended it. He had one close friend and he shunned peer interactions in large groups. He found both school and the neighbourhood fraught, and stayed in his bedroom for long periods. When asked why he did not go to the youth club, he replied, 'Well, there is always someone on your back, you know, giving you a hard time. I go there when there isn't a lot of people around. I just don't like the pressure.'

Male 'homebirds' are subject to a different kind of feminization from that of the apprentices. The home signifies not just social rootedness but also a gendered female space. One of the young men from the estate once referred to Deano as a 'mother's boy'. Deano certainly strongly identified with his mother and often contributed to domestic work. A different notion of masculinity develops, contrasting with the competitive forms found in public contexts. Deano moved between these gendered domains, although not without ambivalence and stress.

The wind-ups are intimately tied up with particular expressions of masculinity. However, this does not mean that young women are not involved in these forms of behaviour. Young women can take on masculine identities as 'tomboys'.

The 'tomboy' label is applied to young women who adopt 'male' forms of self-presentation and participate in social interactions on an equal footing with their male peers without stigma. However, the participation of young women in this masculine culture decreases when young women turn away from public expressions of masculinity and embrace what McRobbie has termed an adolescent 'culture of femininity' (1981, 1982). This decline is directly connected with the growing importance of heterosexuality in adolescent relations, whose impact means that masculine and feminine identities are both clearly differentiated and more tightly policed. Young women who continue to participate in masculine rituals are liable to have their heterosexuality questioned.

It has been suggested that the impact of heterosexual cultures of masculinity and femininity place young women in a bedroom culture and young men in a street culture (McRobbie 1981, 1982). Mirza (1992) has challenged the idea that this model applies to the position of black women. While black and white young people may share elements of experience, such elements may not account for other aspects of gendering nor accommodate the racisms implicit in whiteness.

The different masculinities found in adolescent communities in south London are generated as young people move between social spaces. Clearly, there is no single, uniform working-class masculinity, but a variety of masculinities determined situationally. Young people position themselves simultaneously in relation to gender, ethnicity and race. It is to these issues that I now turn.

YOUNG MEN, RACISM AND INTER-RACIAL DIALOGUE

The part of south London in which I did fieldwork has a long history of migration (see Back 1991b), mainly from the Caribbean, from the 1950s onward. By 1981 black people constituted 25 per cent of the overall population of the borough and in some districts between 40 per cent and 50 per cent. In addition, small numbers of people settled from Pakistan, India, Africa, Greek and Turkish Cyprus, and during the 1980s a large number from Vietnam.

A dimension of my fieldwork was the degree to which racism structured the relationship between a white researcher and black and white respondents.[5] As with gender differences (Back 1992), the trust black young people offered me was always contingent. Paradoxically, south London is associated with both the most extreme manifestations of racism and some of the most profound moments of inter-racial dialogue. These twin processes are most evident in youth styles. As Hebdige points out (1974a, 1974b, 1979, 1981, 1983), the impact of black culture on white young people is not uniformly progressive: for example, skinhead style incorporates Jamaican music, yet proclaims white power and white pride. In this case black culture was an emblem of white chauvinism (Mercer 1987); the appropriation of black cultural forms was allied with an imperial notion of national pride.[6]

The taking on of black style and language has resulted in a radical reconfiguration of white working-class culture in multiethnic locales (Chambers 1976; Gilroy and Lawrence 1988). It is vital to appreciate that folk antiracism can be generated in the context of these encounters, but it is also necessary to identify the particular gendered constructions of race that white young men, in particular, find attractive.

Black icons? The doubling of fear and desire

The man who adores the Negro is as sick as the man who abominates him.

(Fanon 1967)

Young white people of south London have an intimate relationship with black forms of speech and style. Interaction within multiracial peer groups has opened up black cultural practices to white appropriation. While this process is most profound on the multiethnic estate, it is also found within the adolescent community of the predominantly white estate. Amongst young whites there exists a continuum of identifications with black culture from the most rudimentary usage of creole to cases where young white men and women expressed a desire to *be* black (Back 1991b).

Stuart Hall suggests: 'Just as masculinity always constructs femininity as double – simultaneously Madonna and Whore – so racism constructs the black subject: noble savage and violent avenger' (1988: 28). As in Hall's formulation, in south London adolescent communities, black young men were sometimes viewed by whites – both male and female – as innovators of prestigious youth styles. Yet at the same time black young men could equally be characterized as undesirable, dangerous and aggressive. Many black young men talk of cases where white adults 'hold on to their bags tightly' or 'put their heads down and walk away'. As Tim points out here:

> White people fear black people. Lotta people out there don't know black people. It's only what they hear and read in the newspapers. Walking down the road you see white ladies holding onto their bags tight as you pass them, as if you are gonna rob dem.

Such reactions relate to a gendered construction of black masculinity which includes fantasies about black male heterosexuality, sexual potency and violence. From a black perspective these notions of fear and desire are both restricting and unrepresentative. bell hooks, writing on her experience of growing up in the American south, comments: 'whiteness in the black imagination is often a representation of terror' (1992: 342).

While the stereotypes of black masculinity are embraced by some, many of these young men feel constrained and alienated by the mythology of 'black macho'. Wilson, aged 17, comments,

> Yeah, there is this expectation to be this big black macho thing. Some people play to that, that's OK if they want to do that. But I think that's like making black people to be like, you know, closer to the beast. It's pure wickedness. There's a lot of stuff about how black men treat women and that. It is true that some black men are pure idiots but to make it like saying all black men are this, or all black men are that is just rubbish.

The important point here is that black men are not passive subjects in the face of this kind of racialized and gendered stereotyping. They engage in alternative discourses in which they sometimes manipulate and invert the stereotypes which in other circumstances they would completely reject (Back 1991b).

Young men are characterized in these racist discourses as having oversized penises and predatory desires, while young women's sexuality is viewed as addictive for white men. Delora, aged 17, refers directly to this process: 'Yeah, I remember one white boy saying about going out with black girls, it was like, what did he say – "Once you go black, you never turn back." Like black girls are supposed to be some sex machine.' Delora points to the well-known process by which racism makes black sexuality an element of white fantasy. What is common to these images is that they share a reductive biologism, which fixes black sexuality in the realm of natural attributes. As Hall has commented, it is impossible to understand contemporary racism(s) without 'crossing the questions of racism irrevocably with the questions of sexuality' (1988: 29).

The existence of an interlocked dualism of 'fear and desire' is an essential feature of white constructions of black masculinity. This syndrome was acted out during a visit by our Floodplain estate basketball team to Great Yarmouth. I was the only white player.

We played two games, the second of which we lost by the smallest of margins. The team contested the result and was disqualified from the tournament. I have no doubt that the decision was influenced by racism on the part of the white organizers. Winston, the team captain, said: 'I don't say this often, Les, but these people are racist.' Pauline, the team coach, said, 'The people here will do that if we don't behave properly ... they say, "What do you expect from them ghetto boys?"'. Yet these young men were hardly children of the ghetto; they were all employed, some in white-collar jobs, or studying.

On Saturday evening a dance was held. The team attended with mixed feelings. The irony of the situation was that during the course of the evening the organizers ran a 'best-looking player' competition, and it was won by one of our team. Suddenly black became beautiful! There was a suggestion that as a protest Derek should not accept the prize. However, this did not happen and the team celebrated a strange victory. While our white hosts could allow young black people to be individually glamorous, collectively the same young blacks were threatening. This comes close to what Hall, inspired by the suggestive comments made by Franz Fanon, calls the 'doubling of fear and desire' (1988: 28).

White working-class masculinities and racialized hierarchies

Although non-racist sensibilities are communicated to whites through the process of cultural dialogues (Hewitt 1986; Jones 1988), the 'fear and desire' couplet can also be present. For white young men, the imaging of black masculinity in heterosexual codes of 'hardness' and 'hypersexuality' is one of the core elements which attract them to black masculine style. However, the image of black sexuality as potent and 'bad' is alarmingly similar to racist notions of dangerous/violent 'black muggers'. When racist ideas are most exposed, in situations where there is intimate contact between black and white men, stereotypical ideas can be reproduced 'dressed up' as positive characteristics to be emulated. White identification with black people can become emmeshed within the discourse of the 'noble savage', which renders blackness exotic and reaffirms black men as a 'race apart'.

Staples (1982), writing about black masculinity in America, has shown that while these themes are at the core of classical biologizing racist ideologies, some black men have none the less embraced them. Staples locates this process within the wider context of racial subordination in American society, where the 'macho' gender role underpins the survival strategies of the ghetto 'hustler'. What appears to be the case in south London is a convergence between these processes and the white working-class macho displayed in the policing of a local territory. Whites create a racialized image of black masculinity assembled from fragments of their own experience; the image of blackness is a white artefact. The result is that a particular version of black heterosexual masculinity is adopted in the styles and rituals of white men without necessarily transforming the whites' use of racist discourses. This may have specific pay-offs with regard to white attitudes towards black men. Certainly, it does not alter the wider racist environment. That is, appropriation of black styles may occur simultaneously with more profound and politicized dialogues and within complex exchanges of all kinds.

Previously I have shown that the notions of race and racism adopted by the young men in south London are contradictory and ambiguous (Back 1991a, Back 1993). Although in the predominantly white working-class estate there exists a widely held view that racism and prejudice are wrong, young whites repeatedly use racist discourse to characterize black people outside the area. Racist name calling is prevalent and used in the wind-ups. In this sense there is a clear relationship between the ritual expression of masculine identities and popular racism: the former provides the platform for the latter.

The use of racism in these strategic settings violates the widely held view that it is 'out of order' to use racism or bring colour into multiracial peer interactions. Indeed, the contradictory nature of these ideas allows black young people to gain acceptance by non-blacks on occasion and to resist forms of racism which exist within these peer settings. However, the situation is very different for the newly settled Vietnamese refugees. In many ways, Vietnamese youth operate outside the linguistic and cultural exchanges that take place in multiracial peer groups and constitute a subordinate youth group; what Hewitt (1990: 141) has termed a sociolinguistic underclass.

White young men justify the absence of the Vietnamese young people by asserting that they 'like to keep themselves to themselves' – they 'won't mix'. However, it is clear that their lack of participation in friendship groups is a consequence of racist encounters.

In the course of fieldwork a Vietnamese boy, Tanyi, started to come into the club with two white boys, Cliff and Jack. Cliff and Jack were from established 'estate families'. Cliff's father was reputed to have been a supporter of the National Front in the 1970s and vehemently opposed the settlement of the Vietnamese on the estate. The three boys were said to 'hang around together' on the estate and in the youth club.

The three boys often came to the club to play football and pool. Sometimes Tanyi's Chinese/Vietnamese origins were mentioned in wind-ups, most frequently in terms of a stereotype of 'Orientals' proficient in martial arts. On one occasion when the three boys were playing pool Cliff rolled the pool cue over his shoulder and adopted a fight stance in front of Tanyi. He then withdrew, saying, 'I'd better watch it. Tanyi would make Bruce Lee [the famous martial arts hero] take up pool.' All three boys laughed at this. While Tanyi was accepted as part of the peer group, his 'difference' was often referred to in these exchanges, demonstrating that his presence was contingent on Cliff's and Jack's approval. The three boys used their masculinity as a common register around which to build friendship. In this sense, wind-ups as forms of play were expressions of this process at work (Back 1990). However, these friendships do not last long.

After two months there was tension between Tanyi, Cliff and Jack. Once, a new worker at the club entrance asked Tanyi to spell his name. Cliff said, 'Just put Tony'. Anglicization of names is common amongst British Asian young people who move in white peer groups. On this occasion I think that Cliff's 'naming claim' was of greater significance. It signalled an increasing resentment towards Tanyi's 'difference'. This change also manifested itself in their interactions within the club. Cliff challenged Tanyi in wind-ups more often and subsequently the boys spent less time together. Three weeks later Tanyi stopped coming to the club.

Cliff and Jack told me that Tanyi had decided to 'go back to his own kind'. A few days later I saw Tanyi. He said:

> I was jus[t] sick of the way they treat me. You know, 'yellow' this 'yellow' that, 'Chink' this 'Chink' that. I decided that I didn't want them to use me as something to play with. See they say we don't come to club because we don't want to – but would you want to be treated like that? I go to the club when they have Vietnamese disco on Sundays but no more in the week.

In the face of this kind of harassment it is hardly surprising that the Vietnamese young people are reluctant to enter into close relationships with other young people in the area. The question is: why can young black people gain access to a contingent insider position while the Vietnamese cannot? The answer lies in how racism and gender intersect in the two cases. Despite references to an imagined relationship between 'Orientals' and martial arts, Vietnamese young men are typically vilified as feeble, soft and effeminate, while black men are constructed in the terms of the fear and desire couplet. In short, the internal configurations of white working-class masculinities define the parameters of racist exclusion.

When I met Chas in 1987, he was 14 years old. He is white, lived on a predominantly white estate, but was intimately involved with black musical cultures. He had adopted the full blazonry of black style – a gold-capped front tooth, 'tram lines' shaved into the sides of his blonde hair, and a medallion with the symbol of Africa in red, gold and green. He was unequivocal about the issue of colour. 'It's pure wickedness to cuss people's colour. . . . Like my black friends have as much right to be here as I have.' However, the politics of Chas' posturing did not extend beyond his particular image of blackness. His model of racial hierarchies became clear when we passed a Vietnamese refugee and her son. Chas turned to me: 'I can't stand the Chinks. Their cooking stinks and they keep themselves to themselves like. They don't want to mix.' I asked, 'But isn't that just as bad as saying that all black people are muggers?'. He replied, 'Na! That's not the same at all! My black mates wouldn't let people walk over them the way the Vietnamese do – do you know what I mean? Black people have nuff respect for who they are. If you said things to dem you'd get nuff licks [physical retribution].'

In this short episode the articulation between gender and racism is clear. Black and 'Oriental' youth are characterized by white working-class youth in terms of a set of gendered oppositions. The terms of inter-racial dialogue are set by this process of creating difference: an image of blackness associated with the hardness and assertiveness which is valorized among white working-class males results in the definition of black young men and young women as contingent insiders. By contrast, the young Vietnamese men are feminized and excluded. Black youth are seen as sexually attractive, and, unlike Vietnamese men, are the objects of white fantasies of Oriental hypersexuality (cf. Said 1978).

Franz Fanon showed that in colonial and neo-colonial societies the psychological legacy of racism is complex. He sought to deconstruct the 'white masks' which racism imposed on black people, or, as Bhabha puts it, 'the white man's artifice inscribed on the black man's body' (1990: 188). Bhabha himself suggests that the divisions between Self and Other are always partial, with the result that neither is sufficient unto itself (ibid.: 193). Appropriating Fanon's metaphor, one might also ask why white young men adopt 'black masks'. My answer is that white masculinity does not involve the assertion of a monolithic racialized persona. White young men identify with particular constructions of blackness but reject any form of identification with the feminized images of the 'Oriental'.

CONCLUSION

The white Negro accepts the real Negro not as a human being in his totality, but as the bringer of a highly specified and restricted 'cultural dowry'. In doing so he creates an inverted form of keeping the nigger in his place (Polsky 1961: 313).

Polsky's comment refers to Norman Mailer's famous essay 'The White Negro'. In it he claims to show how white Hipsters in 1950s' America took on black language and style. Or, as Mailer put it, a 'new breed of [white] adventurers, urban adventurers who drifted out at night looking for action with a black man's code to fit their facts' (1961: 285). Polsky's key point is that the Hipster's appropriation of blackness was restricted to a particular stereotype of what being black meant. He suggests the Hipsters did not want black men to be 'Uncle Toms' but they still wanted them to be 'spooks' (Polsky 1961: 313). The point here is that the 'black through white' cultural appropriations I have described in this chapter have a long history. I have argued in this chapter that in order to evaluate these appropriations it is necessary to cross our analysis of racism with a politics of masculinities.

There is no one notion of masculinity found in white working-class culture in south London but rather a constellation of masculine rituals, practices and identities. These notions of masculinity are racialized in complex ways. Part of this process results in white men and women taking on black cultural forms of style and communication. While acknowledging that this experience may communicate egalitarian discourses resulting in a grounded dissection of racial inequality (Hewitt 1986; Jones 1988; Back 1991b), I have concentrated on how this form of appropriation can also result in more complex forms of racism. The notions of blackness which white young men, in particular, identify with may simply be the artefacts of a complex form of white identity. White young men create these images which are assembled from fragments of experience and discourse, then project them on to the bodies of black people. These attributes are not the external features of difference but the re-assimilation of its shadow, a selective construction of blackness confined within the parameters of whiteness. The gendering of blackness and oriental otherness places black and Vietnamese young men in different positions in white male 'common sense'. I argue this process is at the root of new expressions of racism in discourse and action. This process is not monolithic; rather these processes are at work with varying degrees of impact and importance. I may have endowed them with too much explanatory weight and emphasis. Yet I maintain that to appreciate the contingencies of the politics of inter-racial dialogue it is necessary to appreciate the particular crossing of racism and gender. It is only then, for instance, that we can begin to understand why it is that Vietnamese young men and women in this part of south London are so viciously harassed.

Moreover, the processes which result in the 'fear and desire' couplet have important implications for the partial muting of forms of popular racism, and help to explain why young black men can win inclusion among white youths. Yet it is the way in which this process is mediated by notions of masculinity that explains the emergence of new and complex forms of racialized hierarchy. If we are to challenge racism successfully in the domain of popular discourse, we must place an understanding of gendered processes at the centre.

NOTES

I owe an enormous debt of gratitude to many people for helping me to create this chapter. An early version of it was given at a seminar series on racism and gender convened by Ali Rattansi at City University, London. I would like to thank Ali for his useful comments and encouragement. John Solomos and Parminder Bhachu gave inspiration through example and Caroline Hardman provided insightful comments on an early draft. Lastly, thanks to Pat Caplan for advice on this and countless other matters.

1 Cf. David Jackson's *Unmasking Masculinity* (1990), which is a brave attempt at writing a critical autobiography, drawing inspiration from black women's use of autobiography in political writing, yet doing little to engage with the articulation between racism and masculinity in the substance of the book.
2 I draw on an ethnographic study of racism conducted in 1985–9 focusing on two post-war council estates in south London. One estate has predominantly white, working-class residents. The second is a multiethnic neighbourhood. For a discussion of the methods, aims and results of this research, see Back 1991b.
3 The presence of elaborate word games in monotonous work such as assembly lines has been recorded in a variety of contexts (Roy 1953; Vaught and Smith 1980).
4 The literal meaning of 'wanker' is someone who masturbates. It is commonly used to suggest that someone is a fool, or, in the absence of dominant masculine styles of behaviour, unmanly. In the context of play insults, the meanings of such a term are further multiplied.
5 Here the notion of blackness refers to a social and political construction articulated within, but not confined to, the south London context. It both signifies the specific qualities of black London and also resonates with identifications with the African diaspora. While on some occasions this construct was widened to include political opposition to racism, it was rarely applied to the experience of the Vietnamese.
6 There is a long history of European white people appropriating African cultural forms. Roger Bastide (1978) has shown that even within the most acute forms of racial exploitation the crossing of black cultural forms took place. His analysis of African religions in Brazil points out that the de-Africanization of black people occurred simultaneously with a less profound Africanization of whites. Equally, others have demonstrated that white America has a distinctly African heritage (Philips 1990; Mailer 1961; Hewitt 1983).

Chapter 11

'Real true boys'
Moulding the cadets of imperialism

Helen Kanitkar

> Yours is the Earth and everything that's in it,
> And – which is more – you'll be a Man, my son!
>
> (Kipling 1990, 'If–')

Rudyard Kipling provided a memorable summary of idealized qualities for those destined for positions of military or civil leadership in the far-flung British Empire. The poem 'If–' is fluid, rhythmic and neatly rhymed, easy for schoolboys to commit to memory. Such idealized notions of masculinity were inculcated during the imperial period not only through formal education and training, but also through reading and leisure activities. My focus in this chapter is the entertaining light literature to be found in such annuals as the *Empire Annual for Boys* 1909–19 and story collections of the same genre. These were published at Christmas and intended as lively, but morally instructive, reading for boys attending public schools, where 'manliness', sportsmanship and the team spirit, upright conduct and a horror of effeminate behaviour were lauded. Many of these young men were destined for service in the Empire as army officers or government administrators; numbers of them already had fathers or uncles serving abroad. There are many tales which have as heroes young men holidaying with relatives in various parts of the Empire before going up to Oxford or Cambridge. The clubbable, 'old-school-tie', Officers' Mess world is the background for many stories in these annuals and adventure tales; it is definitely the ethos of the genre.

In these tales, the emphasis is on the masculine values of the late Victorian period and the early years of the twentieth century; a time when, as Gilmore has put it, 'manhood was an artificial product coaxed by austere training and testing' (1990: 18). As elsewhere, 'manhood' was defined in terms of the received notions of the social environment and the age. To achieve it boys underwent rites of passage which separated them from home and the familiar, most particularly from their mothers' care and influence. They passed into the charge of men unrelated to them, and were to suffer the dominance of older boys with authority over them. They were expected to stand on their own feet until the time came for them to exercise authority and power in their turn. The aim was to make 'big men of little boys', as the Boy Scout manuals of the day put it. Often actual tests of courage, judgement and initiative were included in these rituals; similar trials appear in *Empire Annual* stories: a boy may have to stand up to the school bully, or, better still, rescue that unpleasant character from a dangerous situation, the boy thus proving not only his bravery but his mature generosity of spirit as well.

The club, the regimental dinner, the boarding school were worlds which women either did not enter except by special invitation, or were only tolerated in out of necessity as school matrons, maids, cleaners and kitchen staff. Likewise, in these boys' stories, women characters seldom play a part.[1] If they do appear, their roles are circumscribed and used to help to define the hero as bold, honourable and considerate of those weaker than himself – all qualities considered worthy of emulation. For example, women may provide an excuse for a brave rescue by being kidnapped by wild tribesmen or carried away by a swift-flowing river. Arthur Mee, editor of the *New Children's Encyclopedia*, indicates that women operate through their influence on men, but not as direct initiators of action; they have 'great power to stir men to glorious things', they act as the 'gentler soul' at the side of great men; and their 'greatest pride is to be womanly, not manly' and to 'have nothing to do with . . . girls who would be men', as 'the manners of men are not for girls to put on' (Mee 1913b: 749–50).

A woman retains respect only if she accepts circumscription of opportunity and development; when in the Empire overseas, she takes her boundaries with her, for even there her governance is limited to her domestic circle and those who move within it. Stoler (1991) has noted that those women who went to live in the colonies during this period were subject to greater restrictions on their activities than those who stayed in England. They were to be kept away from natural dangers, as well as close contacts with the indigenous peoples, lest understanding and appreciation of local mores lead to the horror of 'going native', bad enough in the case of men, but for women unthinkable. The peripheral role of women in the adventure tales highlights the fact that their involvement in the dangerous situations described would be unlikely, even improper, in real life. Moreover, in the stories, participation of a decisive, outcome-determining type is rare for the subjects of imperial rule in colonial countries. Both were expected to be under 'mature' governance, for their own welfare. Women, members of the lower classes, and 'natives': all may offer excuses for action but they are almost incidental to its outcome.

To be moulded into this imperial masculinity, boys either entered the highly structured, all-male, boarding-school environment or were presented with idealized views of such institutions through 'ripping yarns'. Those boys being prepared for entry to public schools were likely to have moved already beyond the governess's schoolroom, where their sisters and younger brothers attended classes, to the transitional phase of instruction by a tutor. This move signalled a young man's entry into male company, with its associated interests, choices of career and means of advancement in the world. At entry to boarding school new loyalties and points of pride – friendship, school, sports team – were generated, preparing boys for later, greater loyalties to regiment, nation and empire. Readership of 'ripping yarns' extended to boys from a variety of backgrounds a positive and beguiling image of the public-school code, presenting the virtues of a class whose position of undeniable power and privilege was, so these books imply, derived from adherence to its ideals.[2] Three images stand out in this literature as providing appropriate role models for the shaping of imperial masculinity: the sporting boy, the all-white boy and, above all, the Christian boy.

THE SPORTING BOY

The upright, manly boy was one who neglected neither physical fitness nor his school work. *Mens sana in corpore sano* was the pattern set before him. The games recommended were team sports which required qualities of leadership, working together and loyalty.[3] A growing interest in female company, which we might regard as a signal of transition from boyhood to manhood, was certainly nothing to boast of in 1911, or so it would seem from an idealized description of the reader of the *Empire Annual for Boys* published in that year's volume:

> Were you to ask the 'real, true boy' [his favourite read or author] you would get an amazing variety of replies. But . . . one and all would tell you they did not want any 'love rot' in their tales. There is a kind of boy, however, who prefers love stories, and these of a particularly sickly sentimental, and sometimes 'nasty' kind. But these immature and weedy youths are not true boys at all; rather they are of the kind of youth that can be seen, with pale and pimply face, sucking cigarette or cane-top, loafing about and ogling the girls, instead of joining in the sports of their more manly fellows.
>
> (Williams 1911: 281)

That this stereotypical ideal of the 'real, true' sporting boy had spread with the Empire, and become an internalized value even among the Indian intellectual elite, can be seen from letters sent by Jawaharlal Nehru's father to his son while a student at Harrow. Motilal Nehru had firm ideas as to the way his son could acquire the attributes and personality of a 'real man':

> I should like you very much to practise shooting as much as you can. It is one of the most necessary qualifications of a well-educated man . . . what I was thinking of was the practice of college games such as cricket. . . . You can engage the services of a professional as some Harrow boys who can afford it sometimes do. . . . The practice of riding is well worth keeping up and improving upon and I would not grudge you the expense it will involve.
>
> (Kumar and Panigrahi 1982: 82, 79, 83)

The Foreword of the first volume of the *Empire Annual for Boys*, published in 1909, was written by J.E.K. Studd, Captain of the Cambridge University cricket XI in 1884. He could not have put the value of sport higher:

> The bond of sport is one of the strongest and most far-reaching in the British race. It . . . is accepted as almost a hallmark of uprightness. 'To play the game' is constantly quoted as the supreme standard of excellence.
>
> (Studd 1909: 7)

Three sporting values are worthy of cultivation in life: to aim high, never lose heart and to help your neighbour. The sports that figure most frequently in the annuals, whether in factual articles or school stories, are cricket, rugby and association football (which by 1913 was being termed 'soccer', but only in inverted commas). Volumes published during World War I years stress the military exploits and achievements of individual officers, who are represented as coming from a public school/Oxbridge background. They are 'brave, noble fellows' who have won

> grander and more lasting triumphs and more immortal renown than they ever won even on the international field at Twickenham, in the Test Match at Lord's, on the river between Putney and Mortlake . . . . There was no hanging back by these men, no 'waiting to be fetched'.
>
> (Wade 1917: 21–2)

The loss of such sportsmen on the battlefield is mourned, whereas soccer, the game normally associated with the working class in Britain, compares unfavourably with the public school/Oxbridge games as a provider of brave soldiers ready to die for Britain and the empire: 'Soccer football was indeed late in starting, compared with some other sports, when the call came' (Wade 1917: 24). The emphasis on team games and the way they are played at public schools and Oxbridge is yet another pointer to the intended readership of these books.

Mee addresses a wider audience when he emphasizes the process of formation of male loyalties:

> you will bring . . . the willingness to sink yourself in entire forgetfulness, and to place your qualities at the service of the team . . . you will be a *part* of the machine and a part of the force which drives it . . . [with] perfect self-mastery and perfect submission . . . you will realise yourself growing into fullness of manhood . . . . On the playing field . . . only the flower of life, and not the weed, can grow. We must be loyal, or the game is lost . . . . If we are loyal to our team, to our school, we shall be loyal to our village, to our town, and to our country; the very beginnings of patriotism lie in the cap that a schoolboy wears.
>
> (Mee 1913a: 544–6)

Mee urges participation in, rather than mere observation of, team games.

These demand not only fitness and skill but assimilation of such moral values as loyalty, pride in the achievements of oneself and of others, leadership, and the ability to get on with one's peers:

> the playing field is in very truth the High School of [a boy's] life. It is there he finds the great distinctive English qualities that mark a man all over the world. I once heard of a man who came to the university of a great English town from a country in the East. He was cultured, kind, and made friends everywhere; a lovable man. Yet every now and then this lovable man would do something terrible in English eyes; he would make you want to hit him, said my friend. *He had not learned the laws of honour.* Now, no English boy can be a healthy boy and miss the laws of honour.
>
> Seek first the Kingdom of Out-of-Doors . . . one of the first rules of games is to lay the foundation of a full and splendid manhood . . . you will keep . . . the thought that a noble mind should live in a noble body . . . . You would scorn to break the great English rule of Fair Play by playing for a baser motive than the pure love of the game.
>
> (ibid.: 543)

Represented here are national values: those who are trained in them will always carry them in their pursuit of enlightenment of the 'other'. The hero of the public-school story in boys' annuals is almost always the captain of cricket or rugby, or at least a star player of the First Eleven or Fifteen. By contrast, tales lauding missionary activities in Asia or Africa are often accompanied by photographs showing the pupils lined up in the school soccer team, as a representation of the working-class youth. Class and race values are thus institutionalized on and through the sports field.

Mee condemns 'players', those who are paid for their sporting skills, as opposed to 'gentlemen', for whom sport is a serious, but unremunerative, recreation:

> You will scorn the sham sporting spirit of these days, the mania of football, whose victims imagine they are sportsmen because they look on while other people play . . . you will have nothing to do with the fraudulent sport which makes a football team a business and buys and sells men like sheep.
>
> (ibid.: 546)

He continues by describing the depressed areas in which the working classes live, and those who spend their free time in public houses, 'ranks of despair which gather week after week at a big football match, and talk of football as if it were deciding the fate of nations' (ibid.: 546). Such behaviour, such companions, are not worthy of the 'true boy', who is urged to 'Quit you like a man: be strong'.

The virtues of the all-male sporting arena and the 'work' of empire building, which the Annuals so proudly extol, sit rather uncomfortably with the assumption that adult males are married men. The emphasis on the great outdoors and the exotica of empire is obvious; so too the absence of female figures. Especially important is the extra-national nature of the activities described and illustrated. Boys are being encouraged to extend their horizons, to see their future as taking them outside their small island, while nevertheless retaining its ideals and culture. These 'cadets of empire' are being urged to see themselves as a breed apart, not only from those they may dominate later overseas, but also from those of their homeland who differ, whether by class allegiance or gender attributes.

THE 'ALL-WHITE' BOY

> We define ourselves by opposition to others .... Each culture inevitably generates its own perception of what is, either as dream or nightmare, its 'other'.
>
> (Ardener 1989: 162)

The notions of the idealized masculine character common to this period are reinforced by the contemporary popular literature. Prevalent were tales of heroism in lands perceived as exotic, wild and uncivilized; these inspired boys to accept their future roles in maintaining and expanding the Empire. Such images are created not only by the lesser-known writers of the era but also by the likes of Buchan and Kipling. John Buchan's *Prester John* presents the white man's role in Africa:

> I knew then the meaning of the white man's duty. He has to take all the risks. ... That is the difference between white and black, the gift of responsibility, the power of being in a little way a king, and so long as we know and practise it, we will rule not in Africa alone, but wherever there are dark men who live only for their bellies.
>
> (1910: 88)

Kipling reiterates the ideal with tongue-in-cheek cynicism:

> Take up the White Man's burden –
> Send forth the best ye breed –
> Go, bind your sons to exile
> To serve your captives' need.
>
> (1990, 'The White Man's Burden')

'The White Man's Burden' may be jingoistic, but it is jingoism with a cutting edge. A more paternalistic presentation appears in the *Empire Annual* 1910, which presents a story purporting to be by a Ugandan mission schoolboy, describing his daily life and the benefits missionaries have brought. The tale is in fact written by a white missionary and is replete with racist images, evidently adjudged as suitable reading for English boys of the period:

> Of course, we people are all black-skinned, and though we don't look so

nice as you do – at least, so we think – and we used to think God did not like us so much as He does you, or He would have given us white skins. . . . In dress we envy you, for we think you look so much nicer than we do. Michael, one of our fellows, dressed up a little time ago in some borrowed things, and he looked so handsome.

(Hattersley 1910: 57–8, 64)

As if to make sure the writer's point is understood, this tale is accompanied by a photograph of a Ugandan schoolboy standing, with a marked swagger, in shorts, blazer, boater, knee-length socks and walking shoes, carrying under his arm a rolled umbrella.

These representations of superiority are fundamentally racist and held sway throughout the empire, not just in black Africa. Images of 'native adults' are complex – they are seen as swarthy, duplicitous and, most relevant to this discussion, childlike. By contrast the young English boy is preternaturally mature and decisive in an environment that is often actively hostile.

An example of this contrast between the hyper-mature English boy and the adult natives who cannot safely manage their own affairs is to be found in the *Empire Annual for Boys* 1914. This is a story with the emotive title 'The Famine Ghoul', who turns out to be a Hindu grain merchant, repeatedly referred to as 'the Hindu', who has locked up his stocks during a time of scarcity until prices are forced up. Some Muslim beggars, claiming to be descendants of rulers of the area, draw near to the verandah of one of the 'best bungalows' of the plains, where the District Officer's young son and his cousin are relaxing one broiling afternoon. The ensuing conversation is worth quoting in full:

'This is terrible, Dick!' [Jack] exclaimed. 'But what *can* we do?'
'It must drive these poor beggars mad to see us sitting here in cool white and drinking tea, while they. . .'
'The victims of famine! Yes, old man, it must be awful for them.'

(Saxby and Simpson 1914: 110–11)

A rupee is thrown to the beggars, who respond by saying it is food they need; money will buy them little to eat, as the price of food is soaring because of the merchants.

'Oh, the brutes! . . . I never heard of anything so rotten.'
'Government ought to have laws to stop such a thing,' said Jack . . . 'send along a decent monsoon; that's about all that would put things right. The natives live from hand to mouth; they never provide for hard times.'
'Shall I call the boy for more tea?'
'Ah well! I suppose it won't do any good to moan over other people's troubles. Hullo!' and the speaker burst out laughing. 'What has happened to my boy? He's actually running!'

'He's coming homewards – to grub – in haste like a horse,' remarked Dick sarcastically . . . but the Hindu continued in his surprising exhibition.

(ibid.: 111–13)

The servant is hurrying to tell his master that a merchant has been murdered in the bazaar by the starving people, and says that there are threats to do the same to a big grain merchant nearby. Jack interrupts him sharply (it does not do to encourage gossip with servants):

'That'll do, Thumbao; you can go to your work.' He had suddenly risen, and there was a set look about his face that indicated no small purpose ruling him at the moment.

(ibid.: 114)

The young English boys force the merchant to sell his grain at a fair price, so saving his life, and preserving peace under the Raj.

This tale indicates how the Englishman selflessly brings order and a sense of fair play to places where, it would appear, such ideas were hitherto unknown. Important matters have to be dealt with by a manly Englishman who can organize and direct the 'new-caught, sullen peoples,/Half-devil and half-child', as Kipling put it.

In these boys' stories internal qualities are reflected in external appearances; a hierarchy of racial groups, constructed according to a range of desirable/undesirable national characteristics, is apparent. Even pets do not escape the imposition of desirable qualities of personality. Dogs are the most popular, faithful to their masters, lively and sporty by nature, courageous in a crisis and prompt to obey the orders of a higher authority; in short, they embody all the noble attributes of masculinity and are thus worthy companions of real men.

In these adventure tales there is immediate suspicion, usually justified by later events, of anyone who does not look wholly European; a story entitled 'The Puttipore Rivals' (Moore 1912), about two motor car salesmen in India, has as its villain 'a stout, dark-haired man', with 'evidently very little European blood in his veins'. Sure enough, the truth emerges, though the author does try to be generous in his judgement: 'his father was a Frenchman and his mother a native. That, of course, is no reason why he should not be an honourable, decent fellow, but . . . there is not a bigger rogue than he in Puttipore' (ibid.: 120). Initial impressions are proved correct; how differently drawn is his rival, a 'smart young Scotsman'. Others take the same mould, such as the upright individual encountered while holidaying in Scotland: 'a typical young Englishman, good-looking, brave, a keen sportsman' (Wilson 1919: 105).

Some ethnic groups are treated with respect by the authors of this juvenile popular literature. Among them are Sikhs, the tribesmen of the North-West Frontier and Gurkhas, who are seen as exemplifying familiar martial qualities of courage and respect for orderly discipline, both of which are admired by the imperial English. The Gurkhas are 'brave to recklessness', and 'their wonderful dash, faithfulness to their officers, and devotion to duty have won the admiration of the whole British Army' (Danvers-Dawson 1917: 119). That the Gurkhas helped British forces during the Indian mutiny is acknowledged, as is their World War I service. Nevertheless, the author of one article on the Gurkhas cannot avoid some condescending comments. He writes that the Gurkhas have shown a 'generous spirit of courtesy which was worthy of a more enlightened people' and adds, 'they can hardly be called handsome even by their best friends' (ibid.: 120). Certainly the black-and-white illustration accompanying this account represents the Gurkhas most unflatteringly. As they charge from the trenches, brandishing the dreaded *kukri*, the knife that is their favourite weapon, their features are depicted as savagely simian. Lionel Caplan (personal communication) has suggested that Gurkha qualities praised by English officers are those adjudged characteristic of the English public schoolboy of the Victorian and immediately post-Victorian period: they are loyal, quick to respond to a command, brave and upright. Nevertheless, like schoolboys, they are in need of direction; the schoolboy is destined to grow up and command in his turn, but the Gurkhas are not – their adulthood remains unacknowledged, not least because they remain subject to the orders of British officers.

Foreign accents, or the inability to speak grammatical standard English, are irresistible to the authors of these boys' adventure yarns as a source of fun which can belittle the speakers. As we have already seen, such examples can be drawn in plenty from stories of the Empire which incorporate native characters, who fall ready victims to mockery. But there are examples much nearer home. In a tale of the Great War, a French general responds to an English officer who has brought him important news: 'I am ver glad to get dis . . . Et make a great deefference to our plans . . . You vill stay an' haf som' sopper with me, eh?'. The same author draws verbal distinctions between British army officers and NCOs: ''Ere you, Bates and Simpkins, are your revolvers ready? But don't loose off till I do, then stan' up an' let 'em 'ave it! . . . Good sort o' place for a hambush, sir.' Although the speaker is an experienced regular soldier, the subaltern who is in charge of the expedition emerges as the hero and is regarded by his superiors as a fine leader of men. His background is precisely what we might expect in an *Empire Annual* tale:

> when war had broken out, he was still a mere public schoolboy. . . . But when Great Britain threw down the gauntlet . . . Ponsonby, like a good many other young men of his class, determined not to be left out in the cold.
> (MacDonald 1915: 9–10)

Even the choice of surnames implies a hierarchy of rank: Ponsonby is the officer, while the 'Other Ranks' are designated Bates or Simpkins, names characteristic of working or lower middle classes in these stories. Ponsonby, certainly, is never made to appear comic, through speech or action.

Heroes of the Great War are sometimes of very tender age, and there is no hint of the tragedy that the battlefield often brought to a young life; only the glory dazzles and tempts young readers to commit themselves to emulation. The Battle of Mons offers the true tale of a 16-year-old bugler:

> the brave little chap was smiling cheerfully at his soldier friends, though his left arm had been shot away and both his head and feet were bandaged . . . the spectators gave the gallant lad many hearty cheers. . . . Ordered to sound his bugle to encourage the regiment, he did so until he had four bullets in him, and even then he continued to blow till he fell quite unconscious. . . . Yes, every man in the regiment is proud of him!
>
> (Wade 1915: 80–1)

Such virtues are not confined to the white protagonists of imperial rule, however; individuals from among the ruled can also show noble qualities, and stories of these are used to strengthen positive role-models as well as to demonstrate the difference between these noble souis who have acquired such qualities from their rulers and the rest of their people. Conformity to English ideals of honour is what is recognized and admired.

THE CHRISTIAN BOY

The ideals carried by the English imperialists reflect a 'muscular Christianity' which ties in with the other ideals of masculinity to which English boys were expected to aspire. An episode from Eliza F. Pollard's *White Dove of Amritzir* illustrates the refusal of an English District Officer to compromise his faith when confronted with what seems to have been interpreted as religious adoration from the 'natives'. It begins with a group of Sikhs seen worshipping a District Officer who has been sent to the Punjab to 'rule' them. They see him as a reincarnation of Guru Gobind Singh (or so we are invited to believe). This disgusts the District Officer, John Nicolson:

> 'Kasan Singh, how dare you!' . . . the speaker . . . looked down with an expression of mingled anger and pity at a man crouching at his feet, muttering words in a strange tongue . . . he dragged himself to where the officer stood, and then prostrated himself on the ground . . . Nicolson exclaimed – 'Faith! and it's more than a man who calls himself a Christian can stand!'
>
> (Pollard n.d.: 164)

Kasan Singh is sentenced to three dozen lashes for his 'blasphemy', which treatment is presented as provoking even greater adulation for Nicolson from the Sikhs.

According to the imperialists, God had favoured the white man, and

especially the Englishman, through the gift of Christianity. In turn, the white
believers, or at least some of them, came from their homes to bring the gift to
'the heathen in his blindness'. An embarrassingly obvious tale equating
whiteness of complexion with purity of spirit is that of 'All-white' John, a
Christianized New Guinea tribesman whose ambition is to,

> 'Go to heaven, be white mans, be English some day. All white, all white,
> jes' like this', as he shows a picture of an angel; 'All white! All white! . . .
> black fellow no more; all English!' John's black eyes rolled and glistened.
>
> (Bevan 1910: 19)

The refrain 'All white! All English!' is eagerly reiterated throughout the
story; the epithets 'white' and 'English', with all the virtuous qualities John
has been persuaded to perceive in them, appear synonymous. Other New
Guinea tribesmen, effectively condemned in John's own words, are designated: 'men of the hills; black all through; no white in them; devils!'. To the
author, their outward appearance instantly betrays their evil nature: they are
'dwarfish fellows . . . naked, sinewy, ugly, bones thrust through the nostrils
like sharp tusks, they looked more beast than human' (ibid.: 25).

John demonstrates the value of the noble qualities which have come to
him through conversion and his association with 'white English men' by
rescuing them from these New Guinea tribesmen. His clever rescue, however, does not win him credit for intelligence but only for a natural instinct
which is shared with the animal kingdom: '[John] yearned to be "white
mans all through", but Nature had made him black and trained him for years
in every wile of his race' (ibid.: 26). John is a comic figure because of his
manner of speaking English and his over-simplified faith; the story also
describes the gulf fixed between the intelligent, reasoning white and the
instinctual black.

Missionaries are least likely to show regard for the way of life that
surrounds them. They see themselves as there to challenge it, and to 'make
real men' of the boys put in their charge via an English education. A series of
articles by Tyndale-Biscoe (1911: 205–8, 211) on a mission school in Kashmir
is a case in point. The writer first describes the Kashmiri capital in a markedly
unsympathetic manner: 'The inhabitants were crawling about, for people in
the East are not as a rule fast walkers' through the snow in the 'dirty white
city'. The missionary condemns much of what he sees, 'which I had not
dreamt of even in nightmares': people walking not abreast but one behind the
other, according to age, gender, caste and wealth. He has a vision of Srinagar
of the future: 'I saw knights-errant walking about these streets, not at the
gentlemanly bullock pace, but young men of muscle and grit who had
awakened from their lethargy and sleep of years to a life of activity and
manliness', which will be realized by his teaching 'Christian principles and
public school ideas to the boys and young men of Kashmir'. He is impressed
by the work of his colleagues: 'When I have seen these countrymen of mine

. . . just doing their duty without fuss or noise, because they are just what they are, I thank God that I have been born a Christian and an Englishman.'

Rarely does condemnation of the 'other' descend to invective, but occasionally prejudice becomes blatant and venomous, as when a missionary describes some of the pupils in the mission school, the purpose of which is 'to make men – men of true Christian character – out of the material to be found in Kashmir':

> There were 200 or more dirty, smelling Brahman things squatting on the floor devouring with great keenness the wisdom from the West. . . . These Brahmans in embryo were swinging backwards and forwards without ceasing, just like a metronome . . . pressing their dirty little fingers along the lines of grease-bedaubed Persian or Sanskrit reading-book.
>
> (Tyndale-Biscoe 1913: 279)

Tyndale-Biscoe sees the purpose of his missionary experiences in north India as 'to make budding bipeds into such men as we believe Almighty God wishes them to be' (ibid.: 283). There is much in the same vein; success stories are proudly told, in which Brahman boys learn how to help others, regardless of status or caste, developing, through missionary influence, a generosity of spirit towards the elderly, women, beggars and animals. Again it is the accepted values of the Christian west that are held up for emulation. Englishmen must see themselves as having the God-given right, as well as the duty, to govern and control those unable to do so for themselves.

CONCLUSION

These adventure tales were composed for boys living seventy or eighty years ago, and are historically and culturally specific to a period of British history. The boys had inherited what was thought to be a consolidated empire built up and maintained by Englishmen who had idealized service overseas as evidence of loyalty to queen and country. Any historic text is 'bound to the signifying network, the cultural context which produced it' (Ash 1990: 76), yet it cannot be assessed from within that cultural context, but only from the perspective of the present. The *Empire Annuals* and other such books are no longer read by British schoolboys. Superficially, styles of masculinity have undoubtedly changed. However, versions of the dominant masculinities these stories reveal are firmly rooted and reworked on the rugby field, in the club and round the boardroom table. Thus in 1992 *The Times* could quote a committee member of London's Garrick Club on the admission of women members: 'If women members come in, it will change. I don't know in what way, but why should I risk it?' (Barker 1992: 1). Misogyny, chauvinism, class and racist prejudices continue to define a hegemonic masculinity of 'real true men' subscribed to by many of the British establishment.

NOTES

1 Women occasionally figure in stories about an earlier historical period, when their activities are not threatening to the dominant images of masculinity of the early twentieth century.
2 Joseph Bristow (1991) provides a full account of the development and ethos of these schools.
3 A detailed study of the significance of sport in the English public school can be found in Mangan (1981). The same author examines the contribution of imperialist juvenile literature to the development and maintenance of a public school educated colonial elite (1989).

Chapter 12

The paradoxes of masculinity
Some thoughts on segregated societies

Deniz Kandiyoti

In this chapter I discuss the concerns that led me to explore aspects of masculinity in Muslim societies, although these did not form an explicit component of my original research agenda. In the process of assembling material for quite a different project – namely a comparative analysis of women, Islam and the state (Kandiyoti 1991) – insights and hypotheses concerning the construction of masculine identities crept up surreptitiously and eventually called for attention with an insistence that could no longer be ignored. This focus on masculinity led me to revise and amend some of my earlier assumptions about the nature of patriarchy (Kandiyoti 1988a) and to question my reading of materials I had been using. A clarification of my intellectual trajectory is therefore in order as a means of situating my observations, which at this stage remain tentative and exploratory.

Anyone working on questions of modernization and women's emancipation in the Middle East must inevitably come across those 'enlightened', pro-feminist men who were often the first to denounce practices which they saw as debasing to women – enforced ignorance, seclusion, polygyny and repudiation (a husband's unilateral right to divorce his wife). I considered their appearance as unproblematic since a whole panoply of explanations was available for their emergence: the effects of colonial expansion and exposure to the west (Ahmed 1992), the rise of new classes in this context (Cole 1981) and a more universal thrust towards modernity inherent in emergent nationalist projects (Jayawardena 1988).

None the less, I had misgivings about the deeper motivations of male reformers and wondered if they were being self-serving by manifestly bemoaning the subjection of women while in fact rebelling against their own lack of emancipation from communal and, in particular, paternal control (Kandiyoti 1988b). Yet how was I to explain instances where their tone was not merely rational and didactic, but strident or full of rage and disgust? Even in a relatively recent text, Mazhar Ul Haq Khan adopts an impassioned tone to talk about the ravages of the purdah family on the male psyche:

The Purdah husband's treatment of his wife or wives is authoritarian, in some cases actually harsh and sadistic. In fact, if polygamous, he can maintain peace among his wives only by the exercise of strict authority and command. The little children note the frightened flutter in the *zenana* at his appearance, which engenders the same emotions of fear, flight and general avoidance as they notice in their mother or mothers and other inmates of the zenana. This creates an emotional gulf between them and their father.

(1972: 113)

The helpless mother also instils similar emotions in her son and unwittingly moulds him in her own image. Yet the male child has an inordinate amount of power over the secluded mother and comprehends the sources of her helplessness at an early age. This leads to 'a strange, though silent reversal of relationships between the purdah mother and her little son' whereby she depends on him to move through the streets and bazaars, and he may even rebuke her for her conduct and instruct her to observe purdah if there are men around (Khan 1972: 119). The message is clear; the subjection of women through purdah and polygamy ultimately mutilates and distorts the male psyche.

Having identified men as the beneficiaries of existing power differentials between genders, I could only explain this type of discourse as the emergence of a novel male agenda which did not necessarily have as its main concern women's liberation, but rather their own.[1] It is only gradually that I started noticing that, quite often, male reformers were not speaking from the position of the dominating patriarch, but from the perspective of the young son of the repudiated or repudiable mother, powerless in the face of an aloof, unpredictable and seemingly all-powerful father. Was I hearing the rage of an earlier, subordinated masculinity masquerading as pro-feminisim?

What I had overlooked was the fact that some men might have had genuine cause to vent spleen in relation to their formative experiences in the family. I had made the elementary mistake of assuming that they had come into being as full-blown men, as patriarchs themselves, on the flimsy grounds that this role was culturally available to them. Had I shown the necessary sensitivity to the gendered structuring of different stages of men's life cycles in Muslim societies, I would no doubt have perceived the intricate web of confirmatory and contradictory experiences behind what I naively assumed to constitute some seamless adult masculinity.

It was at this point that I came across Bob Connell's work (1987), which resolved some of my difficulties. Connell presents masculinity as a social construction which is achieved within a gender order that defines masculinity in opposition to femininity and in so doing sustains a power relation between men and women as groups. As such, there is no single thing that is masculinity. Power relations among men, as well as different patterns of personality development, construct different masculinities. From my point of view, his most useful suggestion was that gender politics among men involve struggles to define what Connell terms 'hegemonic' or 'socially dominant' masculinity, and that the form of masculinity that is hegemonic at a given time and place involves a particular institutionalization of patriarchy and a particular strategy for the subordination of women.

In my earlier work, I had paid attention to these variations only from the perspective of women's subordination and resistance. I proposed an important, but relatively neglected, point of entry for the identification of different forms of patriarchy through an analysis of women's strategies for dealing with them. I argued that women strategize within a set of concrete constraints that reveal and define what I called the 'patriarchal bargain', which may exhibit variations according to class, caste and ethnicity. I assumed that these patriarchal bargains would exert a powerful influence on the shaping of women's gendered subjectivity and attempted to analyse how women, at different points of their life cycles, accommodate to, subvert or resist particular patriarchal scripts (Kandiyoti 1988a). However, I remained partially oblivious to the dynamics among men because of my implicit belief that patriarchy reproduces itself primarily in the relations *between* rather than *within* genders; this also led me to privilege some institutions (kinship and the family) over others (such as the state and the army). Although I still believe that patriarchy finds its starkest expression in relation to the subordination of women, an adequate explanation of the reproduction of patriarchal relations requires much closer attention to those institutions which are crucially responsible for the production of masculine identities.

Connell's approach opens up the possibility of examining subordinate masculinities and the ways in which certain categories of men may experience stigmatization and marginalization. In the west, this examination has mainly focused on men stigmatized because of their sexual orientation or on the experiences of working-class or black men. In the Third World, the psychological effects of colonization have occupied centre-stage. These effects are often described in the language of gender. This is most explicit in Nandy's treatment of British India, where he notes that western colonialism used a homology between sexual and political dominance and produced a cultural consensus in which political and socioeconomic dominance symbolized the dominance of men and masculinity over women and femininity (Nandy 1983). He contends that some nationalists had to produce compensatory discourses to redeem Indian masculinity which, in fact, amounted to identifying with the aggressor.[2]

How, you may well ask by now, did these incursions into hegemonic and subordinate masculinities alleviate my predicament in relation to Middle Eastern male reformers? Surely, all the forms of subordinated masculinity I referred to are traceable to structural inequalities of class, caste, ethnic location or sexual orientation. What possible relevance could this have to a male elite that was in the vanguard of social change in their societies? Indeed, there may be some relationship in so far as I came to reinterpret their stance, at least partly, as a possible crisis in hegemonic masculinity. This involved, among other things, a rejection of the life-styles implied by their fathers' domestic arrangements.[3] I disagree with those who, like Nandy, attribute such crises to external forces alone, namely the effects of colonialism and western hegemony. I think that insufficient attention has been paid to the internal contradictions of certain types of patriarchy. If there are specific masculinities linked with particular social contexts, then an analysis both of enduring patterns and of change must address itself to a concrete examination of such contexts. I therefore turned my attention to the production of masculinity and the main institutions responsible for it in the Muslim Middle East at the turn of the century, with a a special emphasis on Ottoman Turkey.

DISTANT HUSBANDS AND CHERISHED SONS

Although the family is the obvious starting point for such an enquiry, I had some reservations about the ways in which the construction of gendered subjectivity is commonly addressed. A focus on the family inevitably tempts one to fall back upon some variant of psychoanalytic theory. In a broad-based survey of cultural concepts of masculinity, Gilmore, like many, invokes neo-Freudians to account for the development of masculine identity:

> To become a separate person the boy must perform a great deed. He must pass a test; he must break the chain to his mother. . . . His masculinity thus represents his separation from his mother and his entry into an independent social status recognized as distinct and opposite from hers.
>
> (1990: 28)

Or, as put more bluntly by Stoller and Herdt, 'The first order of business in being a man is: don't be a woman' (1982: 34). Despite the fact that these and similar statements appear to have the ring of universal truth, I found psychoanalytic theory, in both its Lacanian and object-relations variants, of limited usefulness in elucidating culturally specific forms of masculine, or for that matter feminine, subjectivity.[4]

There has also been some dissatisfaction with the category of gender as a tool for social analysis among some feminist anthropologists. Gender, it is argued, obscures as much as it clarifies our understanding of social reality. Ortner (1983) suggests that a gender-based analysis might be less useful than an analysis grounded in analogous structural disadvantages. Rosaldo expresses a similar concern when she states:

> We think too readily of sexual identities as primordial acquisitions bound up with the dynamics of the home forgetting that the selves children

become include a sense of not just gender but of cultural identity and social class.

(1980: 401)

Ortner's concept of structural disadvantage is particularly promising for an understanding of how gender differences interact with other differences (age, class and ethnicity) to produce shifting subjectivities and more fluid constructions of gender. My dissatisfaction with psychoanalytic theory does not stem from the fact that it 'fixes' gender once and for all as a stable, developmental acquisition (constructionists have laboured that point sufficiently, and Lacanians are not in any case guilty of this), but that it cannot fully account for the possible effects of culturally specific types of structural disadvantage.

A rare personalized (as opposed to strictly ethnographic) account of Arabo-Muslim male identity, by Abdelwahab Boudhiba (1985), opens up new possibilities for taking structural disadvantage on board. In his account the mother is presented not just as a woman, but as a woman enmeshed in the concrete gender asymmetries of a sex-segregated, polygynous society. Right from the beginning of her relationship with her son, she brings to bear the psychic burden implied by her structural disadvantage as 'a woman in a precarious position without a son'. This emotional tone is something that psychoanalysis alone cannot fully account for. Rather, the key to the psychological dynamic of the relationship lies elsewhere, in the particular institutional context of the Muslim family and the power relations enacted in it. This is to say, not that this dynamic will be devoid of enduring, intrapsychic consequences, but that it may not be useful to talk about these at the level of generality implied by Gilmore in his rendering of the post-Freudian position. A more fruitful point of entry might be sought at the intersection of specific structural disadvantages and their possible psychic representations. Such an analysis may still be served by the central insights of psychoanalysis, although it would have to include more explicitly the social dimensions of the unconscious.

Where would depictions of family life at the turn of the century fit within such a perspective? There are repeated suggestions in the psychoanalytic literature that in societies with structural patterns that tend to weaken the marital bond, where motherhood (especially of male children) is highly valued while wifehood and daughterhood are debased, intense and ambivalent maternal involvement with sons may result.[5] The implication is that the culturally defined female role has a decisive influence on the experience of maternity. The affective needs of women are assumed frequently to be starved in the conjugal union and feelings for the husband displaced onto the male child, sometimes with the expression of open erotic feelings. However, the son may become the target of both maternal seduction and her repressed rage, as the mother alternately builds him up as an idealized protector and rejects and ridicules his masculine pretensions. This is assumed to make for a narcissistic and insecure masculinity.

The temptation of assuming that such graphically described patterns of structural disadvantage will generate predictable intrapsychic consequences for mothers, who will then foster a particular sense of masculinity in their sons, is attested by the volume of literature in this vein. I could not, in the last analysis, subscribe to it, despite the fact that some ethnographic details on family life in the Middle East corroborate depictions of spousal distance and maternal over-involvement with sons. My resistance echoes Loizos' refusal to entertain a unified concept of 'Greek masculinity' (Chapter 3 in this volume) due to the sheer complexity of the societies in question and the varied contexts in which male roles are enacted.

In the case of my material on Ottoman Turkey, it was quite clear that the few biographic accounts on growing up in a polygynous household emanated from a small, upper-class elite. Indeed, recent work on historical demography confirms that the actual incidence of polygyny in Ottoman times may have been not only very low but also confined to high-ranking government officials and men of religion (Behar 1991). We know very little about household dynamics in other social strata and even less about the formative experiences of men and women in relation to their gendered identities in different contexts. Besides, the mother–son dynamic is but one element of a much more complex picture, which must be taken in its entirety to make sense of the layering of experiences which constitute one's sense of gender. However crucial experiences in the family may be, they are but one instance of a whole range of institutional arrangements which go into the definition of what it means to be a man or a woman. The greatest interest surely lies in the multiplicity of gendered selves, and their interactive nature, and the way they are reconstructed in new institutional settings. In what follows, I explore some avenues for research to help us achieve some sense of this complexity.

REREADING MALE NARRATIVES

With hindsight, it now seems that the best way to have tackled my initial problem with respect to male reformers would have been to re-read a wide variety of sources, especially biographies and novels, for the full range of masculinities they reveal. Such texts have rarely been examined with a view to gaining insights about the authors' formative experiences as men, and the voice of the male child, negotiating and constructing his identity from his childhood experiences, has rarely been heard and recorded. Thus, we must consider how the young boy experiences his maleness in relation to his mother, his sisters and the world of women, and ask what other qualities of masculinity are negotiated through his experiences with men. Most importantly, we must try to piece together how these quite different experiences of his masculinity are brought together, with all the contradictions and ambiguity this implies.

Let me illustrate what such a project might entail by introducing one of the most telling accounts of boyhood I could find in the literature. Boudhiba, a Tunisian author, writes of an experience of childhood which was almost certainly shared by men who grew into adulthood in the Middle East during the late nineteenth and early twentieth centuries. This is the experience of being taken to the public baths (*hammam*) by one's mother. He writes,

> Indeed, it is customary for children to go to the hammam with the women and this continues up to the age of puberty. Since the age of puberty is not the same for everyone, the threshold at which one has 'grown up' is highly flexible; since a mother always tends to see her son as an eternal child and since other women are in no way inconvenienced by the presence of a boy, young or not, and since taking a boy to the hammam is a chore that the father would prefer to leave, for as long as posssible to the mother, the spectacle of fairly old children, more or less adolescent, consorting side by side in their nakedness with women of all ages, is by no means rare.
>
> (1985: 168)

This promiscuity with women continues until such time when the boy, by some inappropriate look, comment, or gesture, signals that the time of exile from 'the kingdom of the mothers' has come.

> What Arabo-Muslim has not been excluded from the world of naked women in this way? What Arabo-Muslim does not remember so much naked flesh and so many ambiguous sensations? Who does not remember the incident by which this world of nakedness suddenly became forbidden? We have been given more than a memory. One could not stop himself pinching that big hanging breast that had obsessed him. Another was banned for being too hairy, for having too large a penis, buttocks that protruded too much, a displaced organ. For the boy the hammam is the place where one discovers the anatomy of others and from which one is expelled once the discovery takes place.
>
> (ibid.)

The transition to the men's *hammam* also means entering the world of adult men in an abrupt and definitive manner, consummating the separation between the sexes institutionalized in Muslim societies.

> To enter the world of adults also means, perhaps, above all, to frequent only men, to see only men, to speak only to men. . . . The body is now literally snatched up by the male world.
>
> (ibid.: 169)

And how is this new body experienced? Unfortunately, male authors seem more explicit about their experiences of the women's *hammam*, and even

Boudhiba gives only the briefest account, though an intriguing one, of the young boy's first experience with men:

> The practices of the hammam are structured in a new way from the moment one is taken from one's mother, so that the first hammam taken with men is like a consecration, a confirmation, a compensation. It is a confirmation of belonging to the world of males. . . . Did not one receive the congratulations of one's father's friends, whom one now meets for the first time scantily dressed and some of whom will not fail to make indecent propositions.
>
> (ibid.: 170)

We are left to ponder what range of feelings the nubile boy might have experienced under the adult male gaze. It is at the point of entry into the male world that he might have felt 'feminized' by virtue of his still immature body, whereas his status as the unquestionable possessor of a penis might have been more secure among women. It is a matter of conjecture whether or not this experience is reactivated throughout men's lives, particularly when they find themselves in all-male contexts which involve hierarchies of power in which they perceive themselves as relatively powerless (for instance, as conscripts in the army and new students in boarding schools).

A paradox of sexual segregation is that it results in young males' prolonged and promiscuous contact with women and abrupt and possibly disturbing entry into the male world. I find Boudhiba's description of the male child's move from the women's to the men's bath-house a powerful metaphor for this transition. It is merely a metaphor, however, since the *hammam* occupies a particular historical position. It is an institution which, in so far as it exists at all nowadays, has a very different character. In the past, it was a specifically urban phenomenon, which presupposed a degree of wealth and development of specialized public facilities which were absent in the pre-modern architecture of private households. None the less, it is also an experience which many now middle-aged men can themselves remember. I recall a male colleague describing how the bath-house attendant chided his mother, saying, 'Next time, why don't you bring his father?', a cliché which tells a woman that her son is too mature to be welcome in the women's *hammam*. The different kinds of femaleness which boys experienced (the uninhibited matriarchs, the pre-pubertal and young nubile girls, the modest and silent new brides) and remembered from this exposure are important, as are the ways in which they related to women in each of these stages in the life cycle. Equally important is the boy's confrontation with other versions of his masculinity, constructed as a subordinate male in the world of adult men in the men's *hammam* where, again, actual embodiment is salient.

Keeping in mind the metaphor of the *hammam* and the complexities it implies, let me return to the problem of re-reading textual sources. Few accounts by male authors – especially if they are autobiographies – are as candid as Boudhiba's writing or as transparent as Khan's prose. The concern with presenting a coherent persona encourages rhetoric and the concealment of personal feelings. This is why the novel, in which authors can speak through their characters in ways in which they would avoid if writing in the first person, is so fruitful as an alternative source in the search for male voices.

As an illustration let me mention a single contemporary example: the male child protagonist, Kamal, in Naguib Mahfouz's *Palace Walk* (1990). In this novel, Mahfouz offers brilliant insights into the ambivalence and confusion of the small boy caught between the maternal world of secluded women and the world of his father and older brothers. The world of his mother and sisters is comfortable and soothing, while the adult male world, the world of his father, is by comparison forbidding and hostile. The figure of the father is one of god-like remoteness and authority, filling Kamal with terror. Yet within the women's world there are crucial differences between the boy's relationship with his mother and with his plain but doting sister, Khadija, and his virtually incestuous interest in his very pretty sister, Aisha.

A dramatic and revealing incident occurs in relation to Kamal's mother Amina. A totally secluded woman who never crossed the threshold of her home, she has a deep longing to visit the mosque of al-Husayn, the outlines of which she can barely discern from her balcony. Her older children are aware of this innocent yearning and encourage her to an escapade on a day when her husband is away on business. With much trepidation she decides to go, in the company of Kamal as her guide. A male child, however young, legitimates a woman's presence in public spaces and Kamal is excited and proud at the prospect of being her chaperon. The visit to al-Husayn proceeds smoothly, but on the way back Kamal, with a particular pastry shop in mind, leads her to a busy street, when his mother, overwhelmed and disconcerted, falls in a faint and gets hit by a car. Kamal, her accomplice, is not only the witness to his mother's panic and pain, but also carries the burden of guilt for somehow having precipitated this tragedy through his untimely desire for sweets. Throughout the domestic drama that follows – his mother returns with a fractured shoulder and confesses to her husband who repudiates her (temporarily, as it later turns out) – Kamal is racked with guilt and terrified on her account. He is definitely part of the 'coalition of the weak' who clamour for her return against his father's obstinacy.

In relation to his pretty sister, Aisha, Kamal is practically love-stricken, so much so that when a suitor comes to take her away he is not only broken-hearted but sees the suitor as a hostile rival for his sister's affections. Kamal's attentive sister becomes unavailable to him when the suitor appears, and in his devastation when she leaves the house in marriage, his affection for her is tinged with protectiveness and sexual jealousy. Suad Joseph, in an ethnography based on Lebanon, makes a strong argument for the centrality of brother/sister relationships in defining a sense of gender. She suggests that Arab brothers and sisters are caught up in relationships of love and nurturance on the one hand, and power and violence on the other, in a manner that reproduces Arab patriarchy (forthcoming).

Mahfouz's novel not only describes the complexities of the boy's experience of the world of women but offers many other insights concerning his relations with adult men. The child's male role models are presented in a multilayered collage, in which some are accessible and benign, while others are forbidding and remote. His older brothers, one studious and idealistic, the other dissolute, offer contrasting versions of adult masculinity, as do his authoritarian father and his sister's mysterious suitor. Moreover, the young boy is befriended by an English soldier billeted next to his house. The child is full of pride in his secret adult friend, who impresses him with his size and his gun. He is deeply wounded when his secret loyalty is exposed as culpable by his older brother's harsh criticism of the British. In short, Mahfouz weaves an exquisitely intricate picture in which to situate the male child's subjectivity.

CONSTRUCTIONS OF MASCULINITY IN MALE/FEMALE INTERACTIONS

The subtlety of the novel refers to something which could also be documented ethnographically, although this is not attempted very frequently. My own observations, based on a village in southwest Anatolia, reveal a range of gendered relations which I suspect to be quite widespread in the rest of Turkey and beyond. In this coastal village, men were away a great deal of the time fishing, sponge-diving or running excursion boats, while the women were busy weaving carpets at home. In one such household, I well remember an 8-year-old lad who, when the sole male in the house with his mother and three older sisters, would appear at the table and shout, 'Is there no one here to bring tea to a man?'. And though his sisters were highly amused by his arrogance and display of machismo, this did not prevent them from playing along and bringing him his breakfast. Even though they may tease him affectionately, it is not unusual for adult women to celebrate a young boy's physical masculinity and to humour him by spoiling him and acceding to his demands. As long as the boy was alone with his mother and sisters, he could play at being the uncontested master of the house. However, when his older brother and father returned, the situation changed drastically. He was pushed around and given menial tasks to do, and all his posturing disappeared. If it had not, he could have expected a thrashing from his father. In short, he was still part of the female domain and of very low status. He was neither yet old enough to take part in the masculine world defined by the work of his father or brother, nor, when they were present, would he dare to show any disrespect to his older sisters, whose privileges due to their seniority would be upheld by the father. The young boy knew his place and he also knew that he had a very small space in which to act out an assertive version of masculinity. While the world of women reaffirms certain attributes of maleness and, at times at least, the young boy can bask in the comfort of being the male child, this comfort and certainty are shattered when he is with adult men. *Vis-à-vis* older males, the little boy is charming, placatory and obedient; in many ways, his behaviour replicates that expected of women in the face of adult male authority. Moreover, there may be an undercurrent of violence in masculinities which emerge in relations between men. Themes of dominance and subordination are much in evidence not only in intergenerational interactions, but also in interactions among peers. In what follows, I shall attempt to examine some sources of the violence, and at times nurturance and altruism, that are enacted between men.

HOSTILITY AND NURTURANCE IN MALE RELATIONSHIPS

Although male violence is by no means specific to any one context, the types of rage enacted in some relations between men in Turkey deserve comment. In everyday interactions, it takes the form of 'being on a very short fuse', so that the slightest disrespect or provocation may result in what appear to be disproportionate consequences. A strong connection exists between class extraction and expressions of aggressive masculinity, with more restrained and verbal styles among the upper classes and more abandoned and physical ones among the popular classes. It is worth exploring whether one variant of this violence may be traced to men who re-create their own early passivity, by forcing others to take the one-down position. This replay of earlier weakness may, by imposing it on others, help men both to relieve and exorcise those experiences. Whatever the character of early childhood weakness in relationships, the situation is likely to reproduce itself through contact with a series of hierarchical, all-male institutions, the most inevitable and ubiquitous being the army, of which the entire male population will have had first-hand experience. As conscripts, all men will have known the experience of utter helplessness in the face of total, arbitrary authority, where each man will have been controlled by the whims of another man and where, in the absence of compliance, public humiliation and physical punishment may follow. This is an area which has not even begun to be explored and which, despite its importance, will be extremely difficult to research. Although men frequently relate and recall their experiences of military service, what appears to be on offer is more often than not an expurgated and idealized retrospective, sometimes performing a thinly disguised reparatory function.

On one of the rare occasions when I was a witness to such a group discussion among men in a village in central Anatolia, there was a striking absence of reports of negative personal experiences. One villager described in graphic detail the brutality of one of his officers whose actions bordered on the sadistic. When asked whether or not he had himself been subjected to harsh treatment, he smiled coyly and said '*Hayir, biz kendimizi sevdirdik*' ('No, we made ourselves liked'). This is not an unusual response. Indulgence from superiors may be earned through diligently making oneself useful, performing a special craft acquired in civilian life, or demonstrating resourcefulness and wit by running special errands, but most of all by maintaining a consistently deferential posture – the placatory and disarming stance of the boy. Although the institution of authority and control in the army must build upon earlier childhood experience, it may also act as a template to reproduce these experiences in the following generations.

There is, unfortunately, very scant research evidence about the nature of intergenerational relations between men. However, a recent study of Istanbul households (Bolak 1990) based on intensive interviews with women breadwinners and their husbands (many of whom were unemployed or intermittently employed) offers, among other things, important clues concerning men's and women's differing orientations to parenting. The primary aim of the study was to illustrate the complexities in the relationship between male breadwinner status, male occupational instability and gender relations at the household level. The situation of women whose income is indispensable to their household's livelihood represents a culturally non-sanctioned form of sexual division of labour, and provides a vantage point for studying the mechanisms for coping with possible disjunctions between the ideology of the male breadwinner and the realities of economic survival. The ways in which men who find themselves marginalized as providers mitigate threats to their masculine identity also offer important insights into gender.

The men interviewed typically expressed their experiences with their fathers in an unfavourable light. Although they stated that they hoped to be better parents themselves, there were signs that the unresolved ambivalence in the father–son relationship was often recapitulated in their own parenting relationship. Some of this ambivalence came out in relation to budget control and spending priorities, with men objecting to purchases their wives made for their children which they considered fancy and superfluous – like better clothes, books and encyclopedias or extra tutoring in some school subjects. Some men explicitly resented sons whom they saw as recipients of luxuries and favours they themselves never had, like the father who objected to the purchase of a pair of sports shoes, saying, 'nobody got *me* shoes like that'. Quibbling over purchases and commodities may be a surface manifestation of the husband's competition with the children over the mother's nurturance, with sons appearing to steal the love and attention they themselves crave. In addition, since many men in the research sample lacked effective control of the household budget they could not, in fact, fully influence their wives' spending priorities.

On the other hand, their preoccupation with proving their masculinity compelled men to try and maintain their community status by holding on to symbolic gestures of manliness, such as entertaining friends lavishly and an inability to reject unwelcome requests for loans. Many wives ended up blaming their husbands for being 'too generous' and diverting precious resources away from the household and especially children's needs. One respondent offered the following account of his motivation for generosity:

> I've been crushed as a kid. I couldn't live my childhood. If a beggar comes to the door, I'd give him 100 liras instead of 10. If a friend of mine needs help, I give him 2,000 liras instead of 500 liras, if I have it. This causes a problem. She [my wife] considers me to be too generous.

The same man, however, rejected his wife's request to take their sons to school in his truck when it snowed, saying, 'My father never took me to school. They should learn to rough it on their own.'

This study also reveals a connection between men's domestic alienation and their tendency to seek confirmation and male companionship outside the home. Thus, male largess outside the household mandates female thrift and good judgement within the home. In some instances this may trigger a vicious circle, whereby women's accusations of irresponsibility further fuel men's desire to establish their masculine credentials with other men through profligate spending, entertaining friends and taking risks at cards. Loizos points to the contrast in Greece between the 'domesticated' masculinity of the responsible householder and that of the 'free-spirited' men whose domain is the coffee-shop (Chapter 3 in this volume). In this Istanbul sample the free, unfettered masculinity enacted in the coffee-shop may have a compensatory value for those who, due to economic circumstances, fall short in the fulfilment of their breadwinner roles.

It must, however, be recognized that so-called status-gaining activities among men certainly also entail forms of male nurturance and altruism which deserve attention in their own right. The solace men may receive from their peers and the nature of their interactions have been little explored in the literature on the Middle East. Yet, especially where the segregation of the sexes is particularly evident, the spectacle of male groups of varying ages and sizes strolling together, sitting at coffee-shop tables and shop fronts or eating and drinking together is one of the most striking and visible features of urban space. Single-sex groups (both male and female) engage in a great deal of expressive behaviour, such as dancing and singing and indulging in physical displays of affection, including hugging and putting arms around shoulders, without being labelled as homosexuals. Expectations of nurturance from male peers may mandate enormous tolerance of all kinds of minor infraction and misbehaviour which involve letting one's guard down, such as getting drunk and maudlin, making a fool of oneself and being carried home by one's mates. In theory, and often in practice, this camaraderie has no strings attached: a great deal of delicacy is involved when men handle other men's displays of vulnerability.

There is much evidence, however, that the function and character of male peer groups change throughout the life cycle, providing distinct arenas for the enactment of different forms of masculinity. In the central Anatolian village referred to earlier, there were three recognized age sets for adult men, corresponding to changes in their social roles, in contrast to the twofold distinction for women between *kiz* (unmarried girl) and *kadin* (married woman). The children were called *bala* (child) irrespective of their gender. *Delikanli* (literally meaning 'those with crazy blood') referred to adolescents and young unmarried men, who enacted a version of masculinity valorizing the untamed and undomesticated. In fact, a certain amount of deviant behaviour was accepted as an inevitable concomitant of this stage. Causing disruptions at weddings, tractor chases, pranks and minor theft produced reactions ranging from amusement to annoyance, but never incurred serious consequences. This stage came to a close with military service, which was closely followed by marriage. The group of adult married men, referred to as *akay* (men), ranged in age from their twenties to their mid-forties and constituted the active group in the village, economically and politically. They were members of the Council of Elders and were clearly in charge of many other village activities. Finally, the *kart akay* (old men) were men whose married sons were mature enough to take over the day-to-day farming, and who could lead more leisured lives. Old men were explicitly expected to show a marked increase in religiosity and often congregated in and around the mosque.

It would be quite inappropriate, however, to elevate any one version of masculinity into some sort of cultural ideal or norm, especially in view of the considerable latitude which exists for actors within each of the three categories before they risk being labelled as deviant. Male homosexuality, on the other hand, always carries that risk and presents interesting puzzles for the management of masculine identities.

THE AMBIGUITIES OF GENDER AND MALE HOMOEROTIC DESIRE

Although existing sources make it very difficult even to piece together a tentative history of sexualities in Ottoman and contemporary Turkey, the work of Resad Ekrem Koçu (1905–75) constitutes a very rich source of material on homosocial and homosexual masculinities. Koçu was a historian and folklorist who, after losing his university post in 1933, devoted his life to popularizing historical writing by contributing to newspapers, writing historical novels and more generally chronicling the life of Istanbul (Eyice 1976). Among these works, his history of the Istanbul Fire Brigade (*Yangin Var! Istanbul Tulumbacilari*, 1981) documents the lore, modes of dress, relationships and types of entertainment of the firemen in what amounts to a tantalizing account of a homosexual subculture in turn-of-the-century Istanbul.

The city was then dominated by delicate wooden buildings and very susceptible to fire. After the abolition of the Janissaries, each neighbourhood had its own brigade of sturdy young men who worked as a team. Running swiftly with bare feet, they carried a huge water container on their backs. These young men were often orphans or youths from impoverished backgrounds for whom the brigade dormitories were a haven in the urban environment, although some joined because they were attracted by this lifestyle. Their colourful nicknames reflect their diverse regional and ethnic origins: Ali the Laz, Hristos the Boatman, Emin the Gypsy, Husnu the Black, Artin the Girl and even English Hidayet (alias Charles Morgan!). The individual biographies of these firemen reveal that they were the object of homoerotic desire expressed in love poetry or verse narratives recounting their lives and prowess. This poetry simultaneously celebrates their 'feminine' beauty (sleek cheeks, thick eyelashes, curly fringe, slender waist and flirtatious manners) and their allure as swift-footed, strong, muscular and above all virile young men. These images defy any active/passive or masculine/feminine stereotypes: For example:

One beauty among a thousand youths
From the Davutpasha Quay
That godless boatman
Has the eyes of a doe
See the imposing beauty
When on his face appears a frown
Braves who fall in love
Such a brave youth must love.

(Koçu 1981: 71)

The youths are portrayed as the objects of desire and competition among older men (both officers in the fire brigade and outsiders whom they met in taverns and coffee-houses), among other youths (who were their peers within the brigade), and among women of the neighbourhood who try to entice them into becoming their lovers. These women are depicted as sexually active and as using their material affluence to send out household slaves and eunuchs to procure a youth by paying for his sexual services. One such lady, piqued by a young fireman who jokingly demanded a golden watch and a diamond ring, reported him to the police for molestation; he received forty lashes on his bare feet. The poet, clearly enamoured of the young man, curses the police commander by saying:

How dare you beat the prince's feet
That are worthy of my kisses.

(Koçu 1981: 363)

At one level, the youths are presented as studs. Yet for older men (the perspective from which Koçu is writing), they are also irresistible for their feminized beauty and berated for their fickleness and cruelty. It is above all youth and beauty that are the object of desire, and the loved one is depicted as elusive and all-powerful. Yet, sociologically, the young men's power is a myth: they were often dependent on a powerful male patron for their livelihood and vulnerable to abuse of all kinds. Some biographies suggest that they often ended their days in abject poverty, in prison, or as victims of crimes of passion.[6] However, there is also ample evidence that for many, homosexuality did not constitute an exclusive life-style, since they went on to marry and have families, sometimes with the blessing and support of their former patrons. What is remarkable here is the extremely complex ways in which these men were eroticized. As youth they combine a whole range of masculinities and femininities – the smooth features and slenderness of adolescence mingled with the vigour and energy of their manliness – that were evoked and selectively mobilized in their portrayal as objects of desire, rendering equally ambiguous the gendering of the desirer.

CONCLUSION

I am acutely aware, as I conclude this chapter, of having exposed the reader to a bewildering array of historical periods and social contexts. This was not, however, meant to be a purely descriptive exercise documenting the temporal, situational and relational relativity of masculine identities, although such an exercise could be justified as an exploratory device. I was also intending to make a strong case for situating masculinities – however fragmented and variegated they may appear – in historically and culturally specific institutional contexts which delimit and to some extent constrain the range of discourses and choices available to social actors. These institutional contexts are the site of material practices which inform and shape gendered subjectivity and yet are subject to constant change and transformation. My very choice of some institutionalized features of the segregation of the sexes as a backdrop for a discussion of masculine identities is an anachronism, especially in Turkey. Generations are growing up who have never known polygyny, actual or potential, and most men who still remember the women's *hammam* will soon pass away. The particular relations of domination, resistance and negotiation inscribed in these settings will also have been transformed, and with them both personal and cultural constructions of what it means to be a man or a woman. I had reasons of my own for wanting to probe into the mental worlds of men of a particular generation; I learned in the process that behind the enduring facade of male privilege lie profound ambiguities which may give rise to both defensive masculinist discourse and a genuine desire for contestation and change.

NOTES

I would like to thank Peter Loizos for his thoughtful and detailed comments on an earlier version of this chapter. To Nancy Lindisfarne and Andrea Cornwall go my warmest thanks for giving me the confidence to explore a *terra incognita* on which much further work needs to be done. Without their encouragement and very hard work this project would not have seen the light of day, although all omissions and errors of judgement are, of course, my own.

1 I was aware of, but dissatisfied with, psychoanalytic accounts, such as the one by Ashis Nandy explaining Indian reformer Rahhamoun Roy's activism against *sati* as a massive (and public) reparation for his ambivalence towards his own mother, overlaid by a broader cultural ambivalence towards women (Nandy 1980).
2 Colonialism was undoubtedly about more than struggles over contending definitions of masculinity, but it is a testimony to the resilience of such imagery that it has also permeated inter-communal conflicts in the post-colonial period in India. Indeed, the Hindu revivalist and fascistic Rashtriya Swayamsewak Sangh (RSS) still plays upon images of emasculated Hindu malehood in contrast to virile and bloodthirsty Muslims and calls for a regeneration of Hindu masculinity (Chhachhi 1991).
3 It is no accident that the modernization of Ottoman society was primarily talked about in terms of a 'crisis' in the Ottoman family (see Duben and Behar 1991). That this modernization also implied changes in masculinity and femininity receives less explicit recognition in the literature.
4 To the extent that Lacanians posit the timeless universality of the Law of the Father (and the Oedipal break) as the major structuring principle of the human unconscious, they come close to an invariant concept of human nature and invite charges of essentialism. Object-relations theorists, who implicitly concede that different organizations of the family and society may yield different patternings of the psyche, display a crippling fear of falling into 'sociologism' and compromising the irreducibility of psychic events. As a result, their ability to integrate the social seldom goes beyond a potentiality.
5 The surprising similarities emerging out of analyses as diverse as those of Obeyeskere on Sri Lanka (1981, 1984) and Nandy on India (1980) are striking.
6 A collection of prison poems (*Zindan Siirleri*) attributed by Koçu to a former fireman, Nusret the Georgian, serving time for the murder of his lover Ismail, depicts a homosexual prison subculture where men sought solace in hashish and sexual intrigue. It seems clear that some elements among the firemen merged into a semi-legal urban fringe.

References

Acosta, A. (n.d.) 'Quem lucra com esta operação?, *Lampião de Esquina*, São Paulo: no publisher.

Acosta Patiño, R. (1979) *Criminología de la Prostitución: Realidad Actual*, Madrid: no publisher.

Ahmed, L. (1992) *Women and Gender in Islam*, New Haven, Conn.: Yale University Press.

Almeida, S.J.A. (1984) *'Míches'*, unpublished MA thesis, São Paulo: University of Campinas.

Altman, D. (1980) 'What has changed in the 70s?', in Gay Left Collective (ed.), *Homosexuality: Power and Politics*, London: Allison & Busby.

—— (1982) *The Homosexualization of America*, Boston: Beacon Press.

—— (1989) *Homosexuality, Which Homosexuality? Essays from the International Scientific Conference on Lesbian and Gay Studies*, London: Gay Men's Press.

Archetti, Eduardo P. (1991) 'Argentinian tango: male sexual ideology and morality', in R. Gronhaug (ed.), *The Ecology of Choice and Symbol. Essays in Honour of Fredrik Barth*, Bergen: Alma Mater.

—— (1992) 'Argentinian football: a ritual of violence?', *The International Journal of the History of Sport*, 9, 2: 209–35.

Ardener, Edwin (1989) 'Comprehending others', in E. Ardéner (ed.), *The Voice of Prophecy*, Oxford: Basil Blackwell.

Ardener, Shirley (1975) 'Introduction', in S. Ardener (ed.), *Perceiving Women*, London: J.M.Dent and Sons.

Asad, Talal (ed.) (1975) *Anthropology and the Colonial Encounter*, London: Ithaca Press.

Ash, Jennifer (1990) 'The discursive construction of Christ's body in the later Middle Ages: resistance and autonomy', in Threadgold and Cranny-Francis (1990).

Bacelar, Jeferson Afonso (1982) *A Família da Prostituta*, São Paulo: Editores Atica.

Back, L. (1990) *Racist Name Calling and Developing Anti-Racist Strategies in Youth Work*, Centre for Research in Ethnic Relations Research Papers 14, University of Warwick.

—— (1991a) 'Social context and racist name calling: an ethnographic perspective on racist talk within a south London adolescent community', *European Journal of Intercultural Studies*, 1, 3: 19–39.

—— (1991b) 'Youth, racism and ethnicity in south London: an ethnographic study of adolescent inter-ethnic relations', unpublished Ph.D. thesis, Goldsmith's College, University of London.

—— (1992) 'Gendered participation: masculinity and fieldwork in a south London community', in Pat Caplan, Diane Bell and Wazir Jahan Karim (eds), *Gendered Fields*, London: Routledge.

—— (1993) 'Youth, race and nation within a predominantly white working-class neighbourhood in south London', *New Community*, 217–33.

Bakhtin, Mikhail (1986) *Speech Genres and Other Late Essays*, Austin: University of Texas Press.

Barber, Karin (1991) *I Could Speak Until Tomorrow: Oriki, Women and the Past in a Yoruba Town*, Manchester: International African Institute.

Barker, Paul (1992) 'Will you join us, ladies?', *The Times* (Life and Times), 6 August: 1.

Barrett, M. and McIntosh, M. (1985) 'Ethnocentrism and socialist-feminist theory', *Feminist Review*, 23: 215–35.

Bastide, R. (1978) *The African Religions of Brazil: Towards a Sociology of the Interpretation of Civilisations*, Baltimore and London: Johns Hopkins University Press.

Baudrillard, Jean (1990) *Seduction*, London: Macmillan.

Behar, C. (1991) 'Polygyny in Istanbul, 1885–1926', *Middle Eastern Studies*, 27, 3: 477–86.

Bennett, Catherine (1993) 'Ordinary madness', *Guardian*, 20 January: 2–3.

Beopoulou, J. (1987) 'Trajets du patrimonie dans une societe maritime Grecque: lieux masculins and feminins dans l'acquisition et la circulation des biens', in *Femmes et Patrimonie dans les Sociétés Rurales de l'Europe Méditerranéenne*, Marseilles: CNRS.

Bernard, H.R. (1976) 'Kalymnos: the island of sponge fishermen', in M. Dimen and E. Friedl (eds), *Regional Variation in Modern Greece and Cyprus: Towards a Perspective on the Ethnography of Greece*, New York: Annals of the New York Academy of Science.

Beteille, André (1990) 'Race, caste and gender', *Man*, 25, 3: 487–504.

Bevan, Tom (1910) '"All-white" John: a story of New Guinea', *Empire Annual for Boys*, 15–29.

Bhabha, H.K. (1990) 'Interrogating identity: the postcolonial prerogative', in D.T. Goldberg (ed.), *Anatomy of Racism*, Minneapolis: University of Minnesota Press.

Biber, Douglas and Finegan, Edward (1989) 'Styles of stance in English: lexical and grammatical marking of evidentiality and affect', *Text*, 9, 1: 93–124 (special issue on 'The pragmatics of affect', ed. Elinor Ochs).

Birman, Patricia (1985) 'Identidade social e homossexualidade no Candomblé', *Religião e Sociedade*, 12, 1: 2–21.

Blanchford, G. (1981) 'Male dominance and the gay world', in Plummer (1981).

Bloch, M. and Parry, J. (eds) (1982) *Death and the Regeneration of Life*, Cambridge: Cambridge University Press.

Blok, A. (1981), 'Rams and billy-goats: a key to the Mediterranean code of honour', *Man*, 16, 3: 427–40.

Bly, Robert (1991) *Iron John: A Book About Men*, London: Element Books.

Boddy, J. (1982) 'Womb as oasis: the symbolic context of pharaonic circumcision in rural northern Sudan', *American Ethologist*, 9, 4: 682–98.

—— (1989) *Wombs and Alien Spirits*, Madison: Wisconsin University Press.

Bolak, H. (1990) 'Women breadwinners and the construction of gender : a study of urban working class households in Turkey', unpublished Ph.D. dissertation, University of California, Santa Cruz.

Boston Women's Health Book Collective (1984) *The New Our Bodies, Ourselves*, New York: Simon and Schuster.

Boudhiba, A. (1985) *Sexuality in Islam*, London: Routledge and Kegan Paul.

Boulay, Juliet du (1974) *Portrait of a Greek Mountain Village*, Oxford: Clarendon Press.

Bourdieu, Pierre (1977) *Outline of a Theory of Practice*, Cambridge: Cambridge University Press.

Bowen-Jones, Carys (1992) 'Men as sex objects', *Marie Claire*, 50: 22–6.
Bowman, G. (1989) 'Fucking tourists: sexual relations and tourism in Jerusalem's Old City', *Critique of Anthropology*, 9, 2: 77–93.
Bradley, Harriet (1989) *Men's Work, Women's Work: A Sociological History of the Sexual Division of Labour in Employment*, Minneapolis: University of Minnesota Press.
Braidotti, R. (1990) 'The problematic of "the feminine" in contemporary French philosophy: Foucault and Irigaray', in Threadgold and Cranny-Francis (1990).
—— (1992) 'On the female feminist subject, or: from "She self" to "she-other"', in G. Bock and S. James (eds), *Beyond Equality and Difference*, London: Routledge.
Brandes, S. (1980) *Metaphors of Masculinity: Sex and Status in Andalusian Folklore*, Philadelphia: University of Pennsylvania Press.
—— (1981) 'Like wounded stags: male sexual ideology in an Andalusian town', in Ortner and Whitehead (1981).
—— (1992) 'Sex roles and anthropological research in rural Andalusia', in J. de Piña-Cabral and J. Campbell (eds), *Europe Observed*, London: Macmillan.
Bristow, J. (1989) 'Homophobia/misogyny: sexual fears, sexual definitions', in Shepherd and Wallis (1989).
Bristow, Joseph (1991) *Empire Boys: Adventures in a Man's World*, London: HarperCollins Academic.
Brittan, Arthur (1989) *Masculinity and Power*, Oxford: Blackwell.
Brod, Harry (1987) *The Making of Masculinities: New Men's Studies*, Winchester, Mass.: Allen and Unwin.
—— (1990) 'Pornography and the alienation of male sexuality', in J. Hearn and D. Morgan (1990a).
Brownmiller, Susan (1975) *Against Our Will*, Harmondsworth: Penguin.
—— (1984) *Femininity*, London: Paladin/New York: Fawcett Columbine.
Buchan, John (1910) *Prester John*, London: T. Nelson & Sons.
Bürger, Peter (1990) 'Aporias of modern aesthetics', *New Left Review*, 184: 47–56.
Butler, Judith (1990) *Gender Trouble: Feminism and the Subversion of Identity*, New York: Routledge.
Campbell, J.K. (1964) *Honour, Family and Patronage: A Study of Institutions and Moral Values in a Greek Mountain Community*, Oxford: Clarendon Press.
Canaan, J. and Griffin, C. (1990) 'The new men's studies: part of the problem or part of the solution?', in Hearn and Morgan (1990a).
Cañas, J.M. (1974) *Prostitución y Sociedad*, Barcelona: Producciones Editoriales.
Cantarella, E. (1991) 'Moicheia: reconsidering a problem', in M. Gagarin (ed.), *Symposion 1990: Papers on Greek and Hellenistic Legal History*, Cologne: Böhlau.
Capel Martínez, R.M. (1986) 'La prostitución en España: notas para un estudio socio-histórico', in Rosa María Capel Martínez (ed.), *Mujer y Sociedad en España (1700–1975)*, Madrid: Instituto de la Mujer.
Caplan, Pat (ed.) (1987a) *The Cultural Construction of Sexuality*, London: Tavistock.
—— (1987b) 'Celibacy as a Solution?', in Caplan (1987a).
Carby, H. (1982) 'White woman listen! Black feminism and the boundaries of sisterhood', in Centre for Contemporary Cultural Studies, *The Empire Strikes Back*, London: Hutchinson.
Cardonega, A. (1942) *História General das Guerras Angolanas*, Lisbon: AGC.
Carpenter, Edward (1919) *Intermediate Types among Primitive Folk*, London: George Allen and Unwin.
Carrigan, Tim, Connell, Bob and Lee, John (1985) 'Towards a new sociology of masculinity', *Theory and Society*, 14, 5: 551–603 in Brod (1987).
Carter, A. (1991) *Wise Children*, London: Vintage.

Cass, V. (1983–4) 'Homosexual identity: a concept in need of definitions', *Journal of Homosexuality*, 9: 2–3.

Chafe, Wallace and Tannen, Deborah (1987) 'The relationship between spoken and written language', *Annual Review of Anthropology*, 16: 383–407.

Chambers' Dictionary (1986).

Chambers, I. (1976) '"A strategy for living": black music and white subcultures', in S. Hall and T. Jefferson (eds), *Resistance Through Rituals*, London: Hutchinson.

Chapman, R. and Rutherford, J.(eds) (1988) *Male Order: Unwrapping Masculinity*, London: Lawrence and Wishart.

Chhachhi, A. (1991) 'Forced identities: the state, communalism, fundamentalism and women in India', in Kandiyoti (1991).

Chimhundu, Herbert (1992) 'Early missionaries and the ethnolinguistic factor during the "invention of tribalism" in Zimbabwe', *Journal of African History*, 33: 87–109.

Chodorow, N. (1974) 'Family structure and feminine personality', in Rosaldo and Lamphere (1974).

—— (1978) *The Reproduction of Mothering: Psychoanalysis and the Sociology of Gender*, London: University of California Press.

Clary, Julian (1992) *How to be a Real Man*, London: Virgin.

Clements, L. (1993) 'Visibility, power and resistance: shifting lesbian identities in contemporary Britain', unpublished extended essay, School of Oriental and African Studies, London.

Clifford, J. and Marcus, G. (eds) (1986) *Writing Culture*, Berkeley: University of California Press.

Clogg, R. (1972) 'The ideology of the "Revolution of 21 April 1967" ', in R. Clogg and G. Yannopoulos (eds), *Greece Under Military Rule*, London: Secker & Warburg.

Cohen, D. (1991) *Law, Sexuality and Society*, Cambridge: Cambridge University Press.

Cohen, P. (1972) *Subcultural Conflict and Working Class Community*, Working Papers in Cultural Studies 2, University of Birmingham.

—— (1988) 'The perversions of inheritance', in P. Cohen and H. Bains, *Multi-Racist Britain*, London: Macmillan Education.

Cole, J. (1981) 'Feminism, class and Islam in turn-of-the-century Egypt', *International Journal of Middle East Studies*, 13: 387–407.

Cole, S.G. (1984) 'Greek sanctions against sexual assault', *Classical Philology*, 79: 97–113.

Collier, J.F. and Rosaldo, M.Z. (1981) 'Politics and gender in simple societies', in Ortner and Whitehead (1981).

Collier, J.F. and Yanagisako, S.J. (eds) (1987) 'Introduction', in their *Gender and Kinship: Essays Towards a Unified Analysis*, Stanford: Stanford University Press.

Comaroff, J.L. (1987–8) 'On totemism and ethnicity', *Ethnos*, 52–3: 301–23.

Combs-Schilling, M. (1989) *Sacred Performances: Islam, Sexuality and Sacrifice*, New York: Columbia University Press.

Connell, R.W. (1987) *Gender and Power: Society, The Person and Sexual Politics*, Stanford: Stanford University Press/Oxford: Polity Press.

Corbin, J. and Corbin, M.P. (1987) *Urbane Thought: Culture and Class in an Andalusian City*, Aldershot: Gower.

Correio da Bahia (1980) 'Prostituição (II): os travestis saõ os novos donos da noite: com amor e siticone', 12 August.

Costa Lima, Vivaldo da (1977) 'A família de santo nos Candomblés Jeje-Nàgôs da Bahia: um Estudo de relaçoes intra grupois', unpublished masters thesis, Universidade Federal da Bahia.

—— (1990) *A Comida O Comer*, unpublished paper presented at the Federal University of Bahia.

Danvers-Dawson, H. (1917) 'Who are the Gurkhas?', *Empire Annual for Boys*, 119–21.

Darmesteter, J. (1888–90) *Chants Populaires des Afghans*, Paris: Ernest Leroux.

Davis, B. (1982) *Life in the Classroom and Playground*, London: Routledge and Kegan Paul.

Davis, J. (1969) 'Honour and politics in Pisticci', *Proceedings of the Royal Anthropological Institute*, 69–81.

Davis, K., Leijenaar, M. and Oldersma, J. (1991) *The Gender of Power*, London: Sage.

Delaney, C. (1986) 'The meaning of paternity and the virgin birth debate', *Man*, 21, 3: 494–513.

—— (1991) *The Seed and the Soil*, Berkeley: University of California Press.

deLauretis, Teresa (ed.) (1986) 'Feminist studies/critical studies: issues, terms and contexts', in her *Feminist Studies/Critical Studies*, Bloomington: Indiana University Press.

Denneny, M. (1983) 'Gay politics: sixteen propositions', in M. Denneny (ed.), *The Christopher Street Reader*, New York: Coward-McCann.

Devereux, G. (1937) 'Institutionalised homosexuality of the Mohave Indians', *General Biology*, 9: 498–527.

Devor, Holly (1989) *Gender Blending: Confronting the Limits of Duality*, Bloomington: Indiana University Press.

di Stefano, C. (1990) 'Dilemmas of difference: feminism, modernity and postmodernism', in L. Nicholson (1990).

Doke, Clement M. (1931a) *Report on the Unification of Shona Dialects*, Hertford.

—— (1931b) *A Comparative Study of Shona Phonetics*, Johannesburg: University of Witwatersrand Press.

Dorsky, S. (1986) *Women of 'Amran*, Salt Lake City: Utah University Press.

Draper Miralles, R. (1982) *Guía de la Prostitución Feminina en Barcelona*, Barcelona: Ediciones Martínez Roca.

Driessen, H. (1983) 'Male sociability and rituals of masculinity in rural Andalusia', in *Anthropological Quarterly*, 56: 125–33.

Dubbert, J.L. (1979) *A Man's Place: Masculinity in Transition*, Englewood Cliffs, N.J.: Prentice-Hall.

Duben, A. and Behar, C. (1991) *Istanbul Households: Marriage, Family and Fertility*, Cambridge: Cambridge University Press.

Dubisch, J. (1976) 'The ethnography of the islands: Tinos', in M. Dimen and E. Friedl (eds), *Regional Variation in Modern Greece and Cyprus: Towards a Perspective on the Ethnography of Greece*, New York: Annals of the New York Academy of Science.

—— (ed.) (1986) *Gender and Power in Rural Greece*, Princeton, N.J.: Princeton University Press.

Dworkin, Andrea (1981) *Pornography: Men Possessing Women*, London: Women's Press.

Eagleton, T. (1991) *Ideology: An Introduction*, London: Verso.

Easthope, Antony (1986) *What a Man's Gotta Do: The Masculine Myth in Popular Culture*, London: Paladin.

Eckert, Penelope and McConnell-Ginet, Sally (1992) 'Think practically and look locally: language and gender as community-based practice', *Annual Review of Anthropology*, 21: 461–90.

Edholm, F., Harris, O. and Young, K. (1977) 'Conceptualising women', *Critique of Anthropology*, 3, 9/10: 101–30.

Eickelman, D. (1989) *The Middle East: An Anthropological Approach*, Englewood Cliffs, N.J.: Prentice-Hall.

Elson, Diane and Pearson, Ruth (1981) 'Nimble fingers make cheap workers: an analysis of women's employment in the Third World Export Manufacturing', *Feminist Review*, 7: 87 107.

Epstein, Julia and Straub, Kristina (eds) (1991) *Body Guards: The Cultural Politics of Gender Ambiguity*, New York: Routledge.

Espiñeira, Gey (1984) *Divergência e Prostituiçao*, Rio: Tempo Brasileira.

Etienne, M. and Leacock, E. (eds) (1980) *Women and Colonization*, New York: Praeger.

Eyice, S. (1976) 'Tarihci ve Folklorist Reşat Ekhem Koçu', *Türk Folklor Arastirmalari*, no. 322, 7641–4643.

Falcón, L. (1967) 'Publicidad para la profesión que no tiene nombre', *Cromosoma X*, 10: 53–8.

Faludi, Susan (1992) *Backlash: The Undeclared War Against Women*, London: Chatto.

Fanon, F. (1967) *Black Skin, White Masks*, London: Grove Press.

Fardon, Richard (ed.) (1985a) *Power and Knowledge*, Edinburgh: Scottish Academic Press.

—— (1985b) 'Introduction: a sense of relevance', in Fardon (1985a).

—— (1990) 'Malinowski's precedent: the imagination of equality', *Man*, 25, 4: 596–87.

Feminist Review (1984) 'Many voices, one chant: black feminist perspectives', 17: special issue.

Fernbach, D. (1981) *The Spiral Path*, London: Gay Men's Press.

Fichte, Hubert (1985) *Lazarus und die Waschmaschine*, Frankfurt: Fischer Verlag.

Foucault, Michel (1977) *Discipline and Punish*, Harmondsworth: Allen Lane.

—— (1978–86) *The History of Sexuality*, 3 vols, Harmondsworth: Penguin.

—— (1981) 'The order of discourse', in R. Young (ed.), *Untying the Text*, London: Routledge and Kegan Paul.

—— (1984) in Paul Rabinow (ed.), *The Foucault Reader*, Harmondsworth: Penguin.

Foxhall, L. (1989) 'Household, gender and property in classical Athens', *Classical Quarterly*, 39: 22–44.

—— (1991) 'Response to Eva Cantarella', in M. Gagarin (ed.), *Symposion 1990: Papers on Greek and Hellenistic Legal History*, Cologne: Böhlau.

—— (forthcoming a) 'The law and the lady: women and legal proceedings in classical Athens', in L. Foxhall and A. Lewis (eds), *The Contexts of Law in Ancient Greece*, Oxford: Oxford University Press.

—— (forthcoming b) 'Monumental ambitions: the significance of posterity in ancient Greece', in N. Spencer (ed.), *New Directions in Classical Archaeology*, London: Routledge.

Fraser, N. and Nicholson, L. (1988) 'Social criticism without philosophy: an encounter between feminism and postmodernism', *Theory, Culture and Society*, 5: 373–94.

Friedman, S. and Sarah, E. (1982) *On the Problem of Men*, London: Women's Press.

Friedl, E. (1962) *Vasilika: A Village in Modern Greece*, New York: Holt, Rinehart and Winston.

Fry, Peter (1977) 'Mediunidade e sexualidade', *Religião e Sociedade*, 1, 1: 105–23.

—— (1982) *Para Inglês Ver*, Rio: Zahar Editores.

Garber, Marjorie (1991) *Vested Interests*, New York: Routledge.

Garfinkel, Harold (1967) *Studies in Ethnomethodology*, Englewood Cliffs, N.J.: Prentice-Hall.

Gatens, Moira (1983) 'A critique of the sex/gender distinction', in J. Allen and P. Patton (eds), *Beyond Marx? Interventions After Marx*, Sydney: Intervention.

Geertz, C. (1983) *Local Knowledge*, New York: Basic Books.

Ghalem, A. (1984) *A Wife for my Son*, London: Zed Books.

Gilbert, Sandra M. (1983) 'Soldier's heart: literary men, literary women, and the Great War', *Signs* 8: 422–50.

Gilmore, D. (ed.) (1987a) 'Introduction: the shame of dishonour', in D. Gilmore (ed.), *Honour and Shame and the Unity of the Mediterranean*, Washington: American Anthropological Association.

—— (1987b) *Aggression and Community: Paradoxes of Andalusian Culture*, New Haven and London: Yale University Press.

—— (1990) *Manhood in the Making: Cultural Concepts of Masculinity*, New Haven and London: Yale University Press.

Gilmore, M. and Gilmore, D. (1979) ' "Machismo": a psychodynamic approach (Spain)', *Journal of Psychological Anthropology*, 2: 281–300.

Gilroy, P. and Lawrence, E. (1988) 'Two tone Britain: white and black youth and the politics of anti-racism', in P. Cohen and H. Bains (eds), *Multi-Racist Britain*, London: Macmillan Education.

Gilsenan, M. (1976) 'Lying, honor, and contradiction', in B. Kapferer (ed.), *Transaction and Meaning*, Philadelphia: Institute for the Study of Human Issues.

Giovannini, M. (1981) 'Women: a dominant symbol within the cultural system of a Sicilian town', *Man*, 16, 3: 408–26.

—— (1987) 'Female chastity codes in the circum-Mediterranean: comparative perspectives', in Gilmore (1987a).

Goddard, V. (1987) 'Honour and shame: the control of women's sexuality and group identity in Naples', in Caplan (1987a).

Goffman, I. (1961) *Asylums*, New York: Anchor, Doubleday and Co.

Good, B. (1977) 'The heart of what's the matter: the structure of medical discourse in a provincial Iranian town', unpublished Ph.D. dissertation, University of Chicago.

Goodale, J. (1971) *Tiwi Wives*, Seattle: University of Washington Press.

Gough, J. (1989) 'Theories of sexual identity and the masculinization of the gay male', in Shepherd and Wallis (1989).

Greenberg, David (1988) *The Construction of Modern Homosexuality*, Chicago: University of Chicago Press.

Grosz, E. (1987) 'Notes towards a corporeal feminism', in J. Allen and E. Grosz (eds), *Feminism and the Body*, 5: 1–16, special issue of *Australian Feminist Studies*.

—— (1990) 'Inscriptions and body-maps: representations and the corporeal', in Threadgold and Cranny-Francis (1990).

Hacking, I. (1983) *Representing and Intervening: Introductory Topics in the Philosophy of Natural Science*, Cambridge: Cambridge University Press.

Hall, S. (1988) 'New ethnicities', *Black Film/British Cinema*, Institute of Contemporary Arts Documents 7, London: ICA/BFI.

Hanmer, Jalna (1990) 'Men, power and the exploitation of women', in Hearn and Morgan (1990a).

Harding, S. and Hintikka, M.B. (eds) (1983) *Discovering Reality: Feminist Perspectives on Epistemology, Metaphysics, Methodology, and Philosophy of Science*, Dordrecht: D. Reidel.

Harris, E. (1990) 'Did the Athenians regard seduction as a worse crime than rape?', *Classical Quarterly*, 40: 370–7.

Harris, Olivia (1981) 'Households as natural units', in Young *et al.* (1981).

Hart, A. (1992) 'No condom sense: health promotion, HIV and "high-risk" groups/ behaviour', *Anthropology in Action*, 12: 12–14.

Harvey, D. (1989) *The Condition of Post Modernity: An Enquiry into the Origins of Cultural Change*, Oxford: Basil Blackwell.

Hattersley, C. W. (1910) 'From the heart of Africa: a Mengo boy to English boys', *Empire Annual for Boys*, 57–66.

Hautzinger, Sarah (1991) 'Policing violence against women in Salvador da Bahia, Brazil', unpublished paper presented to the Program in Atlantic History, Culture and Society, Johns Hopkins University.

Hearn, Jeff (1992) 'The personal, the political, the theoretical: the case of men's sexualities and sexual violence', in D. Porter (ed.), *Between Men and Feminism*, London: Routledge.

Hearn, J. and Morgan, D. (eds) (1990a) *Men, Masculinities and Social Theory*, London: Unwin Hyman.

—— (1990b) 'Men, masculinities and social theory', in Hearn and Morgan (1990a).

Heath (1991) 'American war aims', *Independent*, 26 February: 18.

Hebdige, D. (1974a) 'Aspects of style in the deviant subcultures of the 1960s', unpublished MA thesis, Centre for Contemporary Cultural Studies, University of Birmingham.

—— (1974b) *Reggae, Rastas and Rudies: Style and the Subversion of Form*, Stencilled paper 24, Centre for Contemporary Cultural Studies, University of Birmingham.

—— (1979) *Subculture: The Meaning of Style*, London: Methuen.

—— (1981) 'Skinheads and the search for a white working class identity', *New Socialist*, September: 38.

—— (1983) '"Ska tissue": the rise and fall of Two Tone', in S. Davis and P. Simon (eds), *Reggae International*, London: Thames and Hudson.

Hegland, M. (1992) 'Wife abuse and the political system: a Middle Eastern case study', in D.A. Counts, J.K. Brown and J.C. Campbell (eds), *Sanctions and Sanctuary*, Boulder: Westview.

Henriques, J., Hollway, W., Urwin, C. Venn, C. and Walkerdine, V. (1984) *Changing the Subject: Psychology, Social Regulation and Subjectivity*, London: Methuen.

Herdt, G. (1981) *Guardians of the Flutes: Idioms of Masculinity*, New York: McGraw-Hill.

—— (ed.) (1984) *Ritualized Homosexuality in Melanesia*, Berkeley: University of California Press.

—— (1987) *The Sambia. Ritual and Gender in New Guinea*, Case Studies in Cultural Anthropology, New York: Holt, Rinehart and Winston.

Herskovits, Melville J. (1966) *The New World Negro*, Bloomington: Indiana University Press.

Herzfeld, M. (1985) *The Poetics of Manhood: Contest and Identity in a Cretan Mountain Village*, Princeton, N.J.: Princeton University Press.

—— (1991) 'Silence, submission, and subversion: towards a poetics of womanhood', in Loizos and Papataxiarchis (1991).

Hewitt, R. (1983) 'Black through white: Hoagy Carmichael and the cultural reproduction of racism', *Popular Music 3*, Cambridge: Cambridge University Press.

—— (1986) *White Talk, Black Talk: Inter-Racial Friendship and Communication Amongst Adolescents*, London: Cambridge University Press.

—— (1990) 'A sociolinguistic view of urban adolescent relations', in F. Rogilds (ed.), *Every Cloud has a Silver Lining*, Studies in Cultural Sociology 28, Hostebro: Akademisk Forlag.

Highfield, R. (1992) 'Goodbye macho man?', *Daily Telegraph*, 30 November: 16.

Hirschon, R. (1978) 'Open body, closed space: the transformation of female sexuality', in S. Ardener (ed.), *Defining Females: The Nature of Women in Society*, London: Croom Helm.

Hobart, M. (1989) 'The patience of plants: a note on agency in Bali', *Review of Indonesian and Malasian Affairs*, 24, 2: 90–135.

Hochschild, Arlie Russell (1983) *The Managed Heart: Commercialization of Human Feeling*, Berkeley: University of California Press.

Hodge, J. (1989) 'Feminism and post-modernism: misleading divisions imposed by the opposition between modernism and post-modernism', in A. Benjamin (ed.), *The Problems of Modernity*, London: Routledge.

Hodza, Aaron C. (1982) *Mitupo Nezvidao Zvamadzidza*, Zimbabwe: Longman.

Hollway, Wendy (1984) 'Gender difference and the production of subjectivity', in Henriques *et al.*, (1984).

hooks, b. (1982) *Ain't I a Woman? Black Women and Feminism*, London: Pluto Press.

—— (1992) 'Representing whiteness in the black imagination', in L. Grossberg, C. Nelson and Treicher (eds), *Cultural Studies*, London: Routledge.

Housman, A.E. (1988) *Collected Poems and Selected Prose*, London: Penguin.

Humphries, M. (1985) 'Gay machismo', in Andy Metcalf and Martin Humphries (eds), *The Sexuality of Men*, London: Pluto Press.

Hunter (1989) 'Women's authority in classical Athens', *Echos du Monde Classique/ Classical Views*, 8 (1): 39–48.

Idris, Y. (1978) 'The shame', in his *The Cheapest Nights*, London: Heinemann.

Independent, (1991) 'Victims of sexual prejudice in uniform', 11 July: 29.

—— (1992) 'Prisoner's inquest told of sex attack', 10 March: 16.

Iossifides, M. (1991) 'Sisters in Christ: metaphors of kinship among Greek nuns', in Loizos and Papataxiarchis (1991).

Jackson, D. (1990) *Unmasking Masculinity: A Critical Biography*, London: Unwin Hyman.

Jameson, F. (1983) 'Postmodernism and consumer society', in H. Foster (ed.), *Postmodern Culture*, London: Pluto Press.

Jameson, M. (1990a) 'Domestic space in the Greek city-state', in S. Kent (ed.), *Domestic Architecture and the Use of Space*, Cambridge: Cambridge University Press.

—— (1990b) 'Private space in the Greek city', in O. Murray and S. Price (eds), *The Greek City*, Oxford: Oxford University Press.

Jamous, R. (1981) *Honneur et Baraka*, Cambridge: Cambridge University Press.

Jayawardena, K. (1988) *Feminism and Nationalism in the Third World*, London: Zed Books.

Jeater, Diana (1993) *Marriage, Perversion and Power: The Construction of Moral Discourse in Southern Rhodesia*, Oxford: Oxford University Press.

Jeffreys, S. (1984) ' "Free from all uninvited touch of man": woman's campaigns around sexuality', in L. Coveny (ed.), *The Sexuality Papers: Male Sexuality and the Social Control of Women 1880–1914*, London: Hutchinson.

Jiménez de Asúa, L. (1929) (3rd edn) *Libertad de Amar y Derecho a Morir: Ensayos de un Criminilista sobre Eugenesia, Eutanasia, Endocrinología*, Madrid: Historia Nueva.

Jones, S. (1988) *Black Culture, White Youth: The Reggae Tradition from JA to UK*, Basingstoke: Macmillan.

Joseph, S. (forthcoming) 'Brother/sister relationships: connectivity, love and power in the reproduction of Arab patriarchy', *Ethnos*.

Kandiyoti, D. (1988a) 'Bargaining with patriarchy', *Gender and Society*, 2, 3: 274–90.

—— (1988b) 'Slavegirls, temptresses and comrades: images of women in the Turkish novel', *Feminist Issues*, 8, 1: 33–50.

—— (ed.) (1991) *Women, Islam and the State*, London: Macmillan.

Kanter, Rosabeth Moss (1977) *Men and Women of the Corporation*, New York: Basic Books.

Kaplan, G.T. and Rogers, L.J. (1990) 'Scientific constructions, cultural productions: scientific narratives of sexual attraction', in Threadgold and Cranny-Francis (1990).

Keller, Evelyn Fox (1990) 'Gender and science', in McCarl Nielsen (1990).

Kenna, M. (1976) 'Houses, fields and graves: property and ritual obligations on a Greek island', *Ethnology*, 15: 21–34.

Kennedy, John (1978) 'Circumcision and excision ceremonies', in J. Kennedy (ed.), *Nubian Ceremonial Life*, Cairo: American University of Cairo Press.

Kessler, Susan J. and McKenna, Wendy (1978) *Gender: An Ethnomethodological Approach*, New York: John Wiley.

Khan, M.H. (1972) *Purdah and Polygamy: A Study in the Social Pathology of Muslim Society*, Peshawar: Cantt.

Kimmel, Michael (1987) *Changing Men: New Directions in Research on Men and Masculinity*, California: Sage.

—— (1990) 'After fifteen years: the impact of the sociology of masculinity on the masculinity of sociology', in Hearn and Morgan (1990a).

Kinni-Olusanyin, Esi (n.d.) 'The prominence of women in Yoruba and Fon religion', unpublished paper presented to the Department of Theatre Arts, University of Ibadan, Nigeria.

Kipling, Rudyard (1990) *The Complete Verse*, London: Kyle Cathie.

Kochman, T. (1972) 'Black American speech events and language programs for the classroom', in C.B. Cazden, V.P. John and D. Hymes (eds), *Functions of Language Use in the Classroom*, New York: Teacher College Press.

Koçu, E. (1981) *Yangin Var! Istanbul Tulumbacilari*, Istanbul: Ana Yayinlari.

Kumar, R. and Panigrahi, D.N. (1982) *Selected Works of Motilal Nehru, Vol. 1 (1899–1918)*, Bombay: Vikas.

Kurz, Irma (1986) *Malespeak*, London: Jonathan Cape.

La Fontaine, J. (1981) 'The domestication of the savage male', *Man*, 16, 3: 333–49.

Lakoff, G. and Johnson, M. (1980) *Metaphors We Live By*, Chicago: University of Chicago Press.

Lamo de Espinosa, E. (1989) *Delitos sin Víctima. Orden Social y Ambivilencia Moral*, Madrid: Alianza.

Landes, Ruth (1940) 'A cult matriarchate and male homosexuality', *Journal of Abnormal and Social Psychology*, 25: 386–97.

—— (1967) *A Cidade das Mulheres*, Rio: Civilizaçao Brasileira.

Leacock, Seth and Leacock, Ruth (1972) *Spirits of the Deep: A Study of an Afro-Brazilian Cult*, New York: Natural History Museum.

Leonardo, Michaela di (1991) *Gender at the Crossroads of Knowledge: Feminist Anthropology in the Postmodern Era*, Berkeley/Los Angeles: University of California Press.

Lepine, Claude (1978) *Contribuição ao Estudo do Sistema de Classificação dos Tipos Psicologicos no Candomblé Ketu em Salvador*, São Paulo: USP.

LeVay, Simon, (1992) 'Are homosexuals born and not made?', *Guardian*, 9 October: 30.

Lever, A. (1986) 'Honour as a red herring', *Critique of Anthropology*, 6, 3: 83–106.

Lewis, I.M. (1971) *Ecstatic Religion*, Baltimore: Penguin.

Lindisfarne-Tapper, N. (1991) 'Local contexts and political voices', *Anthropology in Action*, 10: 6–8.

Loizos, P. (1975a) *The Greek Gift: Politics in a Cypriot Village*, Oxford: Blackwell.

—— (1975b) 'Changes in property transfer among Greek Cypriot villagers', *Man*, 10, 4: 503–23.

Loizos, P. and Papataxiarchis, E. (eds) (1991) *Contested Identities: Gender and Kinship in Modern Greece*, Princeton N.J.: Princeton University Press.

Lutz, Catherine (1986) 'Emotion, thought and estrangement: emotion as a cultural category', *Cultural Anthropology*, 1, 3: 287–309.

—— (1990) 'Engendered emotion: gender, power and the rhetoric of emotional control in American discourse', in L. Abu-Lughod and C. Lutz (eds), *Language and the Politics of Emotion*, Cambridge: Cambridge University Press.

Lyotard, J.-F. (1984) *The Postmodern Condition: A Report on Knowledge*, Manchester: Manchester University Press.

McCleod, E. (1982) *Women Working: Prostitution Now*, London: Croom Helm.

MacCormack, C. and Strathern, M. (eds) (1980) *Nature, Culture and Gender*, Cambridge: Cambridge University Press.

MacDonald, Henry (1915) 'Through! A tale of the Great War', *Empire Annual for Boys*, 9–25.

McElhinny, Bonnie (1992) 'I don't smile much anymore: gender, affect and the discourse of Pittsburgh Police Officers', in M. Bucholz, K. Hall and B. Moonwoman (eds), *Locating Power: Proceedings of the 1992 Berkeley Conference on Women and Language*, Berkeley: Linguistics Department (Berkeley), University of California.

—— (1993) 'How gender talks: dialects and discourse as symbols of professional identity on the Pittsburgh Police Force', Ph.D. dissertation, Stanford University.

MacIntosh, Mary (1968) 'The homosexual role', reprinted in Plummer (1981).

MacKey, Eva (1991) 'Revisioning "home"work: feminism and the politics of voice and representation', unpublished MA term paper, University of Sussex.

McNay, Lois (1992) *Foucault and Feminism*, Oxford: Polity Press.

McRae, Edward (1985) 'O militante homosexual no Brasil', unpublished Ph.D. thesis, University of São Paulo.

McRobbie, A. (1981) 'Just like a Jackie story', in A. McRobbie and T. McCabe (eds), *Feminism For Girls*, London: Routledge and Kegan Paul.

—— (1982) 'Jackie: an ideology of adolescent femininity', in B. Waites, T. Bennet and G. Martin (eds), *Popular Culture: Past and Present*, London, Croom Helm/ Open University Press.

Mageo, J.M. (1992) 'Male transvestism and cultural change in Samoa', *American Ethnologist*, 19, 3: 443–59.

Mahfouz, N. (1990) *Palace Walk*, New York: Doubleday.

Mailer, N. (1961) 'The white negro: superficial reflections on the hipster', in N. Mailer, *Advertisements For Myself*, London: André Deutsch.

Malti-Douglas, F. (1991) *Woman's Body, Woman's Word*, Princeton, N.J.: Princeton University Press.

Mangan, J.A. (1981) *Athleticism in the Victorian and Edwardian Public Schools*, Cambridge: Cambridge University Press.

—— (1989) 'Noble specimens of manhood: schoolboy literature and the creation of a colonial chivalric code', in Richards (1989).

Marriott, McKim (1976) 'Hindu transactions: diversity without dualism', in B. Kapferer (ed.), *Transaction and Meaning*, Philadelphia: ISHI Publications.

Marshall, John (1981) 'Pansies, perverts and macho men: changing conceptions of male homosexuality', in Plummer (1981).

Martin, Emily (1987) *The Woman in the Body*, Milton Keynes: Open University Press.

—— (1992a) 'The end of the body?', *American Ethnologist*, 19, 1: 121–40.

—— (1992b) 'Body narratives, body boundaries', in L. Grossberg, C. Nelson and P. Treichler (eds), *Cultural Studies*, New York/London: Routledge.

Martin, Susan (1980) *Breaking and Entering: Policewomen on Patrol*, Berkeley: University of California Press.

Marvin, Gary (1984) 'The cockfight in Andalusia, Spain: images of the truly male', *Anthropological Quarterly*, 57, 2: 60–70.

Marx, K. (1959) 'The eighteenth Brumaire of Louis Bonaparte', in L. Feuer (ed.) *Marx and Engels: Basic Writings on Politics and Philosophy*, New York: Doubleday Anchor.

Mascia-Lees, F., Sharpe, P. and Cohen, C.B. (1989) 'The postmodernist turn in anthropology: cautions from a feminist perspective', *Signs*, 15, 1: 7–33.

Mee, Arthur (1913a) 'Letters to boys of the future: the boy who loves a game', in his *The New Children's Encyclopaedia*, 6.

—— (1913b) 'Letters to girls of the future: to the girl who is wondering', in his *The New Children's Encyclopaedia*, 7.

Mercer, K. (1987) 'Black hair/style politics', *New Formations*, 3: 33–56.

Mercer, K. and Julien, I. (1988) 'Race, sexual politics and black masculinity: a dossier', in Chapman and Rutherford (1988).

Mernissi, F. (1982) 'Virginity and patriarchy', in A. al-Hibri (ed.) *Women and Islam*, Oxford: Pergamon (special issue of Women's Studies International Forum, 5, 2).

Mies, M., Bennholdt-Thomsen, V. and Von Werlhof, C. (1988) *Women: The Last Colony*, London: Zed Books.

Miller, J. (ed.) (1990) *The Don Giovanni Book*, London: Faber and Faber.

Mirza, H. (1992) *Young, Female and Black*, London: Routledge.

Mitchell, J. and Rose, J. (1982) *Feminine Sexuality: Jacques Lacan and the Ecole Freudienne*, London: Macmillan.

Mohanty, C. (1987a) 'Feminist encounters: locating the politics of experience', *Copyright*, 1: 30–44.

—— (1987b) 'Under Western eyes: feminist scholarship and colonial discourses', *Feminist Review*, 30: 61–88.

Mohanty, C., Russa, A. and Torres, L. (eds) *Third World Women and the Politics of Feminism*, Bloomington: Indiana University Press.

Molyneux, Maxine (1979) 'Beyond the domestic labour debate', *New Left Review*, 116: 3–27.

Moodie, T.D. (1988) 'Migrancy and male sexuality in the South African gold mines', *Journal of South African Studies*, 14 (2): 228–56.

Moore, H.C. (1912) 'The Puttipore rivals', *Empire Annual for Boys*, 118–28.

Moore, Henrietta (1988) *Feminism and Anthropology*, Oxford: Polity Press.

—— (forthcoming) 'The problem of explaining violence in the social sciences', in P. Harvey (ed.), *Sex and Violence: Issues in Representation and Expression*, London: Routledge.

Moore, S. (1993) 'Kiss and don't tell', *Guardian*, 23 July.

Moraga, C. and Anzaldua, G. (eds) (1981) *This Bridge Called My Back: Writings by Radical Women of Color*, Watertown, Mass.: Persephone.

Morgan, Robin (1989) *The Demon Lover: On the Sexuality of Terrorism*, London: Mandarin.

Mott, Luiz (1982) 'Dez viados em questão: tipologia dos homossexuais do cidade de Salvador, Bahia', paper presented to the 13th Reunião da Associação Brasileira da Antropólogia.

—— (1987) *O Lesbianismo no Brasil*, São Paulo: Editora Mercado Aberta.

—— (1988) *Escravidão, Homossexualidade e Demonologia*, Rio: Icone Editores.

Mott, Luiz and Assuncão, Aroldo (1987) 'Gilete na Carne: Etnographia das automutilacões dos travestis da Bahia', *São Paulo: Soc. Dir. Saúde*, 4, 1: 41–56.

MS (1984) 'The pregnant woman's bill of rights', 9: 56.

Murphy, M.D. (1983) 'Coming of age in Seville: the structuring of a riteless passage to manhood', *Journal of Anthropological Research*, 39(4): 376–92.

Musallam, B. (1983) *Sex and Society in Islam*, Cambridge: Cambridge University Press.

Najmabadi, A. (1991) 'Hazards of modernity and morality: women, state and ideology in contemporary Iran', in Kandiyoti (1991).

Nandy, A. (1980) *At the Edge of Psychology: Essays in Politics and Culture*, Delhi: Oxford University Press.

—— (1983) *The Intimate Enemy*, Delhi: Oxford University Press.

Nelson, C. (1974) 'Public and private politics: women in the Middle Eastern World', *American Ethnologist*, 1, 3: 551–63.

Nicholson, L. (ed.) (1990) *Feminism/postmodernism*, London: Routledge.
Nielsen, Joyce McCarl (ed.) (1990) *Feminist Research Methods: Exemplary Readings in the Social Sciences*, San Francisco: Westview Press.
Obeyeskere, G. (1981) *Medusa's Hair: An Essay on Personal Symbols and Religious Experience*, Chicago: University of Chicago Press.
—— (1984) *The Cult of the Goddess Pattini*, Chicago: University of Chicago Press.
Ochs, Elinor (1992) 'Indexing gender', in A. Duranti and C. Goodwin (eds) *Rethinking Context: Language as an Interative Phenomenon*, Cambridge: Cambridge University Press.
Oliveira, Neuza Maria de (1984) 'Travesti: falo des três atitudes diante do falo', *Maria, Maria*, July/August: 3.
—— (1986) 'As "monas" da Casa Amarela: os travestis na espelho da mulher', unpublished Masters thesis, Universidade Federal da Bahia.
Oliveira Marques, A. (1971) *A Sociedade Medieval Portuguesa*, Lisbon: Livraria Sa da Costa.
Ortner, S. (1974) 'Is female to male as nature is to culture?', in Rosaldo and Lamphere (1974).
—— (1983) 'The founding of the first Sherpa nunnery and the problem of "women" as an analytic category', in V. Patraka and L. Tilly (eds), *Feminist Revisions: What Has Been and What Might Be*, Ann Arbor: Women's Studies Program, University of Michigan.
Ortner, S. and Whitehead, H. (eds) (1981) *Sexual Meanings*, Cambridge: Cambridge University Press.
Overing, J. (1986) 'Men control women? The "Catch 22", in the analysis of gender', *International Journal of Moral and Social Studies*, 1, 2: 135–56.
Papataxiarchis, E. (1988) 'Kinship, friendship and gender relations in two east Aegean villages', unpublished Ph.D. thesis, University of London.
Peattie and Taylor (1991) 'Alex', *Independent*, 14 March: 30.
Pereira, Ricardo Calheiros (1988) 'O desperdicio de semen: um estudo do eroticismo entre rapazes', unpublished Masters thesis, Universidade Federal da Bahia.
Peters, E. (1980) 'Aspects of bedouin bridewealth among camel herders in Cyrenaica', in J. Comaroff (ed.), *The Meaning of Marriage Payments*, London: Academic Press.
Pharr, Suzanne (1988) *Homophobia, A Weapon of Sexism*, Inverness: Chardon Press.
Philips, J.E. (1990) 'The African heritage of white America', in J.E. Holloway (ed.), *Africanisms in American Culture*, Bloomington: Indiana University Press.
Piña Cabral, J. de (1989) 'The Mediterranean as a category of regional comparison', *Current Anthropology*, 30: 3.
Pitt Rivers, J. (1965) 'Honour and social status', in J. Peristiany (ed.), *Honour and Shame*, London: Weidenfeld and Nicolson.
—— (1977) *The Fate of Schechem or The Politics of Sex*, Cambridge: Cambridge University Press.
Pleck, J. (1981) *The Myth of Masculinity*, Cambridge, Mass.: MIT Press.
—— (1987) 'American fathering in historical perspective', in M. Kimmel (ed.) *Changing Men: New Directions in Research on Men and Masculinity*, London: Sage.
Plummer, K. (ed.) (1981) *The Making of the Modern Homosexual*, London: Hutchinson/Gay Men's Press.
Polan, Brenda (1988) 'The gender blender', *Guardian*, 29 September: 20.
Pollak, M. (1985) 'Male homosexuality – or happiness in the ghetto', in P. Aries and A. Bejin (eds), *Western Sexuality*, Oxford: Blackwell.
Pollard, Eliza F. (n.d.) *The White Dove of Amritzir*, London: Partridge.
Polsky, E. (1961) 'On Hipsters', in N. Mailer, *Advertisements for Myself*, London: André Deutsch.

Porter, D. (1992) *Between Men and Feminism*, London: Routledge.
Poster, M. (1986) 'Foucault and the tyranny of Greece', in D. Hoy (ed.) *Foucault: A Critical Reader*, Oxford: Basil Blackwell.
Prince, C.V. (1957) 'Homosexuality, transvestism and transsexualism', *American Journal of Psychotherapy*, 11, 1: 80–5.
Pronger, B. (1990) *The Arena of Masculinity: Sports, Homosexuality and the Meaning of Sex*, London: Gay Men's Press.
Ramazanoğlu, Caroline (1989) *Feminism and the Contradictions of Oppression*, London: Routledge.
Ray, Peter (1992) 'It's not natural', *Living Marxism*, 50: 31–2.
Raymond, Janice G. (1979) *The Transsexual Empire*, London: Women's Press.
Reiter, Rayna (ed.) (1975) *Toward an Anthropology of Women*, New York: Monthly Review Press.
Reskin, Barbara and Roos, Patricia (1990) *Job Queues, Gender Queues: Explaining Women's Inroads into Male Occupations*, Philadelphia: Temple University Press.
Ribeiro, R. (1970) *Cultos Afrobrasileiros do Recife*, Recife: Boletim do Instituto Joaquim Nabuco.
Richards, Jeffrey (1989) *Imperialism and Juvenile Literature*, Manchester: Manchester University Press.
Rifaat, A. (1990) 'Honour', in M. Badran and M.Cooke (eds), *Opening the Gates*, London: Virago.
Rogers, Barbara (1980) *The Domestication of Women*, London: Tavistock.
Rogers, C. (1975) 'Female forms of power and the myth of male dominance', *American Ethnologist*, 2: 727–56.
Rorty, R. (1979) *Philosophy and the Mirror of Nature*, Princeton, N.J.: Princeton University of Press.
Rosaldo, M. (1974) 'Women, culture and society: a theoretical overview', in Rosaldo and Lamphere (eds) (1974).
—— (1980) 'The use and abuse of anthropology: reflections on feminism and cross-cultural understanding', *Signs*, 5, 3: 389–417.
Rosaldo, M. and Lamphere, L. (eds) (1974) *Women, Culture and Society*, Stanford: Stanford University Press.
Rouge (1990) 'Class in the 90s', 4: 19.
Roy, D. (1953) 'Work satisfaction and social reward in quota achievement: an analysis of piecework incentive', *American Sociological Review*, 18: 507–14.
Rubin, Gayle (1975) 'The traffic in women: notes on the "political economy" of sex', in Reiter (1975).
Rubinstein, Jonathan (1973) *City Police*, New York: Farrar, Strauss and Giroux.
Sacks, K. (1974) 'Engels revisited: women, the organization of production, and private property', in Rosaldo and Lamphere (1974) (reprinted in Reiter 1975).
Said, Edward (1978) *Orientalism*, London: Routledge and Kegan Paul.
Salmond, A. (1985) 'Maori epistomologies', in J. Overing (ed.), *Reason and Morality*, London: Tavistock.
Sanders, P. (1991) 'Gendering the ungendered body: hermaphrodites in medieval Islamic law', in N. Keddie and B. Baron (eds), *Women in Middle Eastern History*, New Haven: Yale University Press.
Santos, Juana Elbein dos (1988) *Os Nàgô e A Morte*, Petrópolis: Vozes.
Saxby, Argyll and Simpson, E. (1914) 'The famine ghoul', *Empire Annual for Boys*, 110–19.
Schechner, Richard (1985) *Between Theatre and Anthropology*, Philadelphia: University of Pennsylvania Press.
Scott, James C. (1990) *Domination and the Arts of Resistance: Hidden Transcripts*, New Haven: Yale University Press.

Scott, Joan (1989) *Gender and the Politics of History*, New York: Columbia University Press.

Sealey, R. (1990) *Women and Law in Classical Greece*, Chapel Hill and London: University of North Carolina Press.

Sedgwick, E.K. (1985) *Between Men: English Literature and Male Homosexual Desire*, New York: Columbia University Press.

Segal, Lynne (1990) *Slow Motion: Changing Masculinities, Changing Men*, London: Virago.

Segato, Rita Laura (1986) 'Inventando a natureza: família, sexo e gênero nos Xangôs de Recife', in R. Segato (ed.), *Olóòrisá*, São Paulo: EMW Editores.

Seidler, V. (1987) 'Reason, desire and male sexuality', in Caplan (1987a).

—— (1989) *Rediscovering Masculinity*, London: Routledge.

—— (ed.) (1991a) *The Achilles Heel Reader*, London: Routledge.

—— (1991b) *Recreating Sexual Politics*, London: Routledge.

Shapiro, Judith (1979) 'Cross-cultural perspectives on sexual differentiation', in H.A. Katchadourian (ed.), *Human Sexuality: Comparative and Developmental Perspectives*, Berkeley: University of California Press.

Shepherd, G. (1978) 'Transsexualism in Oman?', *Man*, 13, 1: 133–4.

—— (1987) 'Rank, gender and homosexuality: Mombasa as a key to understanding sexual options', in Caplan (1987a).

Shepherd, Simon and Wallis, Mick (eds) (1989) *Coming On Strong: Gay Politics and Culture*, London: Unwin Hyman.

Shore, B. (1981) 'Sexuality and gender in Samoa: conceptions and missed conceptions', in Ortner and Whitehead (1981).

Shorter Oxford English Dictionary (1973) Oxford: Clarendon Press.

Shostak, A. (1987) 'Motivations of abortion clinic waiting room males: "bottled-up" roles and unmet needs', in Kimmel (ed.) (1987).

Showalter, Elaine (1985) *The Female Malady*, London: Virago.

Singer, A. (1973) 'Marriage payments and the exchange of people', *Man*, 8, 1: 80–92.

Skynner, Robin (1992) 'Why don't we talk about it?', *Guardian*, 19 December: 14.

Spender, Dale (1980) *Man Made Language*, London: Routledge and Kegan Paul.

Spivak, Gayati Chakravorty (1981) 'French feminism in international frame', *Yale French Studies*, 62: 154–84.

Staples, R. (1976) *Introduction to Black Sociology*, New York: McGraw-Hill.

—— (1982) *Black Masculinity: The Black Man's Role in American Society*, New York: Black Scholar.

Stevens, John (1992) 'Stiff lips and Windsor knots', *Guardian*, 29 December: 16.

Stolcke, V. (1986) 'New reproductive technologies – same old fatherhood', *Critique of Anthropology*, 6, 3: 5–32.

Stoler. A.L. (1991) 'Carnal knowledge and imperial power: gender, race and morality in colonial Asia', in di Leonardo (1991).

Stoller, Robert (1976) *Sex and Gender*, London: Hogarth Press.

Stoller, R. and Herdt, G.H. (1982) 'The development of masculinity: a cross-cultural contribution', *Journal of the American Psychoanalytic Association*, 30: 29–59.

Strathern, M. (1972) *Women in Between: Female Roles in a Male World: Mount Hagen, New Guinea*, London: Seminar Press.

—— (ed.) (1987) *Dealing with Inequality*, Cambridge: Cambridge University Press.

—— (1988) *The Gender of the Gift*, Berkeley: University of California Press.

—— (1991) *Partial Connections*, Savage, Md.: Roman and Littlefield.

Studd, J.E.K. (1909) 'Foreword', *Empire Annual for Boys*: 7–9.

Tamer [Tamir], Zakariyya (1978) 'al-Urs al-Sharqi', in Zakariyya Tamir, *al-Ra'd*, Damascus: Manshurat Maktabat al-Nuri.

—— (1985) 'Snow at the end of the night', in Zakariyya Tamer, *Tigers on the Tenth Day*, London: Quartet.

Tapper, N. (1991) *Bartered Brides*, Cambridge: Cambridge University Press.

Tapper, N. and Tapper, R. (1987) 'The birth of the prophet: ritual and gender in Turkish Islam', *Man*, 22, 1: 69–92.

Tapper, R. (1979) *Pasture and Politics*, London: Academic.

Teixeira, Maria Lina Leão (1987) 'Lorogun: identidades sexuais e poder no Candomblé', in M. Teixeira (ed.), *Candomblé: desvendando identidades*, São Paulo: EMV Editores.

Thaiss, G. (1978) 'The conceptualization of social change through metaphor', *Journal of Asian and African Studies*, 8, 1–2: 1–13.

Threadgold, Terry (1990) 'Introduction', in Threadgold and Cranny-Francis (eds) (1990).

Threadgold, Terry and Anne Cranny-Francis (eds) (1990) *Feminine, Masculine and Representation*, London: Allen & Unwin.

Trevisan, João (1986) *Perverts in Paradise*, London: Gay Men's Press.

Trudeau, Garry (1991) 'Doonesbury', *Guardian*, 23 January: 29.

Turner, Bryan (1985) 'The practices of rationality: Michael Foucault, medical history and sociological theory', in Fardon (1985a).

Tyndale-Biscoe, C.E. (1911) 'Changed lives in Kashmir', *Empire Annual for Boys*, 205–16.

—— (1913) 'More news from Kashmir', *Empire Annual for Boys*, 278–86.

US Department of Justice (1987a) *Profile of State and Local Law Enforcement Agencies*, Washington, D.C.: Office of Justice Programs, Bureau of Justice Statistics.

—— (1987b) *Police Departments in Large Cities*, Washington, D.C.: Office of Justice Programs, Bureau of Justice Statistics.

Vance, C. (1989) 'Social construction theory: problems in the history of sexuality', in Altman *et al.* (1989).

Vaught, C. and Smith, D. (1980) 'Incorporation and mechanical solidarity in an underground coal mine', *Sociology of Work and Occupation*, 7, 2: 159–87.

Verger, Pierre (1988) *Orixás: Deuses Iorubás na Africa e no Novo Mundo*, Salvador: Editores Corrúpio.

Vernier, B. (1984) 'Putting kin and kinship to good use: the circulation of goods, labour and names on Karpathos (Greece)', in H. Medick and D.W. Sabean (eds), *Interest and Emotion: Essays on the Study of Family and Kinship*, Cambridge: Cambridge University Press.

Vidal-Naquet, P. (1981) 'The black hunter and the origin of the Athenian ephebia', in P. Vidal-Naquet (ed.), *The Black Hunter*, Baltimore and London: Johns Hopkins University Press.

Vindicación Feminista (1979) 'La sexualidad femenina', 28: 14–36.

Wade, George A. (1915) 'Boy-heroes in the Great War', *Empire Annual for Boys*, 80–6.

—— (1917) 'Great players fallen in the war', *Empire Annual for Boys*, 21–6.

Ware, V. (1990) 'The good, the bad and the foolhardy: moving the frontiers of British women's history', in F. Rogilds (ed.), *Every Cloud has a Silver Lining*, Studies in Cultural Sociology 28, Holstebro: Akademisk Forlag.

Weedon, C. (1987) *Feminist Practice and Poststructuralist Theory*, Oxford: Basil Blackwell.

Weeks, J. (1977) *Coming Out: Homosexual Politics in Britain, from the Nineteenth Century to the Present*, London: Quartet.

—— (1980) 'Capitalism and the organization of sex', in Gay Left Collective (ed.), *Homosexuality: Power and Politics*, London: Allison & Busby.

—— (1989a) 'Against nature', in Altman *et al.* (1989).
—— (1989b) *Sex, Politics and Society: The Regulation of Sexuality since 1800*, London: Longman.
Weideger, P. (1986) *History's Mistress*, Harmondsworth: Penguin.
Weiner, A. (1976) *Women of Value, Men of Renown*, Austin: University of Texas Press.
Westcott, M. (1990) 'Feminist criticism of the social sciences', in Nielsen (1990).
Westermarck, E. (1914) *Marriage Ceremonies in Morocco*, London: Curzon.
Westley, William (1970) *Violence and the Police*, Boston: MIT Press.
Whitehead, H. (1981) 'The bow and the burden strap: a new look at institutionalized homosexuality in native North America', in Ortner and Whitehead (1981).
Wieringa, Saskia (1989) 'An anthropological critique of constructionalism: berdaches and butches', in Altman *et al.* (1989).
Wikan, Unni (1977) 'Man becomes woman: transsexualism in Oman as a key to gender roles', *Man*, 12, 2: 304–19.
—— (1984) 'Shame and honour: a contestable pair', *Man*, 19, 4: 635–52.
Williams, Christine (1989) *Gender Differences at Work: Women and Men in Nontraditional Occupations*, Berkeley: University of California Press.
—— (1992) 'The glass escalator: hidden advantages for men in the "female" professions', *Social Problems*, 39, 3: 253–67.
Wiliams, H. (1911) 'Four famous authors for boys', *Empire Annual for Boys*: 281–94.
Wilson, J.S. (1919) '"Daftie"', *Empire Annual for Boys*, 105–15.
Winkler, J. (1990) *The Constraints of Desire*, London: Routledge.
Wittgenstein, L. (1963) *Philosophical Investigations*, Oxford: Basil Blackwell.
Wolfram, S. (1985) 'Facts and theories: sayings and believing', in J. Overing (ed.), *Reason and Morality*, London: Tavistock.
Woodhouse, Annie (1989) *Fantastic Women: Sex, Gender and Transvestism*, London: Macmillan.
Woortman, Klaas (1987) *A Família das Mulheres*, Rio: Tempo Brasileiro.
Young, Kate, Wolkowitz, Carol and McCullagh, Roslyn (eds) (1981) *Of Marriage and the Market*, London: CSE Books.
Zinovieff, S. (1991) 'Hunters and hunted: *Kamaki* and the ambiguities of sexual predation in a Greek town', in Loizos and Papataxiarchis (1991).
Zita, J. (1992) 'Male lesbians and the postmodernist body', *Hypatia*, 7, 4: 106–27.

Name index

Subject index